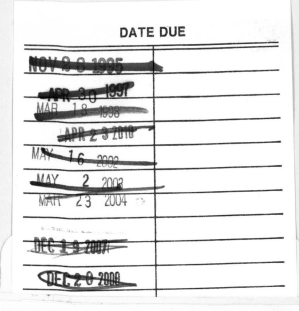

NAZI PROPAGANDA

Z. A. B. ZEMAN

NAZI
PROPAGANDA

75154

Published in association with
THE WIENER LIBRARY

LONDON
OXFORD UNIVERSITY PRESS
NEW YORK TORONTO

Oxford University Press, Amen House, London E.C.4
GLASGOW NEW YORK TORONTO MELBOURNE WELLINGTON
BOMBAY CALCUTTA MADRAS KARACHI LAHORE DACCA
CAPE TOWN SALISBURY NAIROBI IBADAN ACCRA
KUALA LUMPUR HONG KONG

*Printed in Great Britain
Set by Spottiswoode, Ballantyne & Co. Ltd.,
Reprinted lithographically by Alden Press*

FOR DR. ALFRED WIENER

PREFACE

THIS book, which is sponsored by the Wiener Library, is based on the material contained therein.

The reader may like to know a little more about the Library which is named after its founder, Dr. Alfred Wiener, a refugee from Nazi persecution. It is rather more than the collection of books which the name suggests. It is in fact a research institute of contemporary history and specializes in the following subjects: the rise and fall of Nazi Germany; the history of the Weimar Republic; the technique of totalitarian subversion; genocide, especially the destruction of European Jewry; Germany after Hitler; international Fascism; racial and religious discrimination, especially anti-Semitism; group relations; refugee and minority problems; modern Jewish history.

On these subjects, the institute has assembled some 60,000 volumes, which are supplemented by a classified press file starting from 1933, the year of Hitler's advent. Other important sections are the several thousand documents relating to the various Nürnberg trials, an exclusive collection of 1,500 eye-witness accounts and personal memoirs, and finally a picture library.

While no inventory is as yet available of the whole library, four catalogues deal with the following major sections—'Persecution, Terror, and Resistance in Nazi Germany'; 'From Weimar to Hitler: Germany 1918–1933'; 'German Jewry: Its History, Life, and Culture', and 'After Hitler: Germany 1945–1963'. The Wiener Library Bulletin which appears four times a year lists the new acquisitions obtained from many parts of the world.

The Library was established at Amsterdam in 1934 and transferred to London in 1939. It is now the British equivalent of similarly specialized institutes abroad with all of which it maintains useful links, notably the Institut für Zeitgeschichte in Munich; the Rijksinstituut voor Oorlogsdocumentatie in Amsterdam; the Yad Washem Institute in Jerusalem; the Centre de Documentation Juive Contemporaine in Paris; the Istituto Nazionale per la Storia del Movimento di Liberazione in Italia in Milan, and the Zydowski Instytut Historyczny in Warsaw.

From most of its foreign counterparts, however, the Wiener Library, by far the oldest of them, differs in that it is concerned with the past not only as a closed chapter and a memorial, but also in its continuing impact on the present. Readers of Mr. Zeman's book will be able to judge for themselves how far this is true of the particular subject with which he deals.

The present volume is one in a series of Wiener Library publications which was begun by Lionel Kochan's study entitled *Pogrom—November 10, 1938* (André Deutsch), 1957, and continued, in 1961, with a collection of essays entitled *On the Track of Tyranny* (Vallentine Mitchell) and written by a number of prominent scholars including, from this country, Professor Max Beloff, Mr. Alan Bullock, Mr. James Joll, Dr. Eva G. Reichmann.

Our grateful thanks are due to the Wolfson Foundation for the generous assistance which made the writing of this book possible. I should also like to convey our sincere thanks to the Oxford University Press, for their courtesy and co-operation.

C. C. ARONSFELD
Acting Director
The Wiener Library

ACKNOWLEDGEMENTS

THE author is greatly indebted to the staff of the Wiener Library, and especially to Mr. C. C. Aronsfeld, Dr. F. Hájek, Dr. L. J. Kahn, and Mrs. I. R. Wolff for their kind help and for their unfailing interest in his work. The advice on source material given by Dr. A. Hoch and Dr. H. Heiber of the Institut für Zeitgeschichte in Munich was extremely helpful, and Mr. Alan Bullock, Mr. Norman Collins, and Dame Rebecca West made valuable suggestions for the improvement of the manuscript. Its preparation for the publishers was efficiently carried out by Mrs. C. Bennett.

CONTENTS

PREFACE   vii

ACKNOWLEDGEMENTS   ix

LIST OF ILLUSTRATIONS   xiii

INTRODUCTION   1

I   THE CONQUEST OF THE MASSES   9

II   THE STATE AND PROPAGANDA   38

III   THE AGENCIES OF PROPAGANDA ABROAD   54

IV   THE CONSTANT THEMES: THE JEWS AND
THE COMMUNISTS   76

V   NAZI FOREIGN BROADCASTING   104

VI   AUSTRIA: AN APPEAL TO COMPATRIOTS   118

VII   BRITAIN AND SUBVERSION   142

VIII   PROPAGANDA IN THE WAR   158

IX   EPILOGUE   180

BIBLIOGRAPHY
Original Sources   187
National Socialist Publications   187
Autobiographies, Biographies, Diaries   199
Secondary Works   203
Newspapers and Periodicals   209

INDEX   211

ILLUSTRATIONS

Facing page

I 'The String-puller.' 1924   34

IIa Hitler: he alone is not allowed to speak in
    Germany. 1926   35
  b *SS* troopers are forbidden to wear their
    uniforms. 1930   35

III Election poster. 'National Socialism—the
    organized will of the Nation.' 1932   50

IV The Field-Marshal and the Corporal. 1933   51

V 'Russia arms! . . . and Germany?' 1933   82

VI 'They fought and bled for Germany's freedom.' 1932   83

VIIa Respectable Hitler. Forty-four years old,
    Germany's Chancellor. 1933   98
  b Austrian Nazis paint a *Hakenkreuz* on a rock
    face. 1934   98

VIIIa *SA* troopers and *Stürmer* posters. Party Rally,
    Nürnberg. 1935   99
  b 'Jews are not wanted here.' 1935   99

IXa Funeral orator. Dr. Goebbels. 1936   130
  b Goebbels at the Exhibition, 'Ten Years' Fight for
    Berlin'. 1936   130

Xa Austrian plebiscite posters. 1938   131
  b The first Nazi poster in Poland. ' England!
    This is your work!' 1939   131

XIa 'Check to the King!' 1940   146
  b Churchill, a sniper. 1941   146

XII The Soviet *Untermenschen* contrasted with the
    defenders of European civilization. 1941   147

INTRODUCTION

H ITLER's speech to the party rally on 12 September 1936 struck a high note of self-congratulation and compliment to his audience. The Germans were lucky to have found him, he said, as he was lucky to have found them; what obstacles might they not surmount when he himself had 'come from nothing to the head of a nation'?[1] This is not the place to consider the irony, or the accuracy, of the double piece of good fortune Hitler referred to. However, it is beyond dispute that his personal rise to power from obscurity was a notable achievement. As an aspiring politician, Hitler was badly placed. He entered the jungle of German post-war politics with so many handicaps that anyone versed in its ways would have advised him against embarking on a political career at all. His family background was undistinguished; his education was negligible, and it did not provide him with the still highly-prized *Verbindungen*—connexions that would have eased his ascent through the remaining traditional channels; his political attitudes alienated him from the new order established in Central Europe after the Great War. Although his military career in the war was distinguished by the award of an Iron Cross decoration his service, as an Austrian by birth, in the German army did not even secure him German citizenship on the con-clusion of hostilities.

Yet Hitler's rise to political power was amazingly rapid. He ran a public conspiracy against the Weimar Republic; he was a revolutionary only in the sense that he despised the Weimar 'system' and that he never thought in terms of the possibility of a compromise with it. He had no revolutionary tradition be-hind him comparable with that of, say, the Russian Bolsheviks: Hitler and his party created this tradition in Germany.

[1] Max Domarus, *Hitler, Reden und Proklamationen 1932–45*, vol. 1, page 643. Würzburg, 1962.

1

The practice of 'propaganda' became its integral—we may even say central—component. But in the hands of the Nazis it assumed a new significance. In the original meaning of the word propaganda was, first of all, the vehicle for a religious faith, or a political doctrine. This was the sense in which Pope Gregory XV used the term when he founded the *Congregatio de Propaganda Fide* in 1622. Later, the Marxist parties on the Continent used the term in a similar manner; their leaders were in the possession of a doctrine; propaganda was the means of giving it wider currency. The Russian Bolsheviks, on the other hand, drew a sharp distinction between agitation and propaganda. Whereas their agitation aims at influencing the masses, their propaganda is intended for indoctrinating the party *élite* with Marxist-Leninist doctrines. The National Socialists did not find it necessary to make this distinction. The poverty of their ideology was marked: National Socialism was basically an open invitation to an elect nation to indulge in the pursuit and the worship of naked power. And propaganda was an instrument for its achievement. It carried no consistent doctrine, but only an amorphous and opportunist set of ideas.

There can be no doubt that the Nazi ideological equipment could not stand comparison with the philosophies that lay behind the great universal movements in European history, be it Christianity or Marxist socialism. But the Nazis often put forward the claim that theirs was precisely such a movement: it sounded entirely hollow. As a claim to admission among the ranks of the immortals, Hitler's *magnum opus, Mein Kampf*, failed miserably. There were, however, two aspects of political activity in which the National Socialists excelled—party organization and propaganda.

The problems of organization began to occupy the leaders of many European political parties a long time before Hitler went into politics. It had been demonstrated—in the eighteen-nineties by the controversy conducted by the German Social Democrats and then by the split of 1903 inside the Russian Social Democracy —that the shape of a modern political party was closely bound up with its functions. Conspiracy and revolution on the one hand, and, on the other, reform through parliamentary means required totally different kinds of organization. The Nazi party, from its very beginnings until the *Machtergreifung* in 1933, stood in an intermediate position between conspiracy and reform: Hitler neither intended to come to terms with the established régime, nor was prepared, or indeed constrained, to renounce the advantages of running a mass organization. In fact two widely divergent impulses shaped the *NSDAP*; it was a party of revolutionary conspirators as well as a party of the masses. Hitler himself saw it as an exclusive '*élite*' group; he made a distinction between its 'followers' and 'members'. In *Mein Kampf* he wrote that 'the task of propaganda is to attract followers; the task of organization to win members. A follower of a movement is one who declares himself in agreement with its aims; a member is one who fights for it'.[2] He did not want the party to grow too large because 'a movement which enlarges itself *ad infinitum* would necessarily some day be weakened by this procedure'.[3] In this respect, however, he realized that his propaganda itself acted as agent of natural selection: 'the more radical and inciting my propaganda was, the more it frightened off weaklings and ir-resolute characters and prevented their pushing into the first nucleus of the organization'.[4] Propaganda spread the con-spirators' message to the masses, and it helped to widen the 'first nucleus' into a broad organization. But within it, the nucleus retained a separate, and higher, status. An official dis-tinction was later drawn between the *Altkämpfer*, the old Nazis, and the *Parteigenossen*, the regular party members. And in his own way, Hitler remained loyal to the old Nazis after he had seized power: they fared somewhat better than did the old Bolshevik guard under Stalin.

For Hitler, propaganda and organization were closely linked: on the scale of Nazi priorities, the former came first. His skill and interest in propaganda raised him from the ranks after the war, and it gained him entry into the political group that he was to make into his own party. He arrived in Munich in time to witness the meteoric rise and fall of the Bavarian Soviet Republic in April and May 1919, and he acted for a few months as a 'political education officer' to the First Bavarian Rifle Regiment. He had already earned a reputation among his senior officers as a man of

---

[2] *Mein Kampf*, pages 474–5. Translated by James Murphy, London, 1939.
[3] ibid., page 476.   [4] ibid., page 478.

3

2

sound ideas ~~who was capable of~~ impressing them on his friends in the ranks; his task as an agitator was simply to make good Germans—if not good republicans or democrats—from the troops infected with Marxist ideas. In this capacity Hitler came in touch with a small political group called the German Workers' Party, and soon he took charge of its propaganda activities. In the following three years, he transformed this group into a militant revolutionary organization, the National Socialist German Workers' Party, the *NSDAP*, which, early in 1922, included some 6,000 registered members.

Indeed, in the years of his apprenticeship as a politician in Munich, most aspects of political activity were synonymous, to Hitler, with propaganda; it was a way of pulling himself out of 'nothing' into prominence. There are two chapters dealing with propaganda in *Mein Kampf*:[5] on these pages Hitler achieved a level of clarity unequalled in other parts of the book.

Although Hitler rightly regarded the First World War as the proper starting point for an examination of propaganda, the first tentative steps were taken before 1914; young Hitler had an opportunity to observe the pioneers of mass propaganda at work in Vienna before the war. He acknowledged his debt to the 'Marxist Socialists' who, he said, had mastered the instrument and 'knew how to handle it in a masterly way and how to put it to practical uses. Thus I soon came to realize', Hitler added, 'that the right use of propaganda represents an art which was and remained almost entirely unknown to the bourgeois parties. Only the Christian-Socialist movement, especially during Lueger's time, acquired a certain virtuosity with this instrument and it owed much of its success to it'.[6]

In this connexion, Hitler had a revealing observation to make. When discussing the uses of propaganda before the war, he compared two politicians prominent in the Vienna of his youth: Karl Lueger and Georg Schönerer. They were both antisemites—the former only in public, the latter in private as well—but whereas Lueger was a Catholic and a loyal Habsburg subject, Schönerer became a Protestant who worshipped the Prussian dynasty.

---

[5] Chapter 6, vol. 1, deals with war and propaganda, and in chapter 11, vol. 2 he impact of propaganda on party organization is discussed.
[6] *Mein Kampf*, page 156.

Although Hitler approved of Schönerer's politics, he did not let this influence his judgement of the respective worth of the two men as politicians. Schönerer was playing up to upper-middle-class Germans: he lacked 'the force and understanding ... with which to transmit the theoretical knowledge to the masses'.[7] Lueger, on the other hand, had a 'rare gift of insight into human nature and he was careful not to take men as something better than they were in reality'. He ran a mass movement and he realized the value of propaganda: to him, Hitler awarded the higher marks.

The last lesson on the subject of propaganda, before Hitler embarked on his political career, was administered by the Allies during the First World War. He was highly critical of German propaganda during the war and gave all the credit to the Allies. But there is no indication that Hitler made an effort to understand the political and social realities that lay behind the work of the propagandists. As far as propaganda to their own countrymen was concerned, the Germans faced a more difficult task and they were less skilled then their opposite numbers among the western Allies. In Britain especially, the war-time Ministry of Information produced some noteworthy results. It was run by the press-lords—Beaverbrook, Northcliffe, and Rothermere—who were ably assisted by a large number of journalists. These men not only had an intimate knowledge of their public, but their public was more homogeneous than that in Germany, and even more so than in Austria–Hungary. The tensions that rent the Habsburg monarchy in October 1918 and brought about the revolution in Germany in the following month had existed during the war. National hostilities in Austria–Hungary, social antagonisms and profound political dissensions in Germany did not make the work of the propagandist in Vienna or Berlin easy.

Nor was Hitler much concerned with the actual content of propaganda: the fascination the subject exercised on him was largely of a technical nature. He saw propaganda essentially as a problem of political salesmanship in a mass market; he clearly perceived the similarity between selling a product and a politician to the people. For his purposes he had to form a precise estimate of the quality of the material he was going to work with. He

[7] ibid., page 94.

appreciated the possibilities offered by the entry of hitherto
apolitical, uneducated masses into political life. He knew that the
'masses' were indispensable for his aims: he did not believe, as
Jefferson had, that they consisted of individuals capable of
directing their own political destinies, nor did he regard them—as
the Russian *narodniki* had done—as a noble moving force of
national salvation.

Hitler thought of the masses as malleable, corrupt, and cor-
ruptible; their sentiment was 'not complex but simple and consistent'.[8] He answered the question 'to whom has propaganda to
appeal?' in an emphatic manner: it 'must always address itself
to the broad masses of the people'.[9] There was no point in trying
to influence the intellectuals: Hitler conceded that they would be
capable of forming their own opinions. The proper task of propaganda, he argued, was to bring certain subjects within the field
of vision of the masses.[10] He knew that a politically uneducated
mass public was bound to be receptive to emotive appeal rather
than to rational argument. Propaganda had to concentrate on as
few points as possible, it had to hammer them home repeatedly,
it had to present them in terms of black and white. It could afford
to make no concessions to the other side.

But all this was not enough. Hitler knew that the kind of
propaganda he had in mind required stiffening with a large dose of
intimidation and terror. According to his own testimony, he had
first noticed this technique in Vienna before the war: pressure was
brought to bear on the workers to join the trade unions, and
character assassination of political opponents was, in Hitler's
view, one of the main features of the Social Democrat press.[11]
Whatever the case may have been Hitler resolved, early in his
political career, 'to fight poison gas by poison gas';[12] he resolved
that lies had to be countered by still bigger lies, and that terror
cringed when confronted with a still more frightful terror.

By the time Hitler left Landsberg prison in December 1924, the
foundations of National Socialist ideology, as well as the basic
views on the party's two main concerns—propaganda and
organization—had been formulated. Superficially, they did not

[8] *Mein Kampf*, page 161.   [9] ibid., page 158.
[10] ibid., page 158.   [11] ibid., pages 46 and 49.
[12] ibid., page 49.

change much in the subsequent years. The Nazi theorists produced little but glosses on Hitler's views; party organization and propaganda continued to be regarded as forming the hard core of the Nazi scheme of things. In fact, however, all these three aspects of National Socialist activity underwent considerable changes. The ideological content of National Socialist agitation of course followed the demands of political circumstances; the party and its propaganda both gained and suffered, after 1933, from their close connexion with the state. Hitler always avidly grasped at every new instrument of power, be it the army or the administrative machinery of the state. The position of propaganda therefore depended largely on Hitler's main preoccupations at the time. It was only during the *Kampfzeit*, the 'period of struggle' which lasted until 30 January 1933, that propaganda retained its privileged position as the highway to power in the state.

This study is an examination of the part played by the manipulation and control of public opinion in the National Socialists' capture and exercise of power in Germany, as well as of the manner in which Hitler's government employed propaganda in its bid for power abroad. The concept of propaganda is understood here in its broadest sense: in the same sense, in fact, the National Socialists themselves employed it.

The first chapter concerns its role in Hitler's capture of power in Germany; it is followed by a chapter on the accommodation and the role of propaganda within the framework of the National Socialist state. Like the early Soviet rulers, Hitler and his party on the whole preferred the employment of propaganda rather than of diplomacy in regard to the outside world: starting from this proposition, the third chapter deals with the technical arrangements for propaganda abroad. The fourth chapter sets out to illustrate the connexion between National Socialist propaganda at home and abroad, by discussing its two main themes: antisemitism and anti-Communism. Of all the mass media, Goebbels thought broadcasting the most suitable for his purposes: broadcasting in Germany is discussed in chapter II, to the outside world in chapter V. It is very likely that in the course of the Saarland broadcasting campaign in the year 1934 the Nazi propagandists came to appreciate the peculiar merits of

7

the technique of creating a 'bridge' between the Germans inside and outside the Reich: the technique was later employed in other media.

The problems of appealing to the Germans outside the Reich are discussed in the following chapters in greater detail: from the failure of the Nazi *putsch* in Austria, in the summer of 1934, the National Socialist leaders learned one of the most important lessons in regard to propaganda abroad. From 1934 to the outbreak of the war—in the chapters III–VII—our attention shifts mainly to Hitler's foreign propaganda: indeed, so does the interest of the Führer and of the other National Socialist leaders. Inside Germany, apart from persuasion, the National Socialist régime had captured the means of coercion; outside the Reich, however, propaganda remained the chief instrument for the achievement of political aims. Finally, the last chapter deals with the special situation created by the war.

Lenin's dictum that the Soviet state rested on a balance of persuasion and coercion applies to Hitler's Germany just as much as to all the other one-party states Europe has seen in this century: both coercion and persuasion were, and still are, aimed to make the state acceptable to its citizens. It appears that the coercive aspects of one-party states exercise a certain fascination on writers and readers alike. In comparison with the vast literature descriptive of coercion, be it in Nazi Germany or the Soviet Union, the attempts of such states to persuade either their own citizens or those of other countries have received only scant attention.[13] Herein lies the main justification for adding this book to the already voluminous literature on National Socialist Germany. But there are other considerations: the history of National Socialism is now a self-contained unit; in its course a massive attempt at persuasion was made: it is the only one on which documentation is available;[14] because of its lack of ideological content propaganda can be seen to operate, as it were, in its pure form. Also, this was the first time in the history of Europe that one-party propaganda was carried out in a highly industrialized state.

---

[13] There exist two specialist studies of Nazi propaganda, published since the end of the war, in German: one by Dr. Walter Hagemann and one by Dr. Karlheinz Schmeer; Dr. Inkeles's book, *Public opinion in the Soviet Union* 1951, is the only study, in English, of Soviet propaganda.

[14] See Bibliography.

I. THE CONQUEST OF THE MASSES

O N the morning of 20 December 1924, a large Daimler-Benz was parked opposite the entrance to Landsberg prison. The driver and Heinrich Hoffmann, a photographer, were sitting in the car, watching the prison gates. Soon Hitler walked out, a free man after thirteen months of incarceration. Hoffmann was not allowed to photograph him leaving the prison; the three men drove off and then stopped at the gate of the old town wall. There, Hoffmann took several photographs of Hitler, next to the imposing motor car, wearing the familiar belted mackintosh. On the same day, the keen photographer sent the picture to a number of newspapers, with the ambiguous caption: 'Adolf Hitler leaves Landsberg fortress'. It easily lent itself to misinterpretation; indeed, the following day all the newspapers that printed it provided it with dramatic captions, such as 'The first step to freedom' and 'The fortress gate has opened'. Remembering the incident, Hoffmann wrote: 'When I received my copies, I could not help laughing'.[1] The first small dishonesty by propaganda was committed a few hours after Hitler's release from prison.

At this time the party was in a bad way. It had been banned by the Bavarian government; some of its founding members were left behind in prison; some had not been able to return from exile; a few had died. The Nazis who remained at large quarrelled among themselves, and had proved themselves incapable of piloting the party safely through its difficulties. Hitler had to start all over again; he returned from prison rested and full of energy.

He had to revive the party and gather the threads of power once again in his own hands. First of all he had to get the ban on the Nazi movement and its newspaper lifted; he succeeded in doing so a fortnight after his release from prison, during a short

[1] Heinrich Hoffmann, *Hitler was my Friend*, page 61.

9

conversation with the Bavarian Prime Minister. On 26 February, the *Völkischer Beobachter*[2] appeared for the first time after a gap of more than fifteen months. Hitler's name was given as that of the publisher. It printed a proclamation by the Führer on the front page, and an announcement of a great public mass-meeting at the Bürgerbräukeller on the following day, to which all former party members were invited; it was expressly stated that no Jews could be admitted.

Some four thousand Nazis crowded into the large hall from which the ill-fated *putsch* in November 1923 had been launched; the rivalries among their leaders who came as well as among those who did not were deadly. Nevertheless, Hitler's first political meeting was carefully stage-managed. A lot of hand-shaking took place on the platform, and smiling faces bore witness to the good chances for the rebirth and unity of the party. No discussion or questions were allowed; Max Amann had done a lot to make smooth proceedings possible, and he said that Hitler alone was capable of leading the movement. During a speech that lasted over two hours, Hitler proved that he had not lost his touch as an orator. The audience fell under his spell, and it is possible that some of the more prominent members of the movement, who had resented Hitler's ambitions, came round while he spoke.

Indeed, public speaking was, at the time, Hitler's main propaganda weapon. Although he usually put down 'writer' as his profession at this time, he could not hope to make any political capital out of political writing: it was not a suitable means for the kind of persuading Hitler wanted to do, and anyway he was not very good at it. He was convinced that all the important revolutionary events had been brought about not by the written, but by the spoken word. But Hitler had in mind the relation between the orator and his audience; his inability to sway a small number of *individuals* has often been contrasted with his supreme skill in bending large crowds to his will.[3] Hitler was at his most effective when his message reached the listener through a haze of mass hysteria; he preferred convincing individuals through the masses rather than the other way round.

[2] See page 22.
[3] Konrad Heiden, *Adolf Hitler*, page 199.

By 1925 Hitler's public speaking had acquired all the qualities that put him into a class of his own. He was not an impromptu speaker: usually, he prepared his speeches in advance. They do not read very well: their contents alone are not an adequate indication as to the effect they actually created at the time of their delivery. Hitler's power as a speaker lay mainly in the *rapport* he established between himself and his audience. The opening moves of every speech he made were hesitant. The attitude of his body was stiff, he was feeling his way like a blind man; his voice was muted and monotonous. After a few minutes, this apparent unwillingness to communicate gave way to a steadier, louder flow of sentences; the speaker's muscles visibly relaxed, and he was soon to begin using his right arm in gestures that resembled blows aimed at an invisible nail. Then the flow increased into a torrent; the punch-line was delivered in a loud, sometimes hoarse, high-pitched voice; the end was abrupt. A new paragraph, another train of thought, was then introduced in a softer voice, though not in the same halting manner as the opening of the speech; the clockwork was again seen by the spellbound audience to unwind itself, the *crescendo* was once more achieved, and wiped out by a wide sweep of the right arm. The onslaught on the eardrums of the audience was tremendous: it was estimated that the frequency of Hitler's voice in a typical sentence was 228 vibrations per second, whereas 200 vibrations is the usual frequency of a voice raised in anger.[4]

Hitler was not, as we have already noted, interested in converting the intellectuals, and there is no reason to suppose that many came to his early meetings. The larger part of the audience, whose critical powers were only indifferently developed, were soon battered into a state of passive receptiveness by the torrential flow of Hitler's words. During the two hours or longer, he conducted them through a number of highly emotive states; at the conclusion of the speech, they had shared a profound experience with the speaker. He appealed to the emotions rather than to the reason of his audience; in the words of Hjalmar Schacht, 'he could play like a virtuoso on the well-tempered piano of the lower-middle-class hearts'.[5] But what Hitler said mattered far

[4] N.D. Fabricant, *13 Famous Patients*, page 43.
[5] *Account Settled*, page 206. Cf. Alan Bullock, *Adolf Hitler, A study in tyranny*, 1962, page 68.

less than how he said it; he found the right mould for his speeches early in his career, and he never had to recast it.

During his conversation with Bavaria's Prime Minister in January 1925, Hitler doubtless had made a promise to conduct the activities of the party within the limits of legality: no more revolutions and revolutionary agitation. He was, however, used to moving on the border-line of legitimate political activity and conspiracy; as soon as he mounted the speaker's rostrum, he was unable to control his sentiments against the established authority. On 9 March, ten days after his first appearance in the Bürgerbräukeller, Hitler was forbidden to make public speeches in Bavaria, and soon the governments of other federal states followed suit. In the end he was able to speak only in Thüringia, Braunschweig, and Mecklenburg. This did not mean that the movement entirely lost its most effective means of agitation; meetings were arranged in the three states that had not placed the ban on Hitler, or, if they took place elsewhere, they were advertised as closed meetings for party members; the party publishing house printed Hitler's speeches in pamphlet form in large editions.

Nevertheless, the first concentrated Nazi propaganda campaign was in fact occasioned by the ban on Hitler's public speaking. On 20 April 1926 a meeting in celebration of Hitler's thirty-seventh birthday took place in Munich; at the same time, the party organ published a rather flattering drawing of Hitler's head, with two pieces of sticking plaster across his mouth, bearing the inscription 'Ban on speaking'[6] and the caption: 'Alone among 2,000 million people of the world he is not allowed to speak in Germany!' Hitler put in an appearance at his birthday meeting in Munich, but he remained silent; Julius Streicher spoke on the subject 'Why is Hitler not allowed to speak?', and a letter from the Nazi-organized 'Action Committee for the Organization of People's Protest Against the Ban on Adolf Hitler's Speaking'[7] was presented to Hitler. According to the text of the letter, 1,234 propaganda cells of the *NSDAP* had collected signatures for the protest.

[6] *Redeverbot.*
[7] *Aktionausschuss zur Durchführung des Volksprotestes wider das Redeverbot Adolf Hitlers.*

In the following years the Nazis used every means to get the ban lifted. Early in 1927, the legal committee of the *Reichstag* turned down a petition by Dr. Frick, a Nazi deputy; the responsible civil servant said that although the ban was unconstitutional, foreigners could not claim any benefits granted by the constitution.[8] Such pronouncements of course aided the Nazi campaign. It was typical of the corrupt federal government and of the contemptible *Reichstag*, they loudly complained, to treat as a foreigner a man who had been born in the '*Ostmark*'—a term for Austria which reduced that country to the status of a German province—and who had spent four and a half years as a front-line soldier in the German army. After two years, the campaign began paying dividends. On 11 February 1927, Saxony, the last state to have imposed the ban, lifted it; the Bavarian government allowed Hitler to speak in public from 5 March, and, finally, the Prussian authorities did the same in September 1928.

Apart from the ban on Hitler's speaking, the regional governments took a variety of administrative measures against the Nazi movement in the twenties. In June 1925, for instance, public collection of contributions for party coffers was forbidden in Munich; in May 1927 the party was banned in Berlin; in July 1929 the police banned the opening ceremony of the Brown House, the new party headquarters in Munich; at the end of the summer, a trial on charges of high treason of several junior army officers with Nazi leanings took place in Leipzig. But such sporadic attempts as were made never seriously threatened the party's existence; they were only too easily exploited by the Nazi propagandists, who presented them as administrative chicanery directed against a respectable patriotic movement.

The Nazis were not seriously disturbed in their pursuits in the last years of the decade. Their mass-meetings were frequent and carefully arranged around a speech by Hitler or other prominent members of the movement; they did away with any semblance of democratic procedure. The mass of the followers were never consulted by the leaders; they were always confronted with one voice, one will, one opinion; they were never given an opportunity to ask questions. Mass-meetings usually took place, on weekdays and weekends alike, late in the evening—they usually began at

[8] *Sammlung Rehse*, page 254.

8 p.m.—when, as Hitler maintained, man's suggestibility was high, and his resistance at its lowest ebb. The pattern of the Nazi assemblies was developed during these years; their programme was arranged with the precision of a railway time-table. The *Parteitag*—the party rally—was the sum total of the various forms of Nazi meetings, and it was designed to be the crowning experience of party life for the rank-and-file members.

The first and last of these congresses before the unsuccessful Munich *putsch* had taken place in January 1923; by the middle of 1926, the party had recovered sufficiently to hold such a rally. The second *Parteitag* in the history of the *NSDAP* took place in Weimar, on 3 and 4 July. In the afternoon of the first day, some 10,000 Nazis assembled in Marktplatz, the main square in Weimar, and the meeting was concluded by a parade of the party para-military organizations, the *SA* and the *SS*, before Hitler. In the evening of the first day of the Weimar rally, Hitler spoke at the National Theatre on the subject 'Politics, Idea, and Organization': the meeting ran on customary lines. First, the rank-and-file members walked in and took their seats; then the uniformed troopers, carrying their standards, arrived and took up their positions—they were there for decorative purposes as well as to prevent heckling—then the leaders of the movement walked down the centre passage and, last of all, Hitler himself. The tension that had been built up among the audience by the introductory proceedings lasted through the first hesitating sentences of his speech; it was released by the increasing torrent of words.

In August of the following year, another *Parteitag* was arranged, the first of the famous Nürnberg rallies. According to the estimates of the local railway officials, more than 100,000 Nazis were brought to Nürnberg in special trains;[9] fifty members of the Berlin *SA* had marched all the way from the capital to Bavaria. The main programme of the rally was opened by a 'congress of delegates' on Saturday morning, 20 August; the day was closed by an effective innovation: a torchlight procession of the *SA*. Many of the visitors to the rally spent the night sleeping on the floors, thinly covered with straw, of the vast exhibition pavilions at Luitpoldhain; early on Sunday morning they were rewarded by watching their Führer present colours to

[9] *Sammlung Rehse*, page 268.

twelve detachments of the *SA*. Shortly before 11 a.m., some 30,000 *SA* and *SS* troops, together with contingents from Austria and Czechoslovakia, marched past Hitler in the main square.

All the basic features of Nazi stage-management were present at the Nürnberg rally in the summer of 1927. The leader and his speeches, the open-air demonstration and the large indoor meeting; the flags, the insignia, the songs, the *Heil* greetings. These were by no means brand-new techniques of political agitation; what was new, however, was the intensive and calculated use that was made of them. The headpiece of the *SA* standard was a three-dimensional replica of the design on the *Völkischer Beobachter*; it had been used by the *SA* since 1923. Hitler had worked out the design himself, giving careful attention to every detail. He was attracted to the symbol of the eagle apparently because he had found it described, in an antisemitic encyclopaedia, as the 'Aryan in the world of animals'; it was important for him that the headpiece of the design should be 'upwards striving'.[10] The Nazis took over many songs from the *Freikorps'* repertoire, and they acquired their own, a *Tonpoem* rather than a song, in the poem by Dietrich Eckart, a friend of Hitler. It began with the line '*Sturm, Sturm, Sturm,*' and ended with '*Deutschland erwache!*'—Germany awake—the Nazi's favourite battle-cry. It was first sung at the rally in 1923, and it had been carefully rehearsed by Hitler himself. Only much later did the Nazis acquire a ponderous march, the *Horst Wessellied*, for their signature tune.

They also adopted the ancient form of the *Heil* greeting; it had been used by the 'back-to-nature' movement of the *Wandervogel* before the First World War, as well as by a number of nationalist movements, in variations such as '*Im deutschen Namen Heil!*' and '*Sieg und Heil!*'; the Nazis later reduced it to the more succinct '*Sieg Heil*', a formula especially effective as a chant at mass demonstrations. The alternative greeting—*Heil Hitler*—more suitable for encounters between two Nazis—had first appeared on banners during the Munich municipal elections in 1924. Indeed, the show the Nazi movement presented was all the more effective against the matter-of-fact drabness of everyday

[10] Karlheinz Schmeer, *Die Regie des öffentlichen Lebens im Dritten Reich*, page 14.

15

life in the Weimar Republic. It was a splash of bright colour on the subdued background of post-war Germany.

But these were the gentle means of persuasion used by the Nazis. Propaganda alone was not enough for them: we have already noted Hitler's views on its connexions with violence.[11] The same idea was stated openly and concisely by Eugen Hadamovsky, who later became the chief of German broadcasting: 'Propaganda and the graduated use of violence have to be employed together in a skilful manner. They are never absolutely opposed to each other. The use of violence can be a part of propaganda.'[12] This axiom had far-reaching practical consequences for the Nazis. They knew that, if they wanted to carry out their propaganda successfully, they had to dominate the streets. In the words of the *Horst Wessellied*, 'Free the street for the brown battalions'.

When the Nazi movement embarked on its public career early in the decade, the streets belonged to the Communists and the Social Democrats. The National Socialists showed themselves in the public thoroughfares of Munich only fleetingly, being conveyed on lorries to their meetings at one or other of the beer-cellars. But in order to be able to break out into the streets, they had to gain strength as a powerful para-military organization. We have already seen that any disturbance, even mild heckling, had no place in Hitler's conception of political meetings; since the early days of the movement, there were always *Ordner* present, men whose task was to ensure smooth proceedings: they were the chuckers-out of political enemies.

In addition, the bloody encounters played, especially in the early history of the party, an important role in securing publicity for it. In an official textbook for German youth which appeared in Berlin in 1938, the author flatly stated that 'The greatest difficulty of the party lay in the fact that . . . nobody took any notice of it'. Rough methods of keeping order at meetings helped. 'Now at last', the author went on in his bright manner,

the party had found the means to shake the newspapers from their icy reserve! Here was the rope by which it could pull itself from the depths of being ignored to the daylight of 'public opinion'. The

[11] See page 6.
[12] Karlheinz Schmeer, op. cit., page 9.

16

criticism of its endeavours made in the press was very acid and unfriendly, because its wishes and aims were never touched upon. From now on, therefore, every opportunity was grasped to answer even the most insignificant provocation by a neat chucking-out. And lo and behold! From this time on, the bourgeois and the Red press dealt with the bad Nazis almost every day.[13]

The meeting at Munich Hofbräuhaus on 4 November 1921 was officially regarded as the foundation date of the *Sturmabteilungen*.[14] On this occasion, a large number of 'Marxists' came to listen to Hitler's speech, and a clash occurred between them and the Nazis. This was the first *Saalschlacht*—a battle in a political assembly hall—in which the Nazis took part, and there were many bloody engagements to come; it was a gang warfare with its own rules. At this time, the Nazis were not only unable to show themselves in public but they also had a difficult time of it protecting their own meetings against hostile intruders from the street.

The *SA* troops were originally divided into groups of one hundred men, the *Hundertschaften*; by September 1922, eight 'hundreds' were in existence in Munich; on 23 November, the organization of the eleventh unit was completed under the leadership of Rudolf Hess. Hitler intended these units to show the 'Marxists' that National Socialism is 'the future ruler of the street just as it will eventually become the ruler of the state'.[15] Indeed, the domination of the street was, for the Nazis, the key to political power in the state.

In August 1922, several *SA* units demonstrated, together with other extreme right-wing groups, against the law for the protection of the Republic; in October, they ventured unaided into the streets of Coburg, during the celebrations of the *Deutsche Tag*. Hitler arrived in a special train, together with some eight hundred *SA* troopers on 14 October, and they marched into the streets of the provincial town in North Bavaria; after some short, sharp clashes they succeeded in clearing the streets of their political opponents. This was a memorable day for Hitler: ten years later all the surviving participants of the Coburg march received a special decoration.

---

[13] Philipp Bouhler, *Kampf um Deutschland*, pages 46–47.
[14] Ernst Bayer, *Die SA. Schriften der Hochschule für Politik*, page 8.
[15] ibid., page 9.

In 1922 and early 1923, the foundations of Hitler's paramilitary organization were laid. The first application forms for entry into the *SA* were printed, and they put special stress on enquiries into the military experience of the applicant; a rudimentary uniform made its first appearance. Early in 1923 their first standards, designed by Hitler, appeared at the *SA* congress in Munich; two months later, Hermann Göring, the last commander of the famous Richthofen flying squadron in the First World War, took over the command of all the *SA* units.

At this time—in March 1923—a group of eight men was separated from the main body of the *SA*, and set up as Hitler's personal bodyguard under the command of Julius Schreck. It became known as *Stosstrupp Hitler*, the forerunner of the *SS*. When Hitler re-established the party in February 1925, the *SA* was still banned; in the following year, the ban was lifted and the stormtroopers reappeared at the Weimar rally. For the time being, the small *Schutzstaffel* took over the original duty of the *SA*, namely that of *Ordner* at political meetings. In the circumstances, the task of the early *SS* men was extremely difficult, and they had to be recruited from the toughest members of the former *SA*. Hitler was allowed to speak in Saxony and Thüringia,[16] and a large number of meetings were organized there; the two states had strong Communist parties—they were 'at the time entirely red Saxony and Thüringia' in Nazi terminology[17]— and the *SS* often found it difficult to prevent the enemies of the Nazi party from breaking up its meetings. Nevertheless, when the *SA* re-emerged in the course of 1926, its members once more took care of the party meetings, and the *SS*, some two hundred strong at the time, was incorporated into the older organization, and placed under the authority of its Supreme Command. Only three years later, early in 1929, the future began to look brighter for the *SS* men when Heinrich Himmler was asked by Hitler to build the organization into an *élite* corps of the party.

In the meantime, however, Hitler placed his reliance on the *SA*. On 1 November 1926, its Supreme Command was established in Munich, with Franz von Pfeffer, the party leader from

---

[16] See page 12.

[17] Gunter D'Alquen, *Die SS, Geschichte, Aufgabe und Organisation der Schutzstaffeln der NSDAP*, page 202. Neusüss-Hunkel, *Die SS*, page 7.

the Ruhr area, as its head; in the following months, a thorough reorganization of the *SA* was carried out. At the rally of 1927, the stormtroopers arrived in full strength: no dissentient voice was heard either at the party meetings or in the streets of Nürnberg. The Nazis were able to take over the town for the duration of the *Parteitag*. Nevertheless, the place for the meeting had to be carefully chosen, and Nürnberg was a highly suitable location. It was not the capital of a state, and it was surrounded by the provinces with strong Nazi party organizations: it was easily accessible, for instance, to party members from the neighbouring Bayrische Ostmark.[18]

Indeed, the varying local conditions profoundly affected the life of the party in these years. Its main strength was still concentrated in Bavaria; in many other German states the Nazis found themselves faced with a hostile attitude on the part of both the local authorities and the population. There was no question of holding the 1927 *Parteitag* in, say, Berlin, instead of Nürnberg. In May that year, the Prussian authorities banned the party and the *SA*; in a number of other German states, the ban on the *SA* uniform also became operative. The *SA* leaders tried to circumvent these bans as best they could. It was quite simple to ignore the ban on uniforms, and to exploit it for the purposes of propaganda. The National Socialists were able to publicize yet another example of 'chicanery' by the administration; the *SA* troops arrived at their meetings in white shirts, or half naked, or in their underclothes. After May 1927 Dr. Goebbels coined the slogan for the Berlin *SA* '*Trotz Verbot, nicht tot*'—not dead despite the ban'; many of the Berlin stormtroopers went to the Nürnberg rally, and they put on their uniforms in the special trains on the way to Bavaria; some of the forgetful enthusiasts who omitted to change into their civilian clothes on the return journey to Berlin were arrested when they got off the train.

In Berlin, the characteristic *Saalschlachten* of the 'period of struggle' took place just as in other German towns; the battle in the Pharus assembly hall, the 'fortress of Berlin Communism,'[19] on 11 February 1927, was the first of many fierce engagements.

---

[18] A Nazi *Gau*, which consisted of three Bavarian provinces: Oberfranken, Oberpfalz, and Niederbayern.
[19] See pages 26–8.

3

But here, in the German capital, the stormtroopers developed a new technique of offensive warfare. In the late twenties they were faced with powerful opposition, Social Democrat and Communist, among the Berlin workers; they split up into small groups, which met in private flats and then, anonymous in dark streets, proceeded to break up any Communist or Socialist meeting going on. Such commando tactics were suitable and successful in the circumstances; for an effective terrorist activity a small number of men was sufficient, and they could operate regardless of official bans. In the words of an official Nazi pamphlet, the *SA* became 'the fist and the propaganda arm'[20] of the movement; apart from providing very useful publicity for the party, the formation of a political army injected an element of violence into the propaganda effort, an element that appeared indispensable to the Nazi theorists.

In terms of numbers, however, the party was far from being a formidable movement in the years before the economic slump; in 1927, only 72,590 Germans paid their membership dues to the *NSDAP*.[21] But Hitler knew how to display the comparatively small numbers to their best advantage: the overall impression created by the Nürnberg rally was one of a highly disciplined, powerful movement. This was largely due to the *SA* organization which amounted, at this time, to nearly half the total registered membership of the party. And with good stage-management, the march-past of some 30,000 stormtroopers could be spun out to last five hours, and create the impression that the stream of partisans of the new movement was indeed endless. The marchers themselves, on the other hand, achieved a still more intense emotional state than the onlookers. They were proud to be marching under the swastika flag; they were self-assured, superior; they belonged to a select community.[22] Their intoxication bound them more closely together; if marching could have such a powerful effect, fighting the common enemy proved a still stronger tie. The *Saalschlacht*, the street battles, the sudden commando raids, were not merely a means of intimidating political opponents. On this subject, Otto Strasser, a Nazi who had to flee Germany in 1935, wrote from his Canadian exile: 'The battle,

[20] E. Bayer, op. cit., page 8. [21] *Sammlung Rehse*, page 270.
[22] K. Schmeer, op. cit., page 18.

however, rather than destroying the purpose of our meeting, actually strengthened it enormously. All those who still remained in the hall after the fight had taken our side in a sort of spontaneous partnership. The bitter struggle had brought about that spirit of *camaraderie* which is engendered when men go through physical conflict together. A short time before they had been doubtful of us, suspicious, as are all human beings of an offer of something for nothing. Now that attitude was changed. We had become allies if only by force of circumstance.'[23]

While Hitler was on his way to supreme power, the Nazis transformed the streets of German towns into a battlefield. Theirs was, of course, not the only movement that had 'political troops' at its disposal. *Reichsbanner*—an association for the protection of the Republic—commanded a strong fighting section; there was the ex-servicemen's *Stahlhelm* and the Communist *Rotfront-Kämpferbund* and the *Antifaschistischer Kämpf-bund*; the Bavarian People's Party was a latecomer with its *Bayernwacht*. Indeed, in the words of Mr. Clark, a contemporary observer of Germany's political scene:[24] 'if one had the military imagination, the parties seemed like phantoms and these [i.e. the para-military organizations] the only realities. If they were all let loose the Thirty Years War would rank as a minor catastrophe'. As a weapon of propaganda, the *SA* came to rank perhaps higher than Hitler's speeches. To stimulate emotion and violence, and to benefit by their interaction, were the first aims of Nazi propagandists. They were, however, less successful in translating this method into the terms of the printed word.

We know that writing took for Hitler a much inferior second place to speaking; it was clear that the effect of his speeches, when printed in pamphlet form during the official *Redeverbot*,[25] fell far short of the impact of the actual speech. But Hitler believed, possibly quite mistakenly, in the necessity of owning a newspaper; after all, every political movement ran its own organ. A newspaper was for him a sign that the movement was prospering; it was an advance from the time when the party had to rely on meetings and leaflets only. He developed his views on the press

[23] Otto Strasser and Michael Stern, *Flight from Terror*, page 107.
[24] *The Fall of the German Republic*, page 288.
[25] See page 12.

early in his career, and they were those of a rabid nationalist. One of the points of the party programme that was first expounded at a meeting in Munich on 24 February 1920 dealt exclusively with the press: 'We demand a legislative fight against conscious political lies and their spreading by the press. In order to make the creation of a German press possible, we demand that (a) All editors and writers on newspapers printed in the German language must be compatriots (*Volksgenossen*). (b) State permission will be necessary for the publication of non-German newspapers. They must not be printed in the German language. (c) Every kind of financial backing of German newspapers or influence on them by non-Germans will be forbidden by law, and we demand as punishment for its breach the closing down of the newspaper as well as an immediate deportation of the foreigners who participated in it. Newspapers which oppose public welfare are to be forbidden. We demand a legislative fight against such trends in art and literature that have a corrosive effect on our national life and the closing down of institutions that run counter to the above-mentioned demands.'[26]

Some months after the publication of this programme the party acquired the *Völkischer Beobachter*. The National Socialist organ was some thirty-two years older than the party. In January 1887 a Munich printer began to publish a weekly, the *Münchener Beobachter*, as the trade journal of the local butchers' guild. After an eventful but obscure existence it became, in August 1919, the *Völkischer Beobachter*. It was then run on *völkisch* and antisemitic lines, until, in December 1920, the National Socialist party bought it for 120,000 Marks.[27]

The early history of the Nazi press is closely connected with the development of this paper. The issue of 25 December 1920, which brought the announcement that the paper had been taken over by the *NSDAP*, was printed in 800 copies only; its first Nazi editor was soon succeeded by Dietrich Eckart, the poet, and Alfred Rosenberg, the ideologist of the movement, as joint editors. During the first two years as the organ of the party, the *Völkischer Beobachter* frequently ran into difficulties; it was

[26] Adolf Dresler, Der Führer und die Presse, *Zeitungswissenschaft, Monatsschrift für internationale Zeitungsforschung*, vol. 14, No. 5, 1939.
[27] See the *Wiener Library Bulletin*, September–December 1954.

often confiscated or banned. When it became, in August 1923, a daily, it was still a local Bavarian newspaper; its circulation had, however, risen to some 25,000 copies. After the failure of the *putsch*, the *Völkischer Beobachter* disappeared from the Munich newspaper stands until 26 February 1925; in its special number on that day—the official date of the 're-establishment' of the party—it printed Hitler's exhortation to its readers for the setting up of a press fund. 'If one can judge the value of a newspaper by the hatred of its enemies, then it was the most valuable paper in Germany', Hitler wrote, and he added: 'The hatred of Jews, of the Marxist criminals, of racketeers like Barmat and Kutisker, was poured out on no other newspaper as much as on the organ of the *NSDAP*, the *Völkischer Beobachter*'.[28]

When the newspaper reappeared in February 1925, 10,000 copies were printed; from 4 April onwards, it again became a daily, and its circulation climbed, albeit slowly, until it reached in 1929 the figure of 26,715 copies.[29] In July 1926, the *Illustrierter Beobachter*, the party organ's sister publication, began to appear in the course of the rally in Weimar. The oldest ally of the official Nazi newspaper was Julius Streicher's weekly, *Der Stürmer*, the first numbers of which appeared in Nürnberg in November 1923, shortly before the Munich *putsch*; it also suffered a temporary eclipse after the ban on the party and its press. The circulation of these three newspapers was largely confined to South Germany in the nineteen-twenties; in Berlin, the Strasser brothers, Gregor and Otto, ran their own organ, the *Berliner Arbeiterzeitung*. Hitler disapproved of the *Arbeiterzeitung* as much as he did of its publishers; the balance on the press front in Berlin began to change in Hitler's favour when Goebbels—he had deserted the Strassers and was now giving his full support to Hitler[30]—launched his small weekly, *Der Angriff*, in July 1927. From 1 October 1929, it started to appear twice a week, and from November of the following year daily.

Indeed, until the Nazi success in the elections in September 1930, the party press did not do at all well. In the summer of that year, only six Nazi dailies were printed in the whole of Germany;

---

[28] *Sammlung Rehse*, page 221.
[29] Hans A. Münster, *Geschichte der deutschen Presse*, page 113.
[30] See page 26.

five of them appeared in Bavaria, and one in Schleswig-Holstein. And of the Bavarian daily newspapers, only the *Völkischer Beobachter* had some tenuous claims to be described as a national newspaper. It was then printing a Berlin, as well as a Munich, edition; its circulation was, however, still rather low—84,511 copies were sold in 1930.[31] Apart from the dailies, there were some forty-three weeklies and other periodicals; they commanded—apart perhaps from the *Illustrierter Beobachter*—little influence and a small readership.

The failure of the Nazi press could not be explained by financial and technical difficulties only. Although it had a certain prestige value for the Nazi leaders, it was not a very suitable vehicle for their propaganda. As late as January 1932, Goebbels complained in his diary: 'Only a few flames are burning in Germany. The others only reflect their light. With the newspapers it's worst: we have the best speakers in the world, but we lack nimble and skilful pens.'[32] There was a good reason for this: the movement did not attract many writers and journalists, and anyway, the translation of Nazi propaganda into the cold columns of the printed word was far from easy. The Nazis of course had to make the attempt, and they produced some interesting innovations.

In all their publications, the leader was short, hard-hitting, calculated to attract immediate attention, to strike a responsive chord rather than to stimulate reflection in the reader. The Nazis did not indulge in the long, ponderous, thoughtful leading articles, the hall-mark of the German Socialist press; nor were they tempted to follow the earlier practice of the Social Democrat organs of printing learned tracts on academic subjects. The *Illustrierter Beobachter* was intended to be a popular tabloid newspaper; in its early issues, it exhibited the characteristic features that were to be found, to a greater or lesser extent, in all the Nazi press. It contained news items of course but they were largely dedicated to the greater glory of the movement: the paper first appeared immediately after the rally in July 1926, and it contained impressive photographs of the proceedings in Weimar. Political *reportage* continued to be confined, almost exclusively,

[31] H. A. Münster, op. cit., page 113.
[32] J. Goebbels, *Vom Kaiserhof zur Reichskanzlei*, page 17.

to one subject: the National-Socialist movement marching forward. Pictures of meetings, demonstrations, and processions were always present: reporting on other topics, insofar as it took place at all, was heavily slanted, and since no demand for objective reporting was ever formulated by the Nazis, there was no need to distinguish between fact and comment.

Violence, death and sex also found their place in the Nazi press. Although the party journalists were no prudes, their treatment of these subjects was prudish in a special sense. The London tabloid newspapers, for instance, deal with such items on their own merits: they are reported because they are starkly dramatic and they have an obvious appeal. The Nazi journalists gave them a new twist. The murder of a peaceful citizen caused by jealousy, desire for gain—any of the 'civil' motives—was of no interest to them; the death of an *SA* trooper in a beer-hall fight, on the other hand, was a highly charged subject, which was invariably given a lot of space. Scandalous gossip about the Jews also rated high on the priority list—this form of journalism had been introduced by Julius Streicher in *Der Stürmer*. 'Ritual murder', for instance, was a hardy perennial; it combined anti-semitism, violence, and sex in equal proportions.

Neither truth nor objectivity were regarded as ideals worthy of achievement. The political struggle, the social scene, had to be presented in the simplest terms of black and white. Nevertheless, the Nazis did not rely only on generalizations; both Streicher and Goebbels preferred to concentrate their attacks on individuals instead, and to invest them with all the hateful qualities they could think of. Goebbels in particular developed this technique in *Der Angriff*. He would pick on a member of the Weimar Republic's 'establishment'—Dr. Weiss, the Jewish deputy chief of the Berlin police, was his favourite target—and then heap abuse upon his head, involve him in scandals, and denigrate his character. Goebbels was fortunate in having the services of '*Mjoelnir*', the *Angriff* cartoonist and a poster painter, at his disposal: his simple arguments were ably underlined by suitable drawings.[33]

Goebbels's influence on Nazi propaganda was never confined

[33] Cf. E. Bramstead's article 'Goebbels and *Der Angriff*' in *On the Track of Tyranny*, a Wiener Library publication, edited by Max Beloff, page 49.

to *Der Angriff.* He had been associated with the Strassers, and he had worked for them in the Rhineland, when the two brothers were building up the party organization in that area and in North Germany. They did so independently of Hitler; although he succeeded in avoiding an open breach with them in 1926, theirs was an uneasy truce. Hitler soon began making his own arrangements in the capital: late that year, he appointed Goebbels the *Gauleiter* in Berlin. When he arrived in the capital, Goebbels was entirely Hitler's man; two years later he was appointed the director of propaganda, a key position in the Nazi hierarchy.

When he arrived in Berlin, there was a copy of *Mein Kampf* in his suitcase, personally inscribed by Hitler. We have no reason to suppose that he disagreed with any of the views on the subject of propaganda expounded in the book. He was a more professional speaker than Hitler. His effects were calculated, he was highly adaptable with regard to the mood of his audience, he could switch emotion on and off. He was an accomplished and successful orator, and there was a high charge of cynicism in his performance. In Berlin he faced a difficult task, and in some respects he improved on the high standards of political agitation set by Hitler. He had to break the hold of Communist and Social Democrat organizations on the working-class population of the capital: in Bavaria, Hitler had never faced such a stark situation. Violence and the fight against 'Marxism' went hand in hand as far as Goebbels was concerned, and they were the main features of the bitterly contested 'Battle for Berlin'. Goebbels had no choice but to carry the struggle into the camp of the enemy: the party organization he took over on his arrival was weak, and he had to build it up in the heat of the battle. The shock tactics he used in furthering the Nazi cause in Berlin made the activities of his friends in Bavaria appear leisurely and gentlemanly pursuits.

Goebbels wasted no time in joining the battle. Early in February 1927, he began to advertise a meeting to take place on 11 February, in the Pharus-Saele in the working-class district called Wedding. Glaring posters in red and black ink announced: 'The middle-class state [*Bürgerstaat*] is approaching its doom. A new Germany must be forged: workers of the brain and of the hands, you can decide the fate of Germany. On Friday 11 February, at the Pharus-Saele: Subject: The Break-Down of the Bourgeois Class-State.'[34] The suggestion that the middle-class state was on the way out could hardly have sounded incredible to a Communist; the announcement itself was not very offensive, even to the opponents of the Nazis, and it did not introduce any distinctly Nazi political jargon. But the movement was already known in Berlin, the first blows had been exchanged, and neither side was in doubt as to what exactly the advertised meeting meant. It was a declaration of war.

The Pharus-Saele was a large, suburban emporium of entertainment; it contained a cinema, a theatre, an assembly room, a beer-garden. And so far the Communists had used it for their general meetings; their local organization met there nearly every week. Shortly before 8 p.m. on 11 February, an excited and impatient Goebbels arrived at the meeting; the SS leader reported to him that the hall had been closed by the police at 7.15 because it was too full, and that two-thirds of the audience consisted of members of the Red Front fighting organization. 'This was what we wanted', Goebbels later wrote in his book of recollections. 'The decision must be made here. This way or that. And we were ready to give all we had.'[35] The atmosphere in the hall, filled with tobacco and beer fumes, was tense when Goebbels entered. There were cat-calls and abuse from the audience as soon as it recognized the Nazi *Gauleiter*; there was no doubt that his supporters were in the minority. Some twenty SA troopers surrounded the speaker's platform; when their leader attempted to open the meeting, he was unable to do so. The din in the hall continued and soon fighting flared up. The battle was short and bloody; there are two accounts of what happened after its conclusion. Goebbels himself wrote that the Nazis succeeded in clearing the hall of their enemies unaided. The noise of the *Saalschlacht* was followed by an icy silence, interrupted by the groans of the wounded; there were some Nazi casualties lying on the speaker's platform. According to Goebbels, there were no Nazi first-aid men present.[36] 'Workers-Samaritans' had to be relied on; they were not very sympathetic, and they abused even the stormtroopers who had

[34] J. Goebbels, *Kampf um Berlin*, page 63.
[35] ibid., page 66.
[36] ibid., page 71.

been seriously wounded. According to another account,[37] the police intervened and the Communists dispersed. When order was restored, Goebbels had the Nazi stretcher-cases brought to the platform, and then proceeded to make a speech against the gory background. Be that as it may, there can be no doubt that Goebbels made his speech surrounded by the Nazi wounded, and that he developed, on this occasion, the concept of the unknown *SA* stormtrooper—the martyr and the hero.

Until 1929, the technical equipment at the disposal of Nazi propagandists was rather primitive. The means of mass communication—large-circulation press, films, radio, and television—instruments that now appear indispensable to totalitarian régimes—were usually absent during the rise to power, both in Russia and in Germany, of the totalitarian parties. The Nazis had their 'propaganda lorries', which carried posters and people shouting slogans; they advertised the *Völkischer Beobachter* by means of mock armoured cars. But until the Nazi election victory in 1930, their press and other printed matter did not command mass circulation and, apart from their meetings, the Nazis had no other way of reaching their public; even microphones were not available for their speakers until the later nineteen-twenties. The end of the decade marked the turning point in their fortunes. In October 1929, Stresemann died, and soon afterwards the Young Plan for reparations was ratified by the *Reichstag*; then the economic slump put an end to Germany's short-lived prosperity. While these momentous events were taking place, Hitler entered into an alliance with Alfred Hugenberg. Hugenberg had a varied career behind him: he began it as a civil servant in German Poland; soon after the turn of the century he found his way into industry through family connexions; when he was thirty-seven years old, he was appointed chairman of the directors of the Krupp consortium. He joined Ullstein and Mosse as one of the three largest publishers when he bought the Scherl Verlag in 1916; ten years later he acquired the controlling interest in UFA, the film company which ran its own weekly newsreel as well as an extensive chain of cinemas. He was, however, thwarted by the government in the attempt to bring under his control the nascent German broadcasting system. He developed his political

[37] R. Manvell and H. Fraenkel, *Joseph Goebbels*, London, 1960, page 77.

interests at the same time; a man without strong political convictions, he was, in the view of a contemporary of his, a 'political calculating machine, completely cold, thinking in relative terms only. The point of his endeavour is to possess political power'.[38] Shortly before he met Hitler, Hugenberg became the chairman of the German National Party; the alliance, dating from the autumn of 1929, was highly attractive to both men. Hugenberg had connexions in the world of industry and finance as well as his communications empire on his side; Hitler had direct access to the masses. On the crucial points, their political views did not differ, both men abhorred the Socialists as much as the Versailles Treaty or the Young Plan. Although Hitler was to break this alliance, it fulfilled a very useful purpose for the Nazi movement while it lasted. The *Berliner Lokalanzeiger*, the *Tag*, and the illustrated weekly the *Woche*, were among the newspapers controlled by the Scherl Verlag; Hugenberg also owned influential news and feature agencies. They all gave Hitler favourable publicity; in the *Ufa Wochenschau*, the weekly newsreel, the Nazi movement often found its way, during the Hitler-Hugenberg alliance, on to the screens of the German cinemas.

Despite the efforts of the Nazi leadership, the party had done only moderately well in the years between 1925 and 1928. At the end of 1928, it commanded a following of 108,717 registered members;[39] at the general elections on 20 May, it polled 809,939 votes, and it sent twelve deputies to the *Reichstag*. Its advance showed considerable regional variations: the number of local party organizations in Essen rose only from 9 to 11 and in Düsseldorf from 20 to 21 in those three years. In Berlin the picture looked brighter, largely due to the energetic work by Goebbels; here 28 local organizations existed in 1928 as compared with 9 in 1925. Nevertheless, Bavaria still provided the best recruiting ground for the Nazis. In Franconia, a district that included Nürnberg, the number of local organizations rose from 18 to 36 between 1925 and 1928; in Upper Bavaria from 16 to 23; the Bavarian Ostmark—a district which bordered on Czechoslovakia—registered a record growth from 57 to 115 organizations.[40] In these years the

---

[38] Dr. Wahrmund, *Gericht über Hugenberg*, page 37.
[39] *Sammlung Rehse*, page 289.
[40] Wolfgang Schaefer, *NSDAP*, page 12.

foundations of the party organization were broadened; the two para-military organizations, the *SA* and the *SS*, were joined, at the time of the Weimar rally in 1926, by the *Hitlerjugend*, the Nazi youth organization; the *Frauenorden*, the women's society, was officially incorporated into the party in January 1928.

The characteristic brand of Nazi radicalism had no great appeal to the Germans during a time of comparative prosperity. This was already apparent during 1924—Hitler was in prison at the time—in the course of the two *Reichstag* elections in that year. In May the party still benefited from the aftermath of the inflation, and it received 6·5 per cent of the total poll; in the winter, the number of votes cast for it declined sharply to 3 per cent. After the 're-establishment' of the party in 1925, those sections of the population which derived no benefit from the improving economic situation—salaried men, former officers, white-collar workers as well as small artisans and shopkeepers and the permanently unemployed—continued to be a receptive audience for Nazi propaganda. In those years, the party remained largely confined to the discontented sections of urban population, without making any significant impression in the countryside.

This situation began to change towards the end of 1927. The break-down of the price structure of agricultural produce then occasioned a feeling of panic among small farmers, and the *NSDAP* began to identify itself with their interests. The first moves in this direction were made by the Nazi leaders during the election campaign in 1928; two years later, in the campaign of 1930, their agitation in the countryside was in full swing. Working on the principle that the memory of the masses was exceedingly short, the Nazi propagandists disregarded their previous declarations on agricultural policy; their propaganda effort was nimble and completely opportunist. On 6 March, an 'Official party announcement on the attitude of the *NSDAP* towards the peasantry and agriculture' was published. It quietly dropped the demand for land reform (although the large landowners in East Germany had at first proved impervious to the attractions of the Nazi movement, the alliance with Hugenberg made it necessary for Hitler to protect their interests as well), and it formulated a policy of lighter taxation, the lowering of rents, and the creation of co-operatives under state patronage: a policy that put the task of making agriculture profitable squarely upon the shoulders of the state. At the same time, an 'agricultural department' was formed inside the party, and on 1 June, Walther Darre was made responsible for the organization of the peasantry; three months later, the *NS Landpost*, a special party organ designed for the countryside, appeared for the first time, and an expert adviser was attached to local and district party organizations in the rural areas. The campaign paid a completely satisfactory dividend: in 1930 the peasants supplied the party with 13·2 per cent of its total membership.[41]

During the five years since the 're-establishment' of the party, the Nazi net had been cast over Germany. It could be used to catch more supporters for the movement when a suitable opportunity presented itself: it came in the shape of the economic slump. Before 1930, the party had been a refuge for the socially and economically under-privileged and for the outcasts; now, the isolated islands of discontent were submerged in the flood. In the elections to the *Reichstag* on 14 September—a fatal date in the annals of the Weimar Republic—members of the middle class joined the peasants as the new supporters of the Nazi movement. The republican party system began to break down; the middle class, including those of its sections that had shared in the economic prosperity, began to search for a new political platform. The Nazi movement offered them this.

Although the *NSDAP* claimed to be a socialist party, it did not make an equally spectacular advance among the German working class. Significantly, there were no Nazi trade unions; only when the ranks of the unemployed rose to 4,380,000 at the end of 1930 were the Nazis moved—in January of the following year—to set up an 'economic-political' department. It was led by Otto Wagener, and it absorbed the organization of industrial cells[42] together with its organ, *Das Arbeitertum*.

In a sociological break-down of the German society into its component parts (excluding housewives, pensioners, and students), the workers accounted for 45·9 per cent of the employed population in 1930; they supplied the Nazi party with 28·1 per

[41] Wolfgang Schaefer, op. cit., page 19. [42] *Reichsbetriebszellenorganisation.*

Something for everyone

cent of its membership.[43] But the features of the party that repulsed the workers attracted the big industrialists. For this, the ground had been prepared in 1928, when the party leadership banned the formation of Nazi trade unions; when the industrialists saw themselves threatened by the slump, they found the Nazi party, among the radical movements, by far the most congenial.

At the general elections in 1930, 6,407,397 votes were cast for the *NSDAP*, and it sent 107 deputies to the *Reichstag*, compared with the twelve deputies who had been elected two years earlier; it became the second largest party in the parliament. Indeed, as the slump gathered momentum, the membership of the party continued to grow at a fast rate. The following table shows the rate of increase:

Year	Number of Registered Members	Rate of Increase, Per cent
1928	108,717	149·3
1929	176,426	161·5
1930 (September)	293,000	—
1930 (December)	389,000	221·0
1931	806,294	207·2
1932	1,414,975	175·5[44]

The sharp increase in Nazi membership exactly followed the growth of the numbers of the unemployed until 1931; from then on, the jobless masses of Germany continued to provide the Nazis with their recruiting ground.

The growth of the party was also reflected in the sudden jump in the circulation figures of its press; the number of copies sold of the *Völkischer Beobachter* rose, between 1929 and 1932, at the following pace:

1929	26,715
1930	84,511
1931	108,746
1932	126,672[45]

[43] W. Schaefer, op. cit., page 17. In comparison, the white-collar employers in private firms and self-employed persons—12 and 9 per cent respectively of the total working population—provided the Nazi party with 25·6 and 20·7 per cent of its members.
[44] ibid., op. cit., page 17.
[45] H. A. Münster, op. cit., page 113.

During the same period, the number of Nazi newspapers rose to 121, and they commanded a total circulation of well over a million; in January 1932 a press agency, the *Nationalsozialistische Partei-Korrespondenz*, was set up. During the period of sharp increase in their following, the Nazis were by no means forced to overhaul their methods of propaganda. Speeches, meetings, and rallies still headed the list of priority, and they had precedence over any other form of agitation. The press still remained relegated to second place; only when Nazi activities were jeopardized by one or other of Brüning's emergency laws, did the press—when it was not banned itself— become more important as the only available means of propaganda. Violence in the streets and at political meetings grew more frequent and intense; civil war raged in full view of a powerless government. In addition to the feeling of belonging to a strong and resolute community, the *SA* could now offer food and shelter to thousands of its unemployed members. When all political uniforms were banned on 8 December 1931, the *SA* and the *SS* continued to meet, wearing white or no shirts; in Munich they staged a sit-down demonstration when mounted police attempted to break up their meeting. Since the ban on uniforms was clearly not very effective, the government banned the *SA* and *SS* on 13 April the following year; their homes, kitchens, and other property were impounded. Although it came late, the ban was a serious blow to the Nazi leaders; at this time, Goebbels recorded in his diary: 'When the *SA* troops once again march in their brown shirts, then the whole depression will be overcome, and the enemy will soon fall under our blows.'[46] His wishes were fulfilled: the ban was lifted on 14 June, and violence flared up once again. During the month after the stormtroopers' return to the streets in their uniforms, some thirty of them were killed; one Sunday at Altona, near Hamburg, sixteen people lost their lives and fifty were seriously injured.

The lethal combination of propaganda and terror was carried on in the same manner—although on a larger scale—as in the twenties. But now, after the turn of the decade, Hitler began to lay his hands on the really heavy artillery of technical equipment

[46] Entry on 8 May 1932 in Goebbels's *Vom Kaiserhof zur Reichskanzlei*, page 93.

for propaganda. At first his alliance with Hugenberg helped, both financially and in the field of public relations; Hugenberg's press and film empire rendered Hitler useful services. But the flow of money from German industry into Nazi coffers continued even after Hitler turned, early in 1932, to attack his former ally. Indeed, in the final stage of Hitler's way to power, circumstances conspired to make the ascent easy for him. The technical means for propaganda had been developed, and they became available to Hitler at a time when he disposed of adequate financial resources and when a highly receptive audience existed. During the year 1930 microphones and loudspeakers became the standard equipment of Nazi meetings; without them, the monster meetings—such as those at the Sportpalast in 1932— would have been impossible to organize. The formidable armoury of Nazi propaganda came into play during the two presidential election campaigns in 1932, when Hitler competed for the highest stakes yet of his political career. He was in close consultation with Goebbels, who relieved him of the cares of the detailed organization of propaganda, as well as making a considerable contribution himself to its general direction. Early in February, Goebbels was able to write that 'the election campaign is ready in principle. We now only need to press the button, to set the machine into motion'.[47] The Nazis ran some 34,000 public meetings during the first campaign; they distributed 8,000,000 pamphlets and printed large editions of the party newspapers; striking coloured posters hammered election slogans home. They were simple and effective—a drawing of the profiles of three grimly determined *SA* men, for instance, carried the text: 'National-Socialism, the organized will of the nation'.[48] Since the highest office in the state was being contested, the Nazi propagandists soft-pedalled party differences, and concentrated on identifying their movement with the nation. They also produced, for the first time, their own films, which were usually shown at open-air meetings, as distribution through the usual channels was still proving difficult.

In the first election on 13 March, Hindenburg did not acquire

[47] Entry for 4 February 1932 in J. Goebbels's *Vom Kaiserhof zur Reichskanzlei*, page 38.
[48] *Sammlung Rehse*, page 371.

Anschläge: *Ebenhausen. Langewiesche-Brandt Verlag 1963*

I. The string-puller. 1924

Einer allein von 2000 Millionen Menschen
der Erde darf in Deutschland nicht reden!

IIa. Hitler: he alone is not
allowed to speak in Germany.
1926

IIb. SS troopers are for-
bidden to wear their
uniforms. 1930

an absolute majority, but he led Hitler by more than 7,000,000 votes. Goebbels was desperate; Hitler announced that the second election campaign would be launched at once. The propaganda machinery was overhauled, and new directives were worked out. Many party workers were sent to reinforce the propaganda department in Munich; in his speeches, Hitler switched from carping criticism of the evils of the Weimar 'system' to painting a picture of a happy future for the Germans; Goebbels, on the other hand, promised to devote himself to combating the 'lies' and slander heaped on the Nazis by their opponents.[49] He was not quite happy about the part the Nazi press played in the campaign; on 1 April, he complained in his diary that journalists had made many mistakes, and that they were 'mostly very badly suited for propaganda'.[50] He also employed an effective innovation in this campaign. He had already discussed, early in January, the possibility of using aircraft for the speedy delivery of principal speakers from one city to another;[51] the idea was put into practice only between 3 and 9 April during the second election campaign. Hitler flew in a Junkers D 1720 plane piloted by Captain Hans Bauer, and he visited twenty-one towns in six days. Apart from its practical advantages, the first *Deutschlandflug* had a high propaganda value: no German politician had taken to the air before for the purposes of electioneering; the slogan 'Hitler over Germany' had an effectively ambiguous meaning. The speaker who commanded the largest audiences in Germany was ubiquitous; the energy, the power to hypnotize, the speed of movement, all belonged to a human being with superhuman attributes. As early as February 1932, Goebbels's department distributed 50,000 gramophone records; during the second presidential campaign, the Nazi propagandists made an extensive use of recorded speeches, which were played from vans carrying loudspeakers. Five days after the election of the President—when the election campaign in Prussia was being launched—a speech by Hitler was played at the beginning of the meeting at the Sportpalast on 15 April; Goebbels described the experiment as a 'tremendous success'—*Bombenerfolg*.[52]

Nevertheless, such practices were mere substitutes for radio

[49] *Vom Kaiserhof*, page 63.   [50] ibid., page 79.
[51] ibid., pages 17-18.   [52] ibid., page 82.

35

4

propaganda. Broadcasting was under government control, and time for political broadcasts was sparingly allocated. Aside from two talks—a part of a discussion programme—delivered by the party ideologist Gottfried Feder in 1930 and 1931, the Nazis did not gain access to the German broadcasting system until the summer of 1932. Their protests in the parliament were frequent but ineffective; they followed the Communist example in creating disturbances at public functions which were broadcast. In August 1932, for example, after the opening speech of the Berlin wireless exhibition, the two party radio functionaries, Hadamovsky and Dressler-Andress, sprang to the microphone and shouted 'Long live National-Socialist radio! Heil Hitler!'[53]

Hitler's bid for the highest office in the state failed again in the second presidential election. Nevertheless, the Nazis were now preparing to take up the reins of government; after a year of continuous election campaigns, punctuated by hard political bargaining, Hitler achieved his ambition. On 30 January 1933, the aged President Hindenburg entrusted him with the office of Chancellor. During the eight years since his release from the Landsberg Prison, the rise of Hitler and his movement to prominence and finally to power had been spectacular. Despite the frequent bans on various forms of Nazi activities issued by the governments of the federal states, the central government in Berlin had proved itself incapable of co-ordinating and directing the fight against a movement that threatened the very existence of the democratic system. It was perhaps too late when Chancellor Brüning began to pass one emergency decree after another. By then the Nazis commanded the largest political organization in Germany. It was built up from insignificant beginnings and its early growth—by no means striking compared with the growth of the party after 1929—was largely due to the skilful exploitation of propaganda techniques. By and large, the themes of Hitler's agitation were not as impressive as their delivery. Certain subjects recurred: the Nazis were anti-parliamentary, anti-Marxist, anti-Communist, anti-Liberal, anti-Jewish. They exploited national humiliations: the Versailles Treaty, and the Young Plan for reparations; they placed the blame for the defeat and humilia-

[53] Hans Bausch, *Der Rundfunk im politischen Kräftespiel der Weimarer Republik 1923-33*, page 177.

tion squarely on the Weimar 'system'. But their propaganda, especially when dealing with current political problems, was quick to grasp the main chance, and it remained unhampered by any ideological considerations. It was firmly based on the principles Hitler had developed early in his career. It was not intended to persuade by reasoning; it appealed to the emotions, and it was reinforced by a considerable dose of violence. Although the theory and practice of Nazi propaganda were derivative to a certain extent, Hitler and his star pupil Goebbels had a sure touch in its execution; its cumulative effect has never been surpassed. Finally, in the first three years of the new decade, the Nazis benefited by the economic crisis; the party had a long tradition behind it of being the refuge of the discontented, of the outcasts. And at the time when it was becoming a truly mass-movement it began acquiring the technical equipment for the conduct of mass propaganda. By the end of 1932, the *NSDAP* was ready to assume the highest responsibility in the state.

II. THE STATE AND PROPAGANDA

'IT is like a dream. Wilhelmstrasse belongs to us. The Führer is already working in the Chancellery. We are standing upstairs at the window, and hundreds of thousands of people are passing by in the flaming light of torches before the grey President and the young Chancellor, and they are gratefully acclaiming them. . . .'[1] When Goebbels recorded the events of 30 January he was no less surprised than moved. The young man who had come to the hostile city six years before was now witnessing its final conversion to the true faith: at long last, Germany had awakened. The future promised unlimited possibilities.

The first foundations for the management of the German people by the state had been laid down some time before the day of Goebbels's exultation. He had become the *Reichspropagandaleiter* of the party on 9 January 1929; his chance to strengthen his own position and to extend the powers of his office came in 1932. Its activities overlapped to a great extent with those of the *Reichsorganisationsleitung*—the department of party organization—headed by Gregor Strasser. And when the ever-present problem of Gregor Strasser's position inside the party flared up again in the autumn of 1932, Goebbels seized this chance to reorganize and strengthen the administration of propaganda. He was convinced that Hitler was getting ready to take over power in Germany, and he carried out the reorganization of the propaganda apparatus with this end firmly in his mind. Its main function had been, until then, the efficient transmission of directives down the hierarchy of local organizations; now, Goebbels's main concern was the broadening of the central organization and the dividing of it into specialized sections that could look after every aspect of propaganda.

[1] *Vom Kaiserhof zur Reichskanzlei*, entry on 30 January 1933, page 251.

38

The section dealing with 'active propaganda' (*Amt I*) formed the core of the organization: it dealt with the execution of political agitation, from the monster meetings with their problems of architectural design, accommodation, transport, etc. (there was a special subsection for *Grossveranstaltungen*: the organization of the party rallies was run, however, by an independent permanent office in Nürnberg, which came under the direct supervision of the *Reichspropagandaleiter*) to the small meetings in the countryside. The main subsection, which had a comparatively long history behind it, was concerned with *Rednerwesen*, the direction of public speaking. The office of 'active propaganda' also distributed its own newspaper, *Unser Wille und Weg*, which had been founded in 1931.

Then there were sections dealing with 'culture'—including architecture, Hitler's special sphere of interest—with radio, film, and 'liaison with offices of the state'. These sections were expanded after January 1933; until then, they existed only in a rudimentary form. The same division was perpetuated on the lower levels of party organization: the *Gaupropagandaleiter* was responsible for five sections corresponding to those in the central office on the provincial level; lower down in the hierarchy, there were the *Kreispropagandaleiter*—the district director of propaganda—the *Ortsgruppenpropagandaleiter*, who worked on the level of local party organization, and finally the *Stützpunkt-propagandaleiter*—the cell-leader. All these ranks led a separate existence from the rest of the party organization; the hierarchy was used for transmitting orders downward, and passing information—situation reports, 'audience research', etc.—upwards. Regular monthly situation reports were passed on from the lowest level through the same hierarchy. By 1934, the party propaganda apparatus employed some 14,000 people.[2]

Nevertheless, the machinery that controlled Nazi propaganda activities was carefully concealed from public view. The marionettes were there for all to see, but the strings, and the string-pullers, would have spoilt the illusion. On one occasion, Goebbels had a fit of blinding fury because an illustrated magazine published a picture of a man putting on a record of a triumphal bell chime after a special announcement; at a press conference in

[2] K. Schmeer, op. cit., page 32.

no one saw
through it

Berlin selected journalists were informed that 'problems of stage management [*Regiefragen*] should not on principle come before the public. All that goes on behind the backcloth belongs to stage management.'[3]

Although the internal structure of party propaganda apparatus was often reshaped, and although its functions frequently overlapped with those of other party or, after 1933, state departments, it gave Goebbels a unique position of power. It was further strengthened when he became, in March 1933, the first Nazi Minister of Popular Enlightenment and Propaganda.

The possibility of backing up propaganda by the full weight of the machinery of the state was exploited to the full by the Nazis shortly after Hitler's appointment as Chancellor. Coercion could be substituted, when necessary, for persuasion; the terror that had been inflicted on the Germans by the stormtroopers before 1933 could now be meted out by the state. On the evening of 27 February, fire raged inside the *Reichstag*. It is immaterial whether it was started by a demented Dutch Communist pyromaniac or by the Nazis themselves, or independently by both; the fact remains that the Nazi action against their political opponents was swift and ruthless. By no means partisans of parliamentary institutions, the Nazis used the *Reichstag* fire as a pretext for their first move towards large-scale political repression. They declared it to be a Communist plot, the beginning of a Communist revolution. On the day after the fire, Hindenburg was made, by Hitler, to sign a decree for the protection of 'the People and the State', which suppressed those sections of the constitution relating to civil liberties, and authorized the central government to assume, whenever necessary, complete power in the federal states.

The *SA* troopers now appeared in the role of the defenders of the state. They were used as a supplementary police force for arresting thousands of their fellow-countrymen; the first concentration camps were set up. The Communists suffered first and foremost; the Social Democrats, and the leaders of the liberal parties, soon joined them in the camps. The last semi-democratic elections took place in an atmosphere of terror. The Nazis had suppressed most of the newspapers run by their political enemies;

[3] K. Schmeer, op. cit., page 28.

they now had the broadcasting system at their disposal. Despite these advantages and their attempt to extract the full propaganda value from the threat of a Communist revolution,[4] the Nazis did not gain a clear majority. They polled 43·9 per cent of the total vote. Only when the fifty-two deputies of Hugenberg's German National Party were added to the 288 National Socialist deputies did Hitler's government achieve a marginal majority in the *Reichstag*.

But this was only a minor obstacle. A few days after the elections Goebbels was appointed, on 13 March, the Minister of Popular Enlightenment and Propaganda. A stream of letters and well-wishers began to pour into the office of the new Minister: this was not a routine appointment, as no such office had existed before. A week later, Hitler saw the Enabling Law through the *Reichstag*; it gave his government dictatorial powers. In these circumstances, the main aim of Nazi propaganda was to achieve the identification of the party with the state. The opening of the new *Reichstag*, on 21 March, served this purpose admirably. It was stage-managed by Goebbels, and the garrison church at Potsdam provided a suitable setting. The place had powerful historical associations: Frederick the Great was buried here, it was a reminder of Prussia's past. Among such memories there was no place for democratic, parliamentary ideals; the tradition was authoritarian, underscored by past military glory. The Nazis turned up in force, and so did the living relics of the Empire in their splendid uniforms of a bygone age. Hindenburg made a speech to the deputies assembled in the garrison church; he was followed by Hitler. Again, the same image as on 30 January occurred to Goebbels.[5] The grey, old President with the young Chancellor: the past and the future of Germany were united in the present moment; Germany's honour was restored, and the shameful recent memories were safely buried.

Goebbels was a busy man in the first months after the formation of Hitler's government. The Nazi leaders no longer saw their party as one of the competitors in the political arena; the point now was to eliminate all competition, while completing a watertight *Gleichschaltung* of every aspect of political activity. And not

[4] See chapter 4, *passim*.　　　　[5] *Vom Kaiserhof*, page 285.

only that: every facet of national life had to be inspired from a single source and directed by a central authority. In their own view, the Nazis possessed the only infallible panacea.

Propaganda occupied, as we have observed, a focal position in the Nazi scheme of things when the party was still on the road to power; after 1933, Goebbels's Ministry was placed in a corresponding key position. According to Hitler's decree, published in June, the Minister was responsible for 'all tasks of spiritual direction of the nation'.[6] This vague directive gave Goebbels's Ministry a wide scope. Other departments of state had to give up a variety of their former functions in its favour. The Ministry of the Interior handed over to Goebbels the supervision of radio, films, press, theatre; the protection of works of art and memorials, and the regulation of state celebrations and holidays; the Foreign Ministry had to give up—at any rate in theory—the control of the whole range of propaganda abroad. The organization of the Ministry and the division of tasks inside it corresponded closely to that of the party department of propaganda (*Reichspropagandaleitung*). Apart from the sections for active propaganda, radio, films, press, there were sections dealing with theatre, creative arts, music, and writing. (In the *Reichspropagandaleitung*, all these latter activities came under the direction of the *Kulturamt*.) There were also special sections dealing with propaganda abroad, foreign press, and the *Fremdenverkehrsabteilung*. The last section looked after tourist traffic; for a National Socialist this did not simply mean going abroad for holidays, or foreigners coming to Germany for the same purpose. Although the Nazis erected no 'iron curtain' around Germany, tourism became a political exercise that was closely linked with the overall propaganda effort.

Most of the top positions in the Ministry and in the *Reichspropagandaleitung* were held by the same men; the two institutions in fact merged, at many points, into one apparatus. The key *Abteilung II* acted as the general staff of the Ministry; policy was formulated here, ideas were discussed and worked out in detail; it also included sections dealing with specific tasks, such as the fight against Marxism, the Versailles peace treaties, antisemitic propaganda, eastern and borderland problems. The head

[6] K. Schmeer, op. cit., page 38.

of the whole department was Wilhelm Haegert, who also managed
the liaison section of the *Reichspropagandaleitung*; Leopold
Gutterer, who looked after the section which dealt with large
meetings (*Grossveranstaltungen*) inside the party propaganda
organization, also acted as a principal (*Referent*) in the *Abteilung
II* in the Ministry; Hans Kriegler was head of the departments of
broadcasting both in the Ministry and in the *Reichspropagandaleitung*, as well as acting as the President of the *Reichsrundfunkkammer*. Division of labour between the two organizations was
purely functional, and it did not affect questions of general
policy. The Ministry was, for instance, responsible for the organization of state visits and state celebrations, whereas the *Reichspropagandaleitung* carried out the celebrations of the various
party anniversaries. ꞥꞷ aꞁꞇeꞷꞃnaꞇꞷꞃeꞅ

Centralization of all propaganda activities implied, for Goebbels, the elimination of every alternative source of information.
In this respect, his most difficult task lay in the *Gleichschaltung*—
the achievement of uniformity—of the press. When Hitler became
the Chancellor of the Republic there existed over 4,703 newspapers in Germany; their political make-up was highly different-
iated, they had a long tradition behind them, and some of them
had acquired, in the course of the years, a nation-wide reputation.
They all made heavy demands on the pool of skilled journalists:
Hitler and Goebbels had not been very successful in the competition for their services.[7] The Nazis ran only a small section of
the very diverse press; at the beginning of 1933 they had 121
dailies and periodicals—most of them with low circulation—
at their disposal. By the end of 1934, the situation had drastically
changed. The party then controlled some 436 newspapers directly, and indirectly all the German press.

But the uniformity achieved in those years was by no means
obvious at a first glance. Only the extremists in the movement
advocated a radical suppression of all the former democratic
press, which would put the party, at once, into a monopoly
position.[8] Goebbels was well aware of the difficulties involved in
replacing the variegated press of Germany. He maintained that
the monopoly of direction behind the scenes should continue to

[7] See page 24.
[8] W. Hagemann, op. cit., page 34.

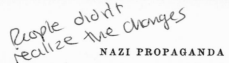

People didn't realize the changes

flow through the traditional variety of channels.[9] Goebbels chose to advance along the line of least resistance. In this way, the readers' habits would not be suddenly broken, and the Nazi journalists would not be faced with a task beyond their powers. The long-term views on the development of the German press— Goebbels very likely shared them with Max Amann, the party publisher, and with Rudolf Hess—were that the *NSDAP* press would eventually come to dominate the field, not so much because of its intrinsic value and merits, but because of the help the party authorities could render it.[10] The Germans could be educated, or perhaps even compelled, to read Nazi newspapers and periodicals.

The slow erosion of the independence of the German press was carried out in a variety of ways. The *Reichstag* fire served as a pretext for the suppression of all Communist newspapers, and a ban on those run by the Social Democrat party. The ruthless suppression of hundreds of newspapers was followed by a more oblique step. The *Wolff Telegraphenbüro* was transformed into the *Deutsches Nachrichtenbüro*, and the other agencies were also brought into line. As well as regulating the flow of news at its very source, Goebbels tackled the problem from the other end, on the editorial level. Official press conferences had been introduced in Germany during the First World War, and in 1919 they became a regular feature of journalists' activities in Berlin. They were run by the *Reichspressechef* or his deputy, and their main purpose was to explain the official attitude of the government on the most important issues of the day to the editors of the national newspapers, and to answer their questions. Soon after Goebbels became the Minister of Propaganda, the conduct of the conferences passed into the hands of the press department of his Ministry. It controlled the admission of journalists to these meetings, as well as the information that was dispensed to them. And under Goebbels's régime, the conference gradually lost its original function—to inform the journalists. This was taken over by the *Deutsches Nachrichtenbüro*, the official news agency, which issued material suitable to serve as the basis for commentaries and leaders. The agency also provided a small circle of

[9] W. Hagemann, op. cit., page 35.
[10] Cf. National Archives, Washington, Record Group No. T.81, documents pertaining to Nazi press policy, especially document No. 28539.

Nazi journalists and party functionaries with strictly confidential material intended for their personal use. The press conference then issued only orders: they came from Goebbels, and he had the whole apparatus of the state behind him if he wished to enforce them. The Nazis attempted to create their own image of an ideal editor: a man who was not a mere technician, but a fighter for their ideals. They had a romantic picture of such a person, which they derived from the 'period of struggle' before 1933; Weiss, the editor of the *Völkischer Beobachter*, described him in the following manner: 'A National Socialist editor never was a journalist exclusively but always and foremost a propagandist, very often a newspaperman, a speaker, and an *SA* trooper in one person. We want editors who will support their Führer and the new Reich not because they have to do so, but because they want to.'[11] In the meantime, however, Goebbels could not rely on cynical journalists being willing to accept his 'ideals'. In the autumn of 1933, the Nazis reinforced their press policy by legislation. The *Schriftleitergesetz*—the law of 4 October—followed the lines that Hitler had first expounded in the party programme some thirteen years earlier.[12] The law declared the office of an editor to be an official position, which could not be held by a person without German citizenship, or who had been deprived of his rights as a citizen, who was a Jew, or who was married to one. When discharging their functions, editors were placed under a variety of restrictions. They were bound by law not to confuse their 'private [good] with the general good in a manner misleading to the public';[13] they were not to print anything that might harm Germany's ability to defend herself, her economy or culture or indeed anything that broke the rules of 'good conduct'. The paragraphs of the law, especially those concerning the functions of the editor, entirely ruled out any possibility of editorial independence; the right to express a personal view of the government was entirely denied to the German journalists. The law gave the Ministry of Propaganda an instrument for the achievement of a complete uniformity of the press: there was no need for censorship because the editor's most important function was that of a censor.

---

[11] From a speech to the journalists' conference at Cologne in November 1935, quoted by W. Hagemann, op. cit., page 39.
[12] See page 22.
[13] *Reichsgesetzblatt* 1933, part 1, page 714.

Goebbels defended the press law in a speech to the journalists on the day of its publication. He argued that the free expression of opinion could seriously threaten the state, and that personal liberty depended on the degree of freedom that 'can be enjoyed by the nation, and the freedom of the individual will be the narrower the greater the dangers are that temporarily threaten the state'.

Only much later—in 1942— did Goebbels explain what he meant by temporary danger: he said that freedom of opinion could be established only when the German nation reached the 'maturity' of the English people, a process that would take at least a century.[14] At the conference on 4 October Goebbels further argued that the state was not able to give up the means of controlling the press, because of the tendency, among the Germans, to take the printed word much more seriously than the spoken word. He talked to the assembled journalists as one of them; he attempted to make the law palatable to them by pointing out that it raised their professional status, and that it strengthened their position in relation to the publisher.

Nevertheless, even in this respect—the relation between the editor and the publisher—the freedom of the journalist to choose his own employer was being gradually whittled down. The operations of Max Amann constituted another line of attack on the independence of the press. He may have disapproved of those clauses of the law that downgraded the relation between the publisher and the editor to a purely contractual basis: nevertheless, by the autumn of 1933, Amann knew that he was well on the way to becoming a dictator of German publishing. In the early years of the party's activity in Bavaria, Max Amann had been its business manager as well as the director of the Franz Eher Verlag, the official Nazi publishing house. As Hitler's personal friend, the proprietor of the Eher Verlag, the chairman of the Union of German Newspaper Publishers, and as the Secretary of the Press Chamber (*Reichspressekammer*), Amann was, by 1933, in a unique position of power. He used it to bring, gradually, a large part of German publishing under his control. His first opportunity came when all of the Communist and Social Democrat press was banned after the *Reichstag* fire: by the end of the year, some 1,500 publishers were robbed of their business. The

[14] W. Hagemann, op. cit., page 37.

decrees issued in April 1935 for the 'preservation of newspaper publishing', for the 'extirpation of newspapers dealing in scandal' etc., offered Amann further opportunities for the reorganization of publishing. Before Amann started building his empire under Hitler's patronage, some 80 per cent of all publishing houses were run as family businesses; their number decreased rapidly, constantly harassed and decimated by the government and by Amann. Even most of the newspapers run by the Scherl Verlag—it was controlled by Hitler's former ally Hugenberg— were gradually swallowed up by Amann's organization. If in 1933 the Nazis ran only 2.5 per cent of all German newspapers, by 1944 82 per cent of the remaining 977 newspapers were controlled, directly or indirectly, by Amann.[15] In 1939 the Amann concern employed 600 editors-in-chief of publishing houses and 3,000 journalists, apart from many thousands of administrative employees.

Although in 1941, on the occasion of Max Amann's fiftieth birthday, Hitler could congratulate his friend on the superlative work he had done for the Nazi idea, the *Gleichschaltung* of the German press had been a slow, costly, and laborious process. By comparison, the control of the film industry and of broadcasting was easier of achievement, and it produced, from the Nazi point of view, more impressive results. For this, there were a number of reasons. Both the privately owned film industry and the state-run broadcasting system were only recently developed as the means of mass communication; they possessed neither the set traditions nor the wide diversity of the press. Although the Nazis had gained little first-hand experience of these media before 1933, Goebbels understood their importance, and he had begun plotting their capture some time before the Nazis came to power.

It has been suggested that the productions of the German film industry in the Weimar Republic prepared the ground for the establishment of the Nazi régime. Mr. Siegfried Kracauer, for instance, concluded his study of the German film *From Caligari to Hitler* with this perceptive paragraph: 'Irretrievably sunk into retrogression, the bulk of the German people could not help submitting to Hitler. Since Germany thus carried out what had

[15] W. Hagemann, op. cit., page 40.

47

been anticipated by her cinema from its very beginning, conspicuous screen characters now came true in life itself. Personified day-dreams of minds to whom freedom meant a fatal shock, and adolescence a permanent temptation, these figures filled the arena of Nazi Germany. Homunculus walked about in the flesh. Self-appointed Caligaris hypnotized innumerable Cesares into murder. Raving Mabuses committed fantastic crimes with impunity, and mad Ivans devised unheard-of tortures. Along with this unholy procession, many motifs known from the screen turned into actual events. In Nürnberg, the ornamental pattern of Nibelungen appeared on a gigantic scale: an ocean of flags and people artistically arranged. Souls were thoroughly manipulated so as to create the impression that the heart mediated between brain and hand. By day and night, millions of feet were marching over city streets and along highways. The blare of military bugles sounded unremittingly, and the philistines from the plush parlours felt very elated. Battles roared and victory followed victory. It all was as it had been on the screen. The dark premonitions of a final doom were also fulfilled.'[16]

Although it is true to say that some films reflected various Nazi tendencies in German life in the pre-Hitler era, and that many of the people connected with the making of films gladly accepted the patronage of Goebbels, German cinemas had largely been showing commercial films, free from any political tendency. High production costs had to be covered by adequate box-office returns: Goebbels attacked precisely these films in a speech to the representatives of the industry in February 1934. He sharply criticized the manner in which German film-making was 'debased' by the dictates of capital, and the low level of the routine film produced purely for the sake of box-office returns; he said that German film-makers must learn to regard their profession as a service, and not as a source of profit.

Some time before this speech, the law for the establishment of a 'Provisional Film Chamber' was published:[17] it was mainly concerned with bringing the film industry into the 'general economic framework' of the state. The film companies began to be heavily subsidized from official funds, and then one after the

---

[16] Page 272, Princeton University Press, 1947.
[17] *Reichsgesetzblatt*, 1933, Part 1, page 483.

other were taken over by the state; the largest of them—Hugenberg's UFA company—was acquired in 1937. In less than five years the film department of the Ministry of Propaganda acquired a monopoly in film production; this policy was accompanied by the gradual elimination of foreign competition for the favours of the German filmgoers. No one could compete with Goebbels as an independent producer.

The Minister rated the value of films as a weapon of propaganda very high indeed; he also had a liking for the world of film, and he gave it a good deal of personal attention. Even well-known directors had to tolerate Goebbels's interference with their business; they often had to make changes in their casts and re-shoot whole scenes at the Minister's bidding. Apart from the propaganda documentaries—films of party rallies, of the Berlin Olympic Games and the heavily slanted newsreels—a number of films with strong political tendencies were made. *Jud Süss* put across the antisemitic message; *Hitlerjunge Quex* glorified the party and its youth; *Friesennot* underlined the trials of the Germans living outside the frontiers of Hitler's state. Indeed, in this *genre*, the Nazis scored some popular successes, which they attempted to match on the stages of the German theatres. The achievement and the technique of film-producing collectives could not however be employed in traditional theatre; individual authors could be neither discovered nor coerced as easily. In theatre, the Nazis had to be content to rely on the old repertoire, and to select from it the plays that suited them best.

Goebbels was attracted to films because they were easier to make and mould and because they reached much wider audiences than live theatre. Nevertheless, their limitations as an instrument of propaganda soon became apparent. Although box-office considerations were done away with, not all the films made in Germany could carry a high charge of Nazi propaganda. A large sector of the industry went on producing entirely apolitical films: indeed, the initial enthusiasm of the Nazi film-makers to put across their message gradually cooled off. Although the Hitler Youth Quex had mercifully perished at the hands of Communist thugs, he was revived during the war. Now a fully grown man, he appeared as Pilot Quex, a figure of comedy rather than of high-minded drama. In this respect, Goebbels failed: the kind of films he criticized in February 1934 continued to be made; the German public had to be amused.

When Goebbels became the Minister of Propaganda, the newspaper and film industries were privately owned: the broadcasting system was, on the other hand, state-run. It had some ten years' history behind it; although it had eluded the grasp of the Nazis before 1933, the imposition on it afterwards of centrally directed uniformity proved comparatively simple. For the Nazi propagandists, the control of broadcasting was the most coveted prize. Indeed, in June 1932 Hitler made his support of von Papen's government conditional on the grant to his party of broadcasting facilities; after that, numerous pronouncements by high party functionaries bore witness to their interest in the medium. At the opening of the radio exhibition in Berlin in August 1933, Goebbels quoted Napoleon, who had described the press as the 'seventh Great Power', and he continued: 'What the press was for the nineteenth century, wireless will be for the twentieth. One could alter the words of Napoleon, and call it the eighth Great Power.'[18]

In Germany, as in many other European countries, the two powers clashed. Mass-circulation press and broadcasting catered for the same public, and their functions—especially as far as the dissemination of news was concerned—were similar. Their rivalry had by no means been resolved before Hitler became Chancellor: the Nazi propagandists later favoured broadcasting at the expense of the press; Goebbels regarded it as a much more effective means of influencing the masses. In a small circle of his collaborators, he expressed the view that the press was an 'exponent of the liberal spirit, the product and instrument of the French revolution', whereas broadcasting was 'essentially authoritarian', and, therefore, a suitable 'spiritual weapon of the totalitarian state'.[19] Since Hitler hardly ever listened to wireless, Goebbels had a greater freedom of action in this than in any other field of propaganda; he also valued the fact that the spoken word disappeared without trace. He often allowed his broadcasters to exploit this liberty. Yet though broadcasting

[18] Quoted by W. Hagemann, op. cit., page 45.
[19] Heinz Pohle, *Der Rundfunk als Instrument der Politik*, page 241. Hamburg, 1955.

III. Election poster. 'National Socialism—the organized will of the Nation.' 1932

Anschläge: *Ebenhausen. Langewiesche-Brandt Verlag 1963*

IV. The Field-Marshal and the Corporal. 1933

was the pampered child of Nazi propagandists, the principle by which it had to give way to the claims of the press to bring important news first—this had been established in the Weimar Republic—was continued. In this respect, Max Amann's influence was decisive: until the outbreak of war speed in the dissemination of news was sacrificed in favour of the established prerogatives of the press.[20]

The new masters of the German broadcasting system laid special stress on the development of 'political broadcasts'— from dramatic poems set to music, composed to glorify the past of the party, to Hitler's speeches. Indeed, the latter were the focal point of Nazi radio programming; as many as fifty speeches by Hitler were transmitted in 1933. But in this respect the Nazi broadcasters had a lot to learn. Hitler's first radio message was followed by a flood of complaints from all parts of Germany; another recording had to be made, this time slower and less slurred, and it was broadcast the following day with better results. The Nazi propagandists learned their lesson; from October 1933, when the Führer announced Germany's departure from the League of Nations, until late in the war, Hitler made no studio broadcast. The contact with the 'masses' was the essential stimulus of his speaking, and its effect was further strengthened by the 'acoustic backcloth': the applause, the rhythmic chant of *Sieg Heil*, the off-stage noises of the large meeting. Without the direct *rapport* with his audience, and without the background it provided, Hitler was a failure as a speaker. He was unable to learn the technique—President Roosevelt in his 'fireside chats' was its master—which confined the speaker in the studio and left him to address a mass audience, but one composed of individuals in the privacy of their homes.

The most impressive achievement of the Nazi broadcasters lay, however, in the creation of this mass audience. In May 1933, German radio manufacturers undertook to produce a cheap, uniform set, the *Volksempfänger*. A few months later, the first 100,000 of these sets reached the market, and in 1934 the power of the transmitters was increased by 30 per cent. When the war broke out, some 3,500,000 sets had been sold.[21] In 1939, 70 per

[20] Heinz Pohle, op. cit., pages 239–40.
[21] ibid., op. cit., page 257.

51

cent of all German households owned a wireless set: the highest
percentage anywhere in the world. But the Nazi policy-makers
were not quite satisfied with this situation: they did not regard
the housewife and her family as a safe enough audience. Compulsory listening was developed alongside the compulsory attendance of meetings and the purchase of Nazi newspapers. Loudspeakers were introduced into factories, and production stopped
when an important party or state broadcast was being transmitted; the completion of the plan for the installation of 6,000
'loudspeaker pillars' in the streets (here the Nazis imitated the
practices introduced by the rulers of Soviet Russia early in the
nineteen-twenties) was interrupted by the war.

Indeed, during the six years of peace they allowed themselves,
the Nazis interfered in every aspect of public and private life to an
extent unknown in Germany's history. The work of the Germans,
their holidays, the new buildings in their towns, the education of
their children, the newspapers they read, the films they saw, and
the radio programmes they listened to bore the Nazi stamp. By
1935, however, behind the propaganda façade, there loomed
three solid actualities of Nazi achievement. While other European
governments were still struggling with the aftermath of the
economic crisis, the Nazis had solved it in Germany; by the Nürnberg laws, the Jews had been deprived of German citizenship;
in the background, there were the means of coercion, the Gestapo
and the concentration camps. Many of the original aims of the
National Socialists had been achieved: power and success were
now living realities, and not merely the objects of veneration
from afar. This of course strengthened the hand of the propagandists: the citizens of the Nazi state were trapped, and they had to
listen to incessant sermons on the excellence of their capture.
Nevertheless, the actual value of propaganda changed, and even
declined, after the National Socialists had reached their goal.
Before 1933, it had served as the main instrument in the drive for
capturing the masses, for laying the foundations for the capture of
power in the state. But once he achieved this power the state,
rather than the party, became Hitler's main object of interest.
The creation of Goebbels's Ministry of course bore witness to the
continued prominence of propaganda in the Nazi system; its
main task, however, was to win popular support for the National

Socialist state. Violence—the reverse side of the propaganda coin —received, as it were, official sanction. From a private army that had operated on the fringes of legality, the *SA* became an executive organ of the state. And soon other agencies of repression became available. At the same time, outside Germany, new horizons opened before Nazi propaganda.

III. THE AGENCIES OF PROPAGANDA ABROAD

WHEN the attention of the National Socialist leaders turned to the foreign scene, their parochial view of life, their circumscribed nationalism, as well as the poverty of their ideology, became more apparent than ever. Their limitations were, in this respect, many and marked. Unlike the Russian revolutionaries, the Nazis had never been given an opportunity to acquire, in exile, a cosmopolitan background. Hitler's acquaintance with the outside world was only slight; his service as a lance-corporal in France during the First World War was his only excursion outside Austria and Germany before 1933. Goebbels's experience of the foreign scene was still more limited, and many other high-ranking Nazis were no better off. Such ignorance put expert knowledge of foreign affairs at a premium. The few leading Nazis with a foreign background, men like Alfred Rosenberg and Rudolf Hess, tended to be automatically regarded as experts on the subject. But, despite these limitations, Hitler's government created a formidable propaganda apparatus abroad; although it often failed in its mission, it had certainly made its mark on the world before the war broke out.

We shall have occasion to notice that, even abroad, the National Socialist propagandists preferred to employ Germans, and especially the German minorities. These were not always available: there were, however, certain constant factors that worked, almost everywhere, in the Nazis' favour. The Nazi movement and its propaganda abroad acted as a catalyst, revealing the deeper ills and deficiencies of European life since the conclusion of the First World War. The conflict had drained the resources of the victorious and defeated states alike, and the long-drawn-out process of Europe's decline from prominence in world affairs had set in. There were also the political and economic complications in its eastern outposts that followed the break-up of the Habsburg Empire, and that did not remain confined to central and eastern Europe; the adoption—and the transformation—of Marxist Socialism by the Russians as the official doctrine of their state, and finally, the economic slump at the turn of the decade: all these factors produced a deep-seated *malaise*, especially among the middle and lower-middle classes of Europe. There was a genuine need for some kind of rejuvenating doctrine, and the Nazis attempted to supply it. Nazi propaganda abroad was mainly directed at the discontented, as it was in Germany.[1] The real and imaginary ills that affected post-war Europe—just as much as the existence of German minorities abroad—facilitated the work of the propagandists in Berlin in their attempt to lift the Nazi movement out of the confines of Germany's frontiers.

After Hitler's seizure of power, the first aim of Nazi propaganda was to make the new régime acceptable abroad: soon they were to embark on a more ambitious course and prepare the ground for expansionist moves. For both these tasks, the new rulers of Germany regarded propaganda, rather than diplomacy, as the more suitable instrument. The Nazis shared with the early Bolshevik rulers of Russia a distaste for traditional diplomacy and a distrust of the diplomats: both movements carried a message that could hardly be contained in diplomatic channels. Hitler described the Foreign Ministry as an 'intellectual garbage dump';[2] jolly Hermann Göring, after posing a rhetorical question to a frightened legation counsellor as to what he did the whole day, said: 'In the morning he sharpens pencils, in the afternoon he goes out to tea somewhere.' Attacks on the conduct of foreign affairs came from several sides—they were launched by Goebbels, Rosenberg, and Hess. They all believed in the efficacy of propaganda, and their belief was reinforced by the fact that the diplomatic apparatus was largely in the hands of men who were not party members.

Hitler inherited the Foreign Minister, Baron Konstantin von

[1] See pages 30–31.
[2] Paul Seabury, *The Wilhelmstrasse*, page 31. University of California Press, 1954.

Neurath, from Schleicher's cabinet: Neurath was a close friend of President Hindenburg, who asked him to continue serving under Hitler. Although—or perhaps because—he did not, in 1933, expect the Nazi revolution to accomplish a great deal, Neurath became a useful servant of the new régime. He was an easy-going man, probably too easy-going: he combined diplomatic skill with laziness and an inability to resist pressure. Until 1936 he was assisted by the State Secretary, von Bülow, another diplomat of the old school. In the nineteen-twenties, the Social Democrat governments had made some unorthodox appointments: by the time Hitler came to power the German nobility had the Foreign Ministry, once again, firmly in its grasp. Few personal changes occurred in 1933; the missions abroad remained virtually untouched. One of the few remaining Social Democrat appointees, Adolf Müller, the German Minister to Berne, served Hitler's régime for more than six months.

Indeed, the Nazi threat that, after their takeover of power 'heads would roll', was received quite stoically in the Wilhelmstrasse: wits inside the Ministry maintained that, as there were no heads in evidence at the office, they could hardly roll.[3] They were not far wrong. The penetration of the Ministry by the National Socialists in the early years of their régime was so slow as to be insignificant. This was true even on the highest level: not until early 1938 did Ribbentrop, a party member, take over the direction of Germany's foreign policy. But just as there were few out-and-out Nazis in the Foreign Ministry, so there were few determined opponents of Hitler. By the end of 1935, Neurath himself had made his peace with the Nazis; professional diplomats were deeply impressed by the easy initial successes of Hitler on the international scene, and they gave him ungrudging support. And although many leading National Socialist politicians did not see it this way at the time, the continuity of the diplomatic service was of the greatest propaganda value to them. They were trying to make their régime respectable abroad: the services of the diplomats were priceless for this purpose. Had the new Nazi government had to create an entirely new representation abroad—as the Bolsheviks had to do after November 1917, when their seizure of power was followed

[3] Ernst von Weizsäcker, *Erinnerungen*, page 109. Munich, 1950.

by wholesale resignations of the Russian diplomatic missions—the impression abroad of a break with the past would have been much deeper, and it would have taken much longer to repair.

Goebbels was, of course, more interested than von Neurath in the subject of propaganda abroad and he was the first leading Nazi to begin sniping at the established positions of the diplomats. A conference concerning propaganda abroad took place at the Chancellery on the afternoon of 24 May 1933. Goebbels opened the meeting by remarking that its purpose was the delimitation of duties between the Ministry of Propaganda and the Foreign Ministry; he pointed out that influencing public opinion abroad was the chief task of his Ministry. He needed large funds for this purpose; larger, indeed, than for propaganda at home. He said that agreement existed on his proposal to send to German missions attachés whose relations with the official representatives and with the domestic authorities would be similar to those of the Military Attachés. But the position of the Press Department of the Foreign Ministry still remained to be clarified.[4]

Neurath had no particular liking for Goebbels, and he resented his attempts to encroach on the functions of the Foreign Ministry. He did not want it to become a clearing house for propaganda and espionage activities;[5] his Ministry had to have its own press department, and if this were incorporated into the Ministry of Propaganda he would have to create a new office for the Foreign Ministry. He suggested that it should therefore remain intact, and that it could enter into a personal union with the Ministry of Propaganda through Walther Funk, the Press Chief and a State Secretary in that Ministry.

At this point Hitler intervened. He agreed with Neurath that the Foreign Ministry could not do without its Press Department, as this furnished the Ministry with the basis for the taking of political decisions. But he was really on Goebbels's side: since public opinion abroad was to be influenced, an entirely new organization had to be created. The Ministry of Propaganda would have to concern itself with the 'most varied methods of

[4] *Docs. Ger. For. Pol.*, series C, vol. 1, page 483, Minutes of the Conference of heads of Departments, Wednesday, 24 May 1933 at 5.0 p.m.
[5] Martha Dodd, *Through Embassy Eyes*, page 249. New York, 1939.

aggression propaganda' and it would have to execute the directives from the political leadership.

Neurath, who spoke again after Hitler, said that the problem of jurisdiction could be solved quite simply: the officials of his Press Department would furnish factual information, but they would not engage in propaganda; the two Ministries would, he suggested, co-operate closely. The Foreign Minister must have known, however, that his position was not very strong and that Goebbels would eventually get his way. Later in the discussion, the distinction that the Foreign Minister was trying to make was blurred by Hitler's and Goebbels's remarks; von Schwerin-Krosigk, the Minister of Finance, agreed that funds for foreign propaganda had hitherto been insufficient, and he promised Goebbels financial backing as soon as his new organization was established. Hitler wound up the conference by pointing out that 'no amount was too high for a good working propaganda establishment'; he said that the Foreign Ministry would have to 'limit itself to its previous traditional activity', and that 'active propaganda abroad' would be taken over by Goebbels's Ministry.

The conference resulted in a compromise: the Foreign Ministry was not to lose much, and Goebbels was given a free hand to create his own organization. But it was not a compromise that could be expected to last. The new Ministry and its chief were more dynamic, and they were in a better position to expand than the long-established Foreign Ministry. Goebbels benefited by Hitler's decree of 30 June 1933,[6] which removed the control of news and information abroad, of art, art exhibitions, sports, and films for export from the Foreign Ministry, and bestowed it on the Ministry of Propaganda. In Berlin, the Foreign Ministry's press conferences declined in importance as the interest of foreign correspondents shifted to those run by the Ministry of Propaganda. Goebbels successfully divested the Foreign Ministry of many of its functions; at the same time, the expenditure on the *Promi*—the affectionate Nazi abbreviation for the Ministry of Propaganda—was rising fast, while that on the Foreign Ministry remained practically static. Compared with other departments of state, the Foreign Ministry was the Nazis' Cinderella: by 1937, they were

---

[6] *Reichsgesetzblatt* of 5 July, no. 75, page 449.

spending on diplomacy less than 0·3 per cent of total government expenditure. In 1934, the government spent 26·1 million marks on the Ministry of Propaganda and 42·8 million on Neurath's Ministry; in the following year, the difference narrowed considerably: 40·8 million and 46·8 million were spent respectively on propaganda and diplomacy. In 1937 Goebbels's Ministry shot ahead with an expenditure of 55·3 million, compared with 49·4 million spent by the Foreign Ministry.[7] Neurath offered, on the whole, little resistance to Goebbels; in a National Socialist government, his was not a wholly safe position.

Nevertheless, from December 1937 onwards, the situation began to change in favour of the Foreign Ministry. In that month, the *Auslandsorganisation*—the Foreign Organization of the party[8] —became a part of the Foreign Ministry; early in the following year, Ribbentrop replaced Neurath as the Minister. Although expenditure on diplomacy did not quite catch up with the amount of money that was lavished on propaganda in the last two years of peace, it rose sharply from 49·4 million marks in 1937 to an estimated sum of 80·8 million in 1939. Ribbentrop was a party member who, unlike Neurath, felt no distaste for propaganda. On the contrary: Ribbentrop's ambition was to prevent the Minister of Propaganda from practising his art abroad. At the time of the Sudetenland crisis, Ribbentrop began by restoring the decimated press division in his Ministry: by the summer of 1939, an open conflict raged between the two departments. It was so acute that on 8 September—eight days after the invasion of Poland—Hitler ordered the Ministers of Foreign Affairs and of Propaganda to agree on a working compromise: this order was in fact not acted on until October 1941, when Goebbels and Ribbentrop signed an agreement on co-operation.[9] By that time, the press division of the *Auswärtiges Amt* consisted of fourteen sections; it was in a position to co-operate or compete on an

[7] N.G. Series No. 4062, secret report of the Ministry of Finance on expenditures of the departments of state, 17 July 1939. The report can be found among the material assembled in Nürnberg for the last of the major trials of war criminals. The accused were mainly German diplomats, and their trial took place in Nürnberg between 6 January and 14 April 1949. Cf. Paul Seabury, op. cit., pages 68 et seq.
[8] For a discussion of the role this institution played in Nazi propaganda abroad, see pages 67–72.
[9] Exhibit RF. 1147, Nürnberg trials, referred to in vol. 7, page 11.

equal footing with the agencies of the Ministry of Propaganda.

But, apart from these two Ministries, there were other institutions interested in propaganda abroad. At the meeting on 24 May 1933[10] Alfred Rosenberg was also present. He had risen to prominence in Hitler's wake; he became the editor of the *Völkischer Beobachter* in 1921 and he was still in the job twelve years later; he marched at his leader's side in Coburg in 1922 and then again to the Munich Feldherrenhalle on the day of the abortive *putsch* in November 1923.

Rosenberg was a Baltic German—he was born in Reval in Estonia—who was educated in Tsarist Russia, and who witnessed the Bolshevik revolution in Moscow. As Julius Streicher was the leading party antisemite, so Alfred Rosenberg was the extreme exponent of anti-Bolshevism among the Nazis.[11] His background qualified him, in his own and other National Socialists' eyes, as an expert on the problems of foreign policy. Indeed, it was symptomatic of the dearth of informed opinion among the party leaders that Rosenberg was given an opportunity to put his views and interests into practice.

On 1 April 1933 he was appointed, by Hitler, the head of the newly created Foreign Political Office (*Aussenpolitisches Amt*) of the party: he attended the meeting on 24 May in this capacity. At the time of its foundation, Rosenberg and other Nazi leaders expected a great deal of the new institution. Three days after Rosenberg's appointment, the *Völkischer Beobachter* explained its editor's new job: 'With the creation of the Foreign Political Office, the particular desires and the unique aspirations of National Socialism will find expression within the area of foreign policy.' At a press conference on the same day, Rosenberg told the assembled journalists that his agency would 'make the German people aware that foreign policy is not a matter for a small caste, but the concern of the entire nation';[12] he declared that the functions of his office would include the treatment of the questions of the eastern and Danubian areas, of German equality, and the training of 'young people who might one day

[10] See page 57.   [11] See page 84 et seq.
[12] *Völkischer Beobachter*, 5 April 1933.

be called upon to participate in the determination of Germany's destiny in foreign policy'. Rosenberg saw himself as the new Foreign Minister: there were rumours in circulation in well-informed circles that the Foreign Political Office was to take over the functions of the Foreign Ministry, and that, anyway, Neurath was on the point of resigning.

The animosity between Rosenberg and Neurath and his Ministry was therefore to be expected. Rosenberg's dislike of the Foreign Ministry was motivated by attitudes similar to Goebbels's animosity towards that institution. There was, however, no love lost between Rosenberg and the Minister of Propaganda either. The tough and incisive Goebbels thought Rosenberg woolly and ineffective; he was highly critical of the ideologist's ability as an administrator. Rosenberg, on the other hand, resented the various propagandist 'excesses' committed by Goebbels and his henchmen; he often complained that they exercised a pernicious influence on public opinion abroad. Remembering his erstwhile party comrade, Rosenberg said of him that he was 'the Mephisto of our once so straightforward movement'.[13] Rosenberg, who never left the straight and narrow path of loyalty to Hitler, thought Goebbels an unreliable man, with a liking for conspiracy and intrigue. Indeed, the personal relations between the two men made co-operation between them and their agencies quite out of the question.

The effectiveness of Rosenberg's apparatus has been seriously over-estimated;[14] Goebbels's view of Rosenberg's administrative abilities was right; in addition, the head of the Foreign Political Office expended a lot of energy on inter-departmental squabbles. In any case, Rosenberg jeopardized the future development of his agency soon after its foundation. In May, he left Berlin on an important mission to London—it was to secure the acquiescence of the English to the Nazi plans for expansion in the East—as Hitler's own emissary. The mission ended in disaster. At the Foreign Office, Rosenberg was coldly received by Sir Robert Vansittart; the swastika-decorated wreath Rosenberg had laid at the Cenotaph was removed by irate members of the British

[13] *Memories of Alfred Rosenberg*, edited by Serge Lang and Ernst von Schenk, page 161. New York, 1949.
[14] Cf. *The Brown Network*, pages 55 et seq.

61

Legion; he received a very bad press, and his efforts to see the Prime Minister failed.[15]

After the fiasco in London, Rosenberg's standing in the party declined. Hitler himself became less readily available: in a covering letter to the Führer with a confidential report on the situation abroad written towards the end of the year, Rosenberg complained that the Chancellery made it impossible for him, on several occasions, to discuss his views with Hitler personally.[16] His position in regard to other agencies dealing with foreign policy, and the *Auswärtiges Amt* in particular, also deteriorated. The funds for the Foreign Political Office were drastically cut down: he could no longer be regarded as a serious rival of either the diplomats or the propagandists. The agency continued its existence in the shadow of its more powerful and experienced rivals. While Rosenberg kept on sending voluminous reports to Hitler, his office organized beer parties for resident diplomats and for visiting dignitaries; it sponsored lectures, and its clerks justified their existence by accumulating a vast library of newspaper cuttings.

Apart from foreign governments and peoples, there existed another important target for National Socialist propaganda. Some 27,000,000 Germans lived outside the frontiers of their mother country. Aside from the solidly German Austria, there were substantial German settlements in Poland and Russia, in Czechoslovakia, Hungary, Rumania, and Yugoslavia. These Germans had a long tradition behind them of settlement in eastern and south-eastern Europe. More recently, the Germans had begun to emigrate to the United States: between 1809 and 1929 more than 6,000,000 German emigrants left for the New World.

Such a large-scale dispersion did not pass unnoticed by German scholars. Since the end of the eighteenth century men like Ernst Moritz Arndt, Friedrich Christoph, Ludwig Uhland, and Jacob Grimm had devoted their attention to German settlements abroad. Indeed, it was natural for scholars to turn to ethnography when the unification of their country was the order of the day. Since the new state was to be based on the nation, questions such as what the nation exactly was, and where it could be found,

[15] See page 145.
[16] *Das politische Tagebuch Alfred Rosenbergs,* page 129.

became urgent problems of academic research. Nevertheless, scholarly work was merely a prelude to political activities; the dividing line between them was often very thin.

By the end of the nineteenth century there existed many societies of the educational or gymnastic kind, designed to sustain the national consciousness of the Germans living abroad. In 1908—at a time when nationalism in Central Europe was becoming more intense and when its organizations were being overhauled—the *Allgemeiner Deutscher Schulverein* (the General Union of German Schools) became the *Verein für das Deutschtum im Ausland (VDA,* the Union of Germans Abroad). The new organization continued to support German schools in 'endangered districts'; in 1908, the Hamburg branch of *VDA* rendered assistance to sixty-two schools in both North and South America. But at the same time, the society widened its scope; it granted a considerable financial subsidy, for instance, to the *Tiroler Volksbund,* an organization dedicated to countering the advance of the Italian irredentist movement in South Tyrol.[17] A few months before the outbreak of the war, an organization similar to *VDA*—the *Deutsches Schutzbund*—was established; during the war two additional institutes were set up in order to advance research in German minorities abroad: the *Institut für Auslandskunde, Grenz- und Auslandsdeutschtum* in Leipzig in 1914, and, three years later, the *Deutsches Auslandsinstitut* in Stuttgart.

The peace treaties of 1919 further stimulated this interest of the ethnographers: apart from the Germans lost to the Reich, a much larger number of them had been deprived of the protection of the Habsburg dynasty; many of these Germans passed under the tougher control of the successor states. Thus millions of new recruits joined the category of *Auslandsdeutsche,* and the activities of the *VDA* had to be considerably expanded. This work was carried on in the Weimar Republic. In 1925 the number of the local groups of *VDA* reached 1,707; by 1931 it had risen to 3,286.[18] Indeed, to say that the Reich Germans knew little about their brethren in Austria, Czechoslovakia, Hungary or Rumania, and that they 'cared less' represents a misreading of the situa-

[17] Ralph F. Bischoff, *Nazi conquest through German culture,* pages 83 et seq. Harvard University Press, 1942.
[18] ibid., page 87.

tion.[19] The study of minorities became a respectable academic subject, taught at many German universities, and the science developed its own terminology. There were the *Grenzdeutsche*, who inhabited ethnically homogeneous areas alongside Germany's frontier; it was assumed that they lived in the states of Austria, Czechoslovakia, or Poland against their will. The *Binnendeutsche*, on the other hand, lived by their consent in countries bordering on Germany, such as Switzerland. The *Inseldeutsche* inhabited compact settlements, and the *Streudeutsche* were scattered farther afield, outside Central Europe. Finally, the Germans living overseas were described as *Überseedeutsche*.

There can be no doubt that the minorities abroad attracted the keen attention of the Reich Germans during the Weimar period. Indeed, it was said of the various societies concerned with the *Auslandsdeutsche* that they helped in 'paving the way for Hitlerian nationalism and the formation of a larger German Reich in central Europe'.[20] And more than that. Very often, the nationalism of the Germans abroad was more intense than that of the Germans at home. While the latter supported the former financially, they were rewarded by the gratifying spectacle of the pure flame of a faith even stronger than their own. The National Socialists of course soon appreciated the opportunities presented to them by this situation.

In this respect, Rudolf Hess, Hitler's deputy, worked harder than any other leading National Socialist. He also possessed the qualifications that seemed auspicious for a Nazi interested in foreign affairs. He was born, in Alexandria in 1896, the son of a German merchant, and educated in Germany and Switzerland. During the war he was wounded twice, while serving on the western front. In 1920, Hess went to the university of Munich to study history, economics, and the new subject of geopolitics. There he came under the influence of Karl Haushofer, an ex-army general and a geographer, the leading German exponent of the 'science' of geopolitics. At the same time, Hess joined the embryonic National Socialist party; he was attracted by this movement after hearing Hitler speak in one of the beer-cellars. In Haushofer's

[19] Cf. A. J. P. Taylor, *The Origins of the Second World War*, page 26. London, 1961.
[20] R. F. Bischoff, op. cit., page 102.

speculations the German minorities abroad played a rather prominent role: his dominant belief was that all the inhabited parts of the globe were governed by a kind of geopolitical law of the jungle. It appealed to the budding Nazi; Hess became Haushofer's friend and assistant. When Hess was arrested with his Führer, after the unsuccessful *putsch* in Munich in November 1923, Haushofer was a frequent visitor to the Landsberg prison. Indeed, a few months after Hitler became the Chancellor, Rudolf Hess began to show a marked interest in German minorities abroad. He circulated a strictly confidential 'record of a decision by the Deputy of the Führer';[21] it was drafted in Munich on 27 October, and it consisted of four points:

(1) All questions regarding the German element beyond the borders (*Grenzdeutsche* and *Auslandsdeutsche*) and questions regarding the strengthening of the whole German community, as well as all related matters within the Reich, are subject to my jurisdiction and supervision.

(2) As a deliberative and executive organ, I have called together the *Volksdeutsch* Council (*Volksdeutscher Rat*) which is headed by Dr. Haushofer, University Professor, Munich.

(3) Dr. Steinacher, Berlin, has primary responsibility for representing the *Volksdeutsch* Council abroad.

(4) The *Volksdeutsch* Council does not appear publicly.

Rudolf Hess.

On the surface, this document was just another piece of evidence of the scramble for power among the party leaders. But it was also the beginning of an attempt to subject all the Germans living abroad to control by the National Socialist party. They should be organized in exclusively Nazi societies; they should be a willing instrument of the policy—whatever it might be at any given moment—of the Nazi government. Hess's associates on the *Volksdeutscher Rat* had a considerable experience behind them of the German minorities abroad. Haushofer's experience had been largely academic; that of Dr. Hans Steinacher was more of a practical nature. He was the chief of the *VDA*, the principal organization of Germans abroad; for several years after the war he had conducted propaganda on behalf of the Germans in several disputed territories of Austria: in Carinthia, in Tyrol,

[21] *Docs. Ger. For. Pol.*, series C, vol. 2, page 49.

and in Ödenburg (Sopron), near the frontier between Austria and Hungary.

Again, Hess's peremptory 'record of a decision' became the centre of a dispute concerning departmental competence. And again—as in the case of Goebbels's earlier attempt to control the *Auswärtiges Amt*'s press section—the Foreign Ministry had to defend itself against encroachments on its own territory. Its cultural Policy Department (*Abteilung VI*) under Senior Counsellor Friedrich Stieve had a section which dealt with German national groups abroad; on 11 November it supplied von Neurath with a brief for his conversation with Hess.[22] By then, Hess had written to the Foreign Minister, and Steinacher had also requested a discussion. Although the Wilhelmstrasse officials were prepared to listen to the ideas of the representatives of the *Volksdeutscher Rat*, they advised their Minister that these discussions could be conducted only on the following basis: 'The *Volksdeutsch* work and the minorities question are very closely linked with Germany's foreign policy in general. The Ministries concerned[23] will be glad to receive from the *Volksdeutsch* Council and to examine any suggestion relating to the furtherance of German nationality work. But the ultimate decision in all *Volksdeutsch* and minorities questions must rest with the Reich government, and specifically with the Foreign Ministry which is responsible for foreign policy.'

The dispute was settled in the end on the lines suggested by the Foreign Ministry. After the conversation with Hess, Neurath was able to inform his officials as well as other Ministries—the Ministry of Propaganda among them—that 'full agreement was reached on the point that the Council shall act only as an advisory body, which has the task of assisting the policies of the responsible ministries in questions relating to the German national community and the minorities. The Government will be able to use the *Volksdeutsch* Council at its discretion'.[24]

Apart from the formation of the *Volksdeutscher Rat*, an institution that was to gather under its wing all the older societies

---

[22] *Docs. Ger. For. Pol.*, series C, vol. 2, pages 107–108.
[23] That is, apart from the Foreign Ministry, those of Interior, Finance, Economics, Popular Enlightenment and Propaganda, and the Prussian State Ministry, the Prussian Ministries of Interior, Ecclesiastical Affairs, and Finance.
[24] *Docs. Ger. For. Pol.*, series C, vol. 2. page 36.

that concerned themselves with Germans abroad, Hess struck out in a different direction. It is possible that, after his brushes with the *Auswärtiges Amt* over the question of the Council, he realized that he had adopted the wrong approach and that the party, rather than government agencies, would show more understanding for his ideas. After all, the party had had connexions abroad before it came to rule the Reich.

Among the earliest Nazi groups abroad were those formed by the German immigrants to the United States and Latin America. Many of the half a million people who emigrated to the United States after the war were young, and they had grown up in Germany in the same conditions as the Nazi movement; some of them had been *Freikorps* members. In Chicago, these right-wing immigrants set up an organization, the *Teutonia*, in 1924; its chairman, who was an ardent follower of Julius Streicher, joined the Nazi party two years later.[25]

In Latin America, the *NSDAP* was making some progress as well: in 1928, a dozen Germans founded a local organization (*Ortsgruppe*) in Paraguay. Although local party organizations were set up in a number of European countries as well as in the Americas, National Socialist ideas cannot be said to have made much impression among the Germans abroad before 1933. They of course ran their national organizations of various political complexions: the Nazi organizations were in a minority among them. But this was enough to arouse the interest of the party members in Germany. In 1930, an office was established in Hamburg by Willy Grothe, a party member who had spent some twenty years in Africa; the function of his office was to keep in touch with German Nazis abroad. In May 1931 it was officially recognized by the party leadership; when Hitler came to power, it had some 3,300 party members on its files.[26]

Soon after the official recognition of the 'foreign division'— *Auslandsabteilung der Reichsleitung der NSDAP*—the office advertised a job in its African department. Ernst-Wilhelm Bohle applied, and got it. Bohle was born in Bradford in 1903; three years later, his father left England for Cape Town to

---

[25] Louis de Jong, *The German Fifth Column in the Second World War*, page 227. London, 1956.
[26] *Trials of the Major War Criminals*, Vol. X, page 13.

67

6

teach physics at the university, and Bohle was brought up and educated there. He was certainly given enough opportunities to become a German nationalist: the Bohle children were forbidden to speak English at home; during the First World War, young Ernst was the only German boy at his Cape Town school. He studied economics in Germany after the war, and from 1924 he worked for a number of business firms.

The work for the party's foreign division suited him: he had personal experience of the life of the Germans abroad, and he had strong views on the question of whether or not they should preserve intact their national identity. He joined the party in March 1932; his devoted work attracted the attention of Rudolf Hess—Hitler's deputy came from a similar background—and Bohle became Hess's protégé. From now on, his rise to prominence was fast. On 8 May, he was put in charge of the foreign division of the party which, by an order of Hess of 17 February 1934, became the *Auslandsorganisation der NSDAP*, usually referred to as *AO*—the Foreign Organization. Bohle knew his was a strong position, and that it could be strengthened still further. Shortly before his official elevation in May 1933, he wrote to a party comrade that his organization controlled 160 groups abroad, that there existed 'great possibilities for its further extension', and that it could render great services to Rosenberg's newly founded *Aussenpolitisches Amt*, as well as to Goebbels's Ministry.[27]

Soon, however, Bohle's organization began to outstrip in importance Rosenberg's amateur foreign office. Bohle was not weighed down by personal animosities and past party feuds; he was an efficient administrator, with good connexions in high party circles. Nevertheless, as the *AO* grew in stature, it came into inevitable conflict with the Foreign Ministry. Friction between the *AO* agents and the diplomats developed, and there was no love lost between Bohle and von Neurath. In his more expansive moments, Bohle regarded his province as a '*Gau* without limits'; in return, the Foreign Minister described Bohle as a 'scoundrel [*Gauner*] without limits.' The conflict did not disappear after December 1937, when the activities of Bohle's

[27] Nürnberg evidence, N.G. 5557, letter from Bohle to Schmeer, Hamburg, 4 April 1933.

organization were officially sanctioned, and he became a Secretary of State in the Foreign Ministry; it continued even after Ribbentrop became Foreign Minister. In his memoirs, Ribbentrop recorded that 'Especially during my early years as Foreign Minister, the activities of the National Socialist Organization of Germans Abroad caused me acute embarrassment, in South America, for instance. There, as elsewhere, such things as processions, uniforms, and rallies created the impression that National Socialism was to be exported. Indeed, however wrongly, the Organization was described as a 'Fifth Column', and furnished President Roosevelt with the grotesque propaganda argument that Germany was trying to establish a foothold in South America, which it would use as a base for action against the U.S.A. In view of these and similar difficulties in many other countries, I often pointed out that while the Organization's aims of keeping Germans abroad together was certainly right, the manner in which this was done entailed disproportionate disadvantages. However, the Organization of Germans Abroad was the pet child of Rudolf Hess, and a shadow was cast over our original friendship by this difference of opinion, and also by the fact that it was not easy to work with Bohle. . . .'[28]

Despite the animosity of the two successive Foreign Ministers and the diplomats, the *Auslandsorganisation* prospered. From humble beginnings in Hamburg it came to administer, by 1934, some 350 groups abroad; three years later, its head office in Berlin employed 700 people, who looked after 28,000 party members abroad, plus 23,000 organized merchant seamen. In the same year, all members of the diplomatic service were organized into an *Ortsgruppe*, another move by the party to tighten its grip on the Foreign Ministry. Indeed, this last arrangement clearly shows the administrative complexities of the Nazi state and, within it, the curious double status of the *AO*. As a State Secretary in the Foreign Ministry, Bohle was directly responsible to the Minister; at the same time, his activities as the leader of the party's Foreign Organization and his responsibility to Rudolf Hess, Hitler's deputy, remained unchanged.[29]

[28] *The Ribbentrop Memoirs*, pages 80–81. London, 1954.
[29] *National Socialism, Basic Principles, Their Application by the Party's Foreign Organization, and the Use of Germans Abroad for Nazi Aims*, page 95. U.S. Department of State, Washington, 1943.

Technically the *AO* remained a province—a *Gau*—of the *NSDAP*, and as such it was divided, like the party itself, into an hierarchy of regional sections. There were eight departments in the *AO* head office; Department I dealt with north-eastern Europe; II with western Europe apart from Great Britain and Ireland; Department III covered Austria, south-eastern Europe and the Near East; IV—Italy, Switzerland and Hungary; V—Africa; VI—North America; VII—Latin America; VIII—Great Britain, Ireland, the Far East, and Australia; a special department dealt with the sailors. There were also departments for teachers, lawyers, government employers, and students abroad, and 'functional offices', such as of foreign trade, culture, a 'speakers' department' which organized festivities in German colonies abroad.[30] At Altona, near Hamburg, the *AO* ran a school, the purpose of which was to instruct Germans from abroad in National Socialist agitation.

There was, however, some confusion as to precisely what kind of Germans the activities of the *AO* aimed at. An official pamphlet, published in Berlin in 1937, flatly stated that the Foreign Organization was concerned exclusively with German citizens living abroad.[31] This was a concession to the growing concern over the activities of the Nazis in the neighbouring countries; there was a convenient ambiguity in modes of expression, and usually no distinction was made between the Germans living abroad and those who remained German citizens. In the Nazi eyes, the question of citizenship was of a purely formal nature; ties of blood and race were assumed to be much stronger.

The main function of Bohle's organization was to unite all Germans abroad under National Socialist leadership; the party had been pursuing the same aim inside Germany before and after 1933. In order to work successfully, the propaganda conducted by the *AO* among the Germans abroad had to be founded on certain basic assumptions. Of these, the most important was the systematic opposition to any form of assimilation. At the *Parteitag der Ehre* in September 1936, where he 'honoured' forty-eight flags of the *AO*'s local groups, Rudolf Hess said: 'The Führer had come in order to hammer into all of us the fact that

[30] Emil Ehrich, *Die Auslandsorganisation der NSDAP*, pages 17 et seq. Berlin, 1937.   [31] ibid., page 7.

70

the German cannot and may not choose whether or not he will be German but that he was sent into this world by God as a German, and that God thereby had laid upon him, as a German, duties of which he cannot divest himself without committing treason to Providence. Therefore, we believe and we know that the German everywhere is a German—whether he lives in the Reich or in Japan, in France or in China, or anywhere else in the world. Not countries or continents, not climate or environment, but blood and race determine the world of ideas of the German.'[32]

It was assumed that the Germans would resist assimilation in their adoptive countries; a divided German community was, however, also undesirable from the National Socialist point of view. Bohle stated this view soon after he had taken the leaderships of the *AO*: 'Today our fighters are often defending desperate posts. They know, however, that at home and abroad only National Socialism can prepare the way for a cohesive Germandom. Only National Socialists who are ideologically well grounded can unite the German colonies, which outside the homeland are often still divided, and create a unity in which the guarantee for support of the homeland by foreign Germandom can be given.'[33]

Since an attempt had to be made to unite all Germans living abroad in supporting Hitler's régime, much of the activity of the *Auslandsorganisation* consisted of propaganda. We shall have an opportunity to examine the techniques employed by the Nazis abroad in greater detail in subsequent chapters; at this point, suffice it to say that the *AO* faithfully reflected the modes of agitation used inside Germany. And since the Nazis were often confronted with hostile governments in foreign countries, their situation resembled that of the party inside Germany before 1933. To a certain extent they continued to use the mixture of propaganda and violence: the *AO* had a special section working on *Gestapo* commissions.[34] The Foreign Organization's agents kept a watchful eye on the activities of the refugees from Nazi Germany; there were many instances of their intimidation.

Indeed, the Germans abroad were regarded in Berlin as the

[32] *Der Parteitag der Ehre*, pages 124 et seq. Munich, 1936.
[33] *Almanach der nationalsozialistischen Revolution*, edited by Wilhelm Kube, page 95. Berlin, 1934.
[34] L. de Jong, op. cit., page 279.

71

best target and, at the same time, a suitable vehicle for National Socialist propaganda abroad. And Bohle was the right man to direct it. Although he came into conflict with the Foreign Ministry, he was too remote from the centre of power in the Nazi state to be suspected, by the Nazi leaders, of empire-building; under the patronage of Hess, he was able to build up the *AO* undisturbed. Even Goebbels, who rarely left an opportunity for criticism of the endeavours of his colleagues unexplored, treated Bohle and his organization kindly. Early in March 1943 he wrote in his diary: 'Bohle gave me a memorandum on foreign propaganda. In it he is highly critical of the so-called propaganda abroad of the Foreign Ministry. This is incredibly bad. The diplomats are not suited to conduct foreign propaganda. I am certain that I could carry out together with the *AO* a wonderful system of propaganda abroad but our diplomats stand in my way.'[35]

While those state and party agencies that dealt in propaganda abroad rarely lived at peace with each other, a large variety of unofficial organizations pursued their activities comparatively undisturbed. They could push forward the more extremist lines of National Socialist propaganda without any regard to their repercussions in the sphere of foreign policy; they can be said to have formed knots of agitation on the periphery of the overall propaganda effort. Some of these unofficial organizations had existed before Hitler came to power; none of them could, however, have continued their activities without at least a tacit approval by the Nazi government; many received official financial support. These organizations specialized largely in anti-semitic, anti-Marxist, and anti-Soviet propaganda: their main interests corresponded to those of Streicher and Rosenberg, the leading party ideologists.

In Erfurt, Colonel Fleischhauer ran one of the most active of these private institutions. Before 1933 he had worked independently of the National Socialists; he entered into a close contact with them after Hitler came to power, and his antisemitic activities prospered. They centred on a bi-monthly newsletter, in three languages, the *Weltdienst*; its first number was published in December 1933. Less than a year later, Fleischhauer organized

[35] L. P. Lochner, editor, *The Goebbels Diaries*, entry for 4 March 1943. London, 1948.

an antisemitic congress; he found it necessary to emphasize in his periodical[36] that Streicher had not summoned the congress, and that the 'pioneers' of antisemitism could not be regarded as 'Hitler agents'. Fleischhauer's Pan-Aryans were non-denominational Christians, on their guard against the Jews and the Freemasons. But Fleischhauer was faced with stiff competition. There was Ernst Pistor in Berlin, who published the newspaper *Der Judenkenner*, and who founded the short-lived *Alliance Raciste Universelle*; the semi-official institute which dealt with eugenics (*Aufklärungsamt für Bevölkerungspolitik und Rassenpflege*) published its house-magazine in both German and English. The *Deutscher Fichte-Bund* was founded in 1914 to propagate German views and aims abroad; when Hitler came to power, the organization survived unharmed: it was easily able to assimilate the attitudes of the new masters of Germany. The activities of the Fichte League in the field of foreign propaganda were intensified in the last two years before the war, and they were largely directed at the English-speaking countries.

There existed many other approved, but unofficial, organizations; many of them were rather elusive, because they frequently changed their names, their leadership, and their address. They once again set off the poverty of the Nazi—or nationalist—ideologies: they dealt in negative doctrines of a limited, sectional appeal. However, an attempt to create a truly international organization was made. In the spring of 1934 an enterprising German lawyer, Hans Keller, founded a society called the 'International Union of Nationalists' (*Internationale Arbeitsgemeinschaft der Nationalisten*); it was based on Zürich, where its expensively produced pamphlets were published. Its first congress took place in Berlin in December; the principal delegates were invited by Goebbels to attend the annual meeting organized by the *Reichskulturkammer* in the Berlin Sportpalast. The delegates came from Warsaw, Paris, Amsterdam, Rome, and elsewhere; most of them were university professors. It was, on the whole, a respectable gathering: perhaps the men who came to it had not realized what purposes they were to be used for. There can be no doubt that

[36] *Weltdienst*, 1 September 1934; Louis W. Bondy, *Racketeers of hatred*, pages 81–82. London, 1946.

Keller sympathized with the Nazis, and that his friends were expected to contribute to making Hitler's government acceptable in their own countries.

Keller regarded the delegates as more representative of their peoples than their respective governments: to make such a distinction is, of course, one of the basic techniques of the propagandist. For Keller it was, however, the central point of his *Weltanschauung*. He maintained that in Europe there existed a 'state' nationalism quite separately from '*völkisch*', or popular, nationalism, and that their identification was the only certain road to national salvation. According to Keller, Hitler had succeeded in healing the rift, and he led the way where others must follow. Keller's 'Third Europe', composed of such rejuvenated states, was clearly a concomitant of Hitler's Third Reich.

But Keller was forced to admit that the 'conceptual instruments' for the discussion of the 'new nationalism' were still lacking.[37] And apart from the elements of the National Socialist doctrine, Keller had nothing to fall back on. He did not, however, have to do all the work himself. Louis Bertrand, for instance, at the time President of the *Académie Français*, wrote in a pamphlet published by Keller[38] that the 'Nationalist International is going to unite the peoples against the Communist International, which is their mortal enemy'.

Anti-Communism was, on the whole, a safer subject than antisemitism. At the first congress of Keller's organization, de Pottere, one of Colonel Fleischhauer's associates from Erfurt (he was using the name of Farmer on this occasion, and he said he represented Hungary) was hard put to it to define the new nationalism in a manner acceptable to the assembled intellectuals. He revealed his true opinions only towards the end of his involved speech. He said then that race alone mattered, and that the Jews, although they could speak German, were not Aryans.[39] Nevertheless, Keller's 'international' did not last long. His attacks on the Italian fascists was perhaps his gravest tactical error: anyway, Keller was too ambitious. The men he

[37] 'Volksgemeinschaft und Völkerfriede', *Sitzungsbericht der Berliner Tagung*, page 8. Zürich, 1935.
[38] *Am Internationalismus gehen die Völker zugrunde*, page 13. Zürich, 1936.
[39] 'Volksgemeinschaft und Völkerfriede', *Sitzungsbericht der Berliner Tagung*, pages 19 and 20.

THE AGENCIES OF PROPAGANDA ABROAD

tried to bring together may have had certain attitudes in common regarding their views of the ills that affected their peoples. This was no substitute for a real community of interests or for the binding force of a coherent ideology. He organized two more congresses: at the end of 1936 the last of his pretentious pamphlets was published.

Perhaps with one exception,[40] the private organizations that attempted to disseminate National Socialist propaganda abroad were not very effective. They never did more than fill in the details in the overall propaganda outline; they were usually patronized by either Rosenberg or Streicher, the ideological extremists, and they often appealed to the lunatic fringe of public opinion outside Germany. The main burden was carried by the state and party agencies; Goebbels continued to exercise the strongest influence on propaganda abroad. He could do so through the press, broadcasting, and films: his control over these media was undisputed. But he regarded foreign propaganda, to a high degree, as an extension of the propaganda at home. He was perhaps too busy inside Germany: at any rate, he was unable to make the distinctions between different types of political environment that are so necessary for the successful conduct of foreign propaganda. There were other highly placed party members—Rudolf Hess or Alfred Rosenberg—who regarded themselves as better qualified for this task, and they built up party and state agencies that played an important role in propaganda abroad. The Foreign Ministry remained the propagandists' principal whipping boy; the enmity between Goebbels and the two successive Foreign Ministers jeopardized a close cooperation between the two government agencies. Hitler took little notice of such rivalries, and he usually let his underlings squabble in peace. Nevertheless, the organizational anarchy in the field of foreign propaganda often made it difficult to disentangle the respective contributions of the various organizations to any given incident or propaganda effect that took place outside Germany. And at the same time, their activities blurred the image abroad of the National Socialist régime: a phenomenon that cannot be said to have always worked out to the disadvantage of Germany's rulers.

[40] For a discussion of the role of the *Antikomintern* see pages 87–92.

IV. THE CONSTANT THEMES: THE JEWS AND THE COMMUNISTS

OUTSIDE Germany, Hitler faced a situation much more delicate and complex than at home. Yet, on the whole, the contents of National Socialist propaganda remained the same whether it was intended for foreign or for domestic consumption. This situation was occasioned by a variety of factors: we have seen that Nazi ideology lacked in international appeal. The leadership of the party was short of men with any kind of experience of the foreign scene: among National Socialists, knowledge of international affairs was at a premium. And, as Hitler's government thought it necessary to make its foreign policy acceptable at home, an additional link was created between propaganda at home and abroad.

Indeed, in the political literature of National Socialism it is impossible to find a body of basic directives dealing with propaganda abroad even remotely resembling those contained in *Mein Kampf*, which concerned propaganda inside Germany. There exist only a few scattered references. In *Mein Kampf*, for instance, Hitler congratulated the Allies on their propaganda effort in the First World War: he was unaware, however, of the fact that the Allied propagandists had been equally impressed by Germany's efforts with regard to Russia.[1] Some time in 1933 Hitler intimated that he had learned from the Bolsheviks, alluding at the same time to Sir Roger Casement and to revolutions, and hoping that 'we shall have friends who will help us in all enemy countries'.[2] But he saw propaganda abroad primarily as an instrument for the achievement of power, just as

[1] Cf. Z. A. B. Zeman, *The Break-up of the Habsburg Empire*, page 184. Oxford University Press, 1961.
[2] H. Rauschning, *Hitler Speaks*, page 19. London, 1939.

76

he had seen propaganda at home before 1933. Discussing the nature of the future war, Hitler is reported to have said: 'The place of artillery preparation for frontal attack by the infantry in trench warfare will in future be taken by revolutionary propaganda, to break down the enemy psychologically before the armies begin to function at all.' And then he added: 'How to achieve the moral breakdown of the enemy before the war has started—that is the problem that interests me.'[3] Nevertheless, the 'moral breakdown of the enemy' was the remote, the ultimate object of propaganda: we shall see that it was achieved only in special political circumstances. For the more routine purposes— including 'projection' of the Nazi state and its ideology—the Ministry of Propaganda was in the main content to translate the key themes of home propaganda to the international plane.

It has been demonstrated that the high antisemitic charge contained in domestic propaganda did not play a decisive part in gaining adherents for the National Socialist movement.[4] Though antisemitism figured prominently in Nazi propaganda, it did not make a significant contribution to Nazi success. Its value lay mainly in the manner in which it was manipulated to satisfy the psychological needs of the Germans. The Jews could be used as scapegoats; antisemitism could be employed as a smoke-screen which served to divert public attention from genuine social and political problems.[5] Ultimately, it could be traced to the Führer's personal predilections: Hitler was an antisemite by conviction.

Although he could calculate and exploit the appeal of anti-semitism in Germany, he miscalculated its value for propaganda abroad. He regarded it as a more than suitable article for export: indeed, he is reported to have said: 'Antisemitism is a useful revolutionary expedient. My Jews are a valuable hostage given to me by the democracies. Antisemitic propaganda in all countries is an almost indispensable medium for the extension of

[3] H. Rauschning, *Hitler Speaks*, page 19. Apart from indicating that these conversations with Hitler date from the period between the beginning of the year 1932 and the end of 1934, Rauschning does not give the precise date of the pronouncement. It is likely, however, that Hitler was more concerned with this kind of problem after, rather than before, January 1933.
[4] This problem has been exhaustively discussed by Dr. E. G. Reichmann in her study *Hostages of Civilisation*. London, 1949. Cf. page 234.
[5] ibid., pages 166–7 and 198.

our political campaign. You will see how little time we shall need in order to upset the ideas and the criteria of the whole world, simply by attacking Judaism. It is beyond question the most important weapon in my propaganda arsenal, and almost of deadly efficiency.'[6]

Hitler's estimate of the value of antisemitic propaganda was mistaken. On balance, the Nazi antisemitic drives abroad had more often a repulsive than an attractive effect. Even in Fascist Italy, there existed little understanding of this special type of Nazi racialism, and still less a desire to emulate it. In a report on the propaganda situation in Italy from October 1933, Scheffer, the *WTB* agency representative in Rome, had to inform the Foreign Ministry that Mussolini had personally received the Chief Rabbi of Milan and that 'Jewish propaganda' was being made, backstage, in Italy: Jewish business circles were, for instance, showing themselves unwilling to buy German goods. Nevertheless, Scheffer had a ready explanation for this state of affairs, an explanation which his masters in Berlin would understand. The Italian, he wrote, 'in whose veins there circulate racially different types of blood, cannot understand the Jewish question in Germany'.[7]

In the National Socialist view of the foreign scene, the Italians, though they were ideologically sound, were racially unrelated to the Germans, and therefore no sanity of views could be expected from them in matters of race. The Nazi view of the British, on the other hand, was the reverse of their image of the Italians: 'Englishmen'—this term usually embraced all the inhabitants of Great Britain—were racially related, although ideologically quite unsound. Hitler did not find in Britain the response to antisemitism he had hoped for. The national newspapers had reported on antisemitic outrages committed by the Nazis even before Hitler came to power: after January 1933 the treatment of the Jews was widely regarded as the testing ground for the intentions of the new government in Germany. The question then asked in many editorials was whether, carrying the new responsibilities of the government, the Chancellor could afford to continue his former policies.

[6] H. Rauschning, *Hitler Speaks*, page 233.
[7] Report from Rome to the *AA*, 10 October 1933, 8677H/E607177-92.

In the following years, even the dailies—such as *The Times*—that carried on the policy of establishing an understanding with Nazi Germany, continued to report on the treatment of Jews in Germany. Indeed, the reports on the pogroms of November 1938 marked the beginning of a strong revulsion, in this country, against Hitler's régime.[8] At the same time, direct antisemitic propaganda did not make an impact of any significance in Britain; it was, on occasions, harmful to the Nazi cause. Goebbels's Ministry never appeared much concerned with this aspect of antisemitic propaganda: the German diplomats in London, on the other hand, realized that it should not be given too much prominence. But they received no guidance from Berlin; they used their own discretion.

As late as 19 July 1939, Dirksen, the Ambassador to London, wrote: 'Having regard to the stolid, tolerant racial character of the British, every antisemitic impulse must be valued all the more highly, since opportunities for disseminating anti-Jewish ideas are very limited.'[9] Apart from Mosley's party, there existed only a few other, more or less antisemitic organizations: Dirksen referred to that of Captain Ramsay (the Tory M.P.), and Lady Hardinge's connexions with such societies. Antisemitic ideas were also expressed in certain right-wing periodicals: Dirksen singled out for mention the low-circulation weekly, *The New Pioneer*; a section of the Catholic press also attacked the Jews, but in an oblique way, in connexion with Bolshevism. Nevertheless, Dirksen wrote, 'antisemitic attitudes are revealed more clearly by conversations with the man in the street than by press-sources'. The rapid increase in Jewish immigration promoted, according to Dirksen, the spread of antisemitism: indeed, he went on to say that 'A further increase of anti-Jewish feeling in Britain can be expected'. There was advice implicit in Dirksen's dispatch to the propagandists that now—less than two months before the outbreak of the war—was the time to begin exploiting antisemitic mood in Britain.

In this country, antisemitic propaganda either had only a marginal appeal, or it was entirely cancelled out by reports on

---

[8] See Lionel Kochan's *Pogrom, 10 November 1938*; London, 1957; especially the last chapter, 'The Reaction Abroad'.

[9] The dispatch was printed in the *Wiener Library Bulletin*, No. 1, 1962.

National Socialist measures against the Jews in Germany. Nevertheless, for a short time and in special circumstances, a heightened receptiveness to antisemitism accompanied, and aided, the breakdown of the established political order in central and eastern Europe. It had shallow roots: set up by the peace treaties on an entirely new basis it had, in 1933, a brief and unsettled existence behind it. In this part of Europe National Socialist propaganda was at its most effective: indeed, it corroded the foundations of the established régimes to such an extent that military conquest later appeared either welcome or easy. We shall have occasion to note that National Socialist propaganda was mainly aimed at the Germans, the *Volksdeutsche*, in this area: Hitler knew that their co-operation was sufficient to severely impair the working of the established order.

In addition the Jewish problem in eastern Europe could be exploited for the purposes of a second line of attack. Indigenous antisemitism, both organized and spontaneous, existed in Rumania and Poland: these two countries contained numerous Jewish minorities.[10] Most of these Jews lived in isolated communities, the progress of their emancipation was slow, and they retained their characteristic features, from religion to dress and mannerisms. The compact Jewish communities both stimulated the pogroms and made them easy to carry out; on a higher social level, the distinction the Jews achieved in commerce, industry, and in the free professions, created resentment among their gentile compatriots. In the nineteenth century, the emergent east-European nationalisms had often contained an antisemitic charge.

Indeed, antisemitism in eastern Europe anticipated, in many respects, the National Socialist attitudes to the Jews; after 1933, under the impact of Nazi propaganda and precept, antisemitism came to play an increasingly important role in the politics of this part of Europe. Early in 1936, for instance, a Jewish newspaper was banned in Poland for publishing insulting references to a National Socialist Minister; in October 1937, Colonel Kowalevski, one of the leaders of the government party,

---

[10] In Poland, there lived some 3,000,000 Jews; in Rumania, the number of Jews amounted to a figure between 500,000 and 750,000. Cf. Hugh Seton-Watson, *Eastern Europe Between the Wars*, page 289. Cambridge, 1945.

told his interviewer from the *Völkischer Beobachter*, after mentioning the brotherly feelings between the Poles and the German minority: 'For us there exists only one difference in the evaluation of the people in Poland: Christian and non-Christian.'[11] From that year until the outbreak of the war, a number of anti-Jewish measures were taken by the government, and discussion of the Jewish problem was artificially stimulated.

In Rumania, the situation in regard to the local Jews developed on similar lines. At the end of 1937, the short-lived government of Octavian Goga and Professor Cuza pursued a pro-German policy combined with ruthless antisemitic measures. It lifted the ban on the import of Nazi propaganda books; Professor Cuza, in an interview with Julius Streicher's *Fränkische Tageszeitung*, demanded a common front of all 'awakened' nations against the Jews and therefore a German-Rumanian *rapprochement*.[12] For some time after the fall of the Goga government, and after the prosecution for treason of Corneliu Codreanu—the leader of the Fascist Iron Guard—the relations between Rumania and Germany deteriorated, while the position of the Jews improved. The antisemitic measures of the former government were not revoked; they remained, for the time being, unimplemented. Nevertheless, after the fall of France, Horia Sima—Codreanu's successor—summed up the situation in the following manner: 'Absolute adherence to the Axis Powers with no swerving from this fundamental principle even if the Axis should be unfair to Rumania, because the present war is really one between the two worlds of Aryans and of Jews.'[13]

Whereas in Poland and Rumania antisemitic propaganda found a ready and receptive audience, in Hungary and Czechoslovakia the situation was, from the National Socialist point of view, less favourable. Many of the 500,000 Hungarian Jews had achieved a high degree of emancipation before 1918; even the antisemitic restrictions imposed under the government of Gömbös, in the years 1933–36, made a clear distinction between the 'Hungarian' and the newly arrived Jews. Only after the autumn of 1938, when Hungary joined Germany in the assault

[11] *VB*, 5 October 1937; Cf. James B. Lunn, *Treachery and Antisemitism*, page 15. London, 1942.
[12] *Fränkische Tageszeitung*, 21 January 1938; James B. Lunn, op. cit., page 19.
[13] ibid., page 21.

81

on the territorial integrity of the Czechoslovak state, was a more ruthless antisemitic policy developed alongside Hungary's increasing dependence on Germany.

In Czechoslovakia, National Socialist antisemitic propaganda remained ineffective in the Czech areas until 1938. Here, the Jews were also better integrated than in Rumania or Poland; Masaryk, the first President, had fought incipient antisemitism under the Habsburg rule. The two Fascist groups—one of them was run by General Gajda, who had played a rather obscure role in the intervention against the Soviet government, and who declared himself, in March 1939, the Führer of the Czechs—commanded only a limited popular appeal. Even Konrad Henlein, the leader of the pro-Nazi Sudeten Germans in Czechoslovakia, thought it advisable to keep antisemitism, for some time, out of his party programme. Only after the Munich agreement in 1938, the growth of antisemitism accompanied, and contributed to, the general demoralization in public life. In Slovakia, an antisemitic party had existed before Munich: it was intensely nationalist and anti-Czech; it became the government party in the independent Slovak state under Hitler's patronage.

Indeed, the exaggerated claim Hitler made for the propaganda value of antisemitism nearly held true in eastern Europe. Here, antisemitism proved a disintegrating and demoralizing force; it accompanied the corrosion of the political system that had been established by the peace treaties, and it accelerated this process. The politicians who were receptive to its appeal thought of antisemitism as of one of the cornerstones of a right-wing popular movement; they also wanted to exploit its value as a diversion of public attention from genuine social problems. In Poland and in Rumania, especially, antisemitism remained—as it had been described in nineteenth-century Russia—an 'idiot's socialism'. In addition, it appealed to those politicans who were either dissatisfied with the post-war settlement, or who were oversensitive to the stresses it had generated: this was particularly true of Slovakia. Antisemitic agitation was of course more effective when it had a corresponding antisemitic mood to exploit. In Hungary Nazi propaganda had to appeal to 'revisionism'—the dissatisfaction with the peace treaty—rather than to the underdeveloped local antisemitism. But whatever the degree of

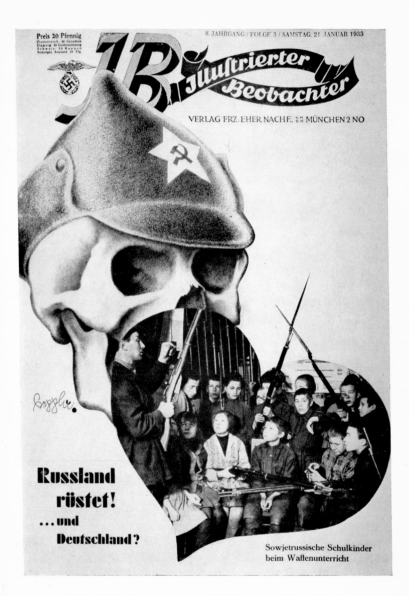

V. 'Russia arms! . . . and Germany?' 1933

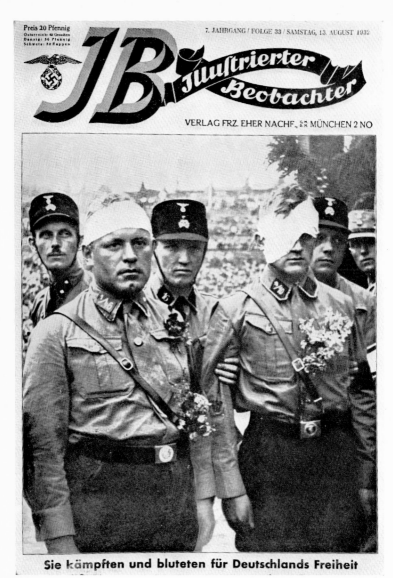

Preis 20 Pfennig
Österreich: 40 Groschen
Danzig: 30 Pfennig
Schweiz: 30 Rappen

7. JAHRGANG / FOLGE 33 / SAMSTAG, 13. AUGUST 1932

JB Illustrierter Beobachter

VERLAG FRZ. EHER NACHF., MÜNCHEN 2 NO

Sie kämpften und bluteten für Deutschlands Freiheit

VI. 'They fought and bled for Germany's freedom.' 1932

development and the reasons for local antisemitism may have been, it always went hand in hand with a policy of understanding with Hitler's Germany, a policy which always presented an assault on the *status quo.*

Anti-Communism was the other article of home propaganda which was vigorously exported. In National Socialist ideology, there existed an organic connexion between the two themes; the conflict with Communism became the battle royal for the National Socialists. Their leaders often said that the movement had grown up in this struggle, in which they expected it to grow stronger and finally to triumph. Certainly, the Communists were, together with the Jews, the main target of Nazi violence and abuse. But whatever the intensity of the actual political engagement may have been, the National Socialists came to look upon it as a propaganda gold mine. The campaign had a wide and varied target. It was aimed, in Nazi terminology, at '*Gesamtmarxismus,*' that embraced all Marxist phenomena, from, say, a Communist cell in a Berlin working-class suburb to the Soviet Union.

On his own evidence, Hitler learned to detest working-class organizations in Vienna before the First World War. There exists no ground for doubting it. In Vienna, he descended far below the level that his lower-middle-class parents' house had provided for him. He looked at his fellow-workers' lives and politics from above: he was among them, but he never regarded himself as one of them. Their organizations were run on Marxist—for Hitler, this meant Jewish—lines; they professed to be international and they showed the young man the way back to his nation.[14] We can assume that Hitler was well on the way to an intense hatred of everything that was even remotely connected with Marxism before he entered politics.

And when he did so, revolution and counter-revolution were very much in the air. He looked on German Social Democracy, another aspect of *Gesamtmarxismus,* as having collaborated in bringing about the defeat and ignominy of the German nation; he witnessed the Communist bid for power in Bavaria. This, and the gradual establishment of Communist rule over Russia, broadened the target without altering, for Hitler, its nature. And Hitler's own views on the subject were doubtless

[14] *Mein Kampf,* page 48.

7

buttressed by the influence of men like Alfred Rosenberg and Max
Scheubner-Richter, German refugees from the Baltic provinces.
By 1921, anti-Communism was firmly established as one of the
major themes of Nazi propaganda.[15] In the summer of that year
posters appeared in Munich inviting its citizens to a public
meeting:

'We German National Socialists demand that the Russian
people be given help, not by supporting its present government,
but by the elimination of its present corrupters. Those who
today give for Russia do not give for the Russian worker but
for his exploiter, the Jewish commissar. German fellow citizens,
come on Thursday 4 August 1921, to the great public giant
demonstration at the Zirkus Krone. Speaker: Herr Adolf Hitler,
on the Dying Soviet Russia.'[16] The National Socialists were now
ready to fight the 'Marxists': the rules of the conflict and its
peculiar characteristics were developed before Hitler left
Munich, at the end of 1923, to serve a term of imprisonment. In a
clash of this kind, marked by physical violence from beginning to
end, the Nazis never concerned themselves too much with the
theories of Marxism. There is no reason to believe that either
Hitler or his leading expert on Russia, Rosenberg, ever read a
single book or article by Marx or Engels.

At first, the German Social Democracy occupied a leading
position among the phenomena of *Gesamtmarxismus*: it was
gradually replaced by Bolshevism. In *Mein Kampf*, Hitler still
treated them as of approximately the same importance; Bolshevism, however, was quite clearly becoming the threat of the
future. In it, Hitler wrote, 'we ought to recognize the kind of
attempt which is being made by the Jew in the twentieth century
to secure dominion over the world'.[17] To this menace, Russia had
already succumbed; it was now 'hanging steadily over Germany'.[18] Otherwise, apart from expressing his disgust with the

[15] Cf. Walter Laqueur, 'Hitler and Russia 1919–23', in *The Survey*, October 1962.
[16] It was one of the posters reprinted in the first edition of *Mein Kampf*. The
poster appendix disappeared from the subsequent editions of the book; in 1939,
in the jubilee edition of *Mein Kampf* which marked Hitler's fiftieth birthday, the
appendix was again reproduced, with the exception of the poster quoted above.
The first moves were then being made in the direction of German–Soviet understanding. See C. Caspar's article—'*Mein Kampf* a Best Seller'—in *Jewish
Social Studies*. New York, January 1958.
[17] *Mein Kampf*, page 539.
[18] ibid., page 538.

'Bolshevization of art' ('If the creative spirit of the Periclean age be manifested in the Parthenon, then the Bolshevist era is manifested through its cubist grimace'),[19] Hitler did not have much to say on the subject. His attitude towards the first victim of Bolshevism—Russia—was ambiguous. He wrote of 'a gang of Jewish literati and financial bandits' (i.e. the Bolsheviks) dominating 'a great people'.[20] But in another context, this great people was demoted to the status of an inferior race. Discussing Germany's eastern policy, Hitler wrote: 'But when we speak of a new territory in Europe today we must principally think of Russia and the border states subject to her. Destiny itself seems to wish to point out the way for us here. In delivering Russia over to Bolshevism, fate robbed the Russian people of that intellectual class which had once created the Russian State and was the guarantee of its existence. For the Russian State was not organized by the constructive political talent of the Slav element in Russia, but was more a marvellous exemplification of the capacity for State-building possessed by the Germanic element in a race of inferior worth. . . . For centuries Russia owed a source of its livelihood as a State to the Germanic nucleus of its governing class. But this nucleus is now almost wholly broken up and abolished. The Jew has taken its place.'[21]

Although Hitler's attitude towards Communism had been firmly established by the time of the 're-establishment' of the party in 1925, there still existed certain striking deviations inside the National Socialist organization. They usually occurred on the Strassers' side of the party: in this connexion, the development of Goebbels's ideas is of interest. While working for the Strassers, Goebbels was a socialist rather than a nationalist: he detested western capitalism more than Bolshevism. The Locarno pact was for him, a 'horrible blend of deceit, meanness, infamy and hypocrisy', which meant that the Germans would become 'the mercenaries against Russia on the battlefields of capitalism'; anyway, Goebbels went on, it was better to 'go down with Bolshevism than live in eternal capitalist servitude'.[22]

[19] *Mein Kampf*, page 221.   [20] ibid., page 274.   [21] ibid., page 533.
[22] H. Heiber (editor), *The Early Goebbels Diaries*, entry for 23 October 1925. London, 1962.

As late as February 1926, Goebbels was horrified by Hitler's views on Russia and Bolshevism, and on private property; in short, by his leader's 'reactionary' attitudes.[23] At the same time Goebbels was fighting hard the 'red rabble' in the streets and at Nazi meetings: the fight, as well as Hitler's offer of a high party office in Berlin, combined to secure his orthodoxy. But he had learned a lot from his adversaries. The posters for his first meeting in Berlin could hardly be distinguished from similar Communist productions.

As the post-war revolutionary tide began to ebb in central Europe, Hitler's interest in fighting the 'Bolshevik threat' increased. In the last years of the decade Nazi agitation against *Gesamtmarxismus*, and Communism in particular, was intensified, until in 1932 it culminated in the creation of an anti-Communist psychosis in Germany. The *Reichspropagandaleitung* started running 'anti-Marxist courses' under the direction of its expert, Paul Meier-Benneckenstein, who later rose, partly because of the importance of his subject, to the Presidency of the *Deutsche Hochschule für Politik*. The courses aimed at the 'achievement of a militant and systematic agitation and propaganda against the *SPD* and the *KPD*'.[24] The 'attack on the Marxist front' took place both before and after January 1933. Before that date, it had camouflaged Hitler's real aim—the achievement of political power—as well as helped him to achieve it; after January, it facilitated Hitler's claim for absolute power. The campaign was highly rewarding: in 1933 some sections of the German body politic, the *Deutschnational* party, the industrialists, and the military, handed power over to Hitler because they believed that he would save the country from Communism.[25]

Of necessity, this agitation had to exaggerate the gravity of the Communist threat. The Nazi propagandists succeeded in creating a pseudo-situation, in which a Communist revolution was imminent. They could not afford to take any note of the facts of the situation. At no elections between 1930 and 1932 did the *KPD*—the Communist Party of Germany—gain more than

[23] *The Early Goebbels Diaries*, entry for 15 February 1926.
[24] *Unser Wille und Weg*, January 1932. Paul Meier-Benneckenstein, *Unser Angriff auf die marxistische Front*.
[25] M. Domarus, op. cit., page 645.

17·6 per cent of the total poll; the party was incapable of waging a conclusive fight with the National Socialists, or indeed with anyone else. Stalin was preoccupied with internal Russian problems; it is probable that he disliked the idea of a united left-wing front in Germany, and that he regarded a nationalist government that would first concentrate on breaking the peace treaties as more suitable for his own ends.[26]

There of course existed some legitimate grounds for a sharp animosity between the Nazis and the Communists. They had fought each other in the streets of Germany for many years; the National Socialists found themselves, during the years of the economic crisis, in direct competition with the Communists for the favours of the industrial workers, who were then deserting the SPD. By grossly exaggerating the Communist threat, the Nazi propagandists forged an extremely effective political weapon. Hitler was described as the saviour of Germany from Communism; what he had done for Germany, he could easily do for Europe.

There existed the same continuity between the campaign against Communism in Germany and abroad as in the case of the drive against the Jews; there existed the same disinterest among the National Socialist leaders as to its precise international implications. In April 1933 Hitler's government turned its attention to the foreign scene; a secret circular was sent out by the Foreign Ministry to all its missions abroad, enquiring into the local propaganda situation.[27] A detailed reply from Moscow arrived in Berlin in August:[28] the Ministry of Propaganda took no notice of it. The report dealt with the possibilities of propaganda to the Soviet Union, and this was of no interest to Goebbels. His main pursuit—at any rate until July 1941[29] was propaganda about the Soviet Union and about Communism for the benefit of third parties. For them, the Communist threat was publicized and inflated.

A few months after the destruction of the German Communist Party in the spring of 1933, the *Antikomintern*—the Union of

[26] Cf. 'Moscow-Berlin 1933', *The Survey*, October 1962.
[27] 26 April 1933; *Presseabteilung*, 86774/E60698383–4.
[28] Report from Moscow to the *AA*, 22 August 1933, 8677H/E607140–161.
[29] See page 167.

German Anti-Communist Societies—was founded under the patronage of Goebbels. Its function was 'to combat the Communist International and its allies',[30] i.e. the Jews, and, as an afterthought, the Freemasons. It was a well-endowed society; soon after its foundation it acquired spacious headquarters in Berlin N W 40, In den Zelten 9ᵃ. It housed the Department Soviet Union—it was also referred to as the Institute for Scientific Research on the Soviet Union (*Institut zur wissenschaftlichen Erforschung der Sowjetunion*)—which was made up of specialists in Russian economy, history, etc., or on propaganda relating to Russia. The department also contained a well-stocked library, a press-cuttings section, and a service for monitoring Soviet broadcasts. In it, propaganda and research were inextricably mixed: but, most important, it was intended to generate propaganda about the Soviet Union, not *to* it. The *Antikomintern*'s second department—the press section—ran various publications, such as the news bulletin which appeared twice a month in German, English, and French, as well as the twice-weekly information sheet on the Soviet Union; the foreign department looked after connexions with similar organizations and private individuals abroad. And finally, there existed a large department for 'antisemitic action': anti-Communist propaganda was, for the National Socialists, unthinkable without its antisemitic concomitant.

Although Communism had been defeated in Germany, its usefulness as a target for Nazi propaganda had by no means ended. From now on, the *Antikomintern* was to serve as 'the most advanced position of the international anti-Bolshevik movement'.[31] The work of the *Antikomintern* was of course firmly based on the official propaganda policy: the organization performed, however, certain important auxiliary functions. It could supply details, whenever necessary, for the rough outlines sketched by the *Promi*; it could lend pseudo-scientific gravamen to the lightweight pronouncements of the propagandists; it could, if need be, appear to pursue a policy independent

[30] A letter from Dr. Klein of the *Antikomintern* to the *Reichssendeleitung*, dated 16 October 1935. *Reichsrundfunkkammer* (*RRK*) papers, file No. 11980, at the Allied Document Centre, Berlin.

[31] *Im Kampf gegen den Weltbolschewismus*, a publisher's report, page 2. Berlin, 1936.

of the party line. During the twenty months after August 1939, when the Stalin-Hitler Pact was operative, the *Antikomintern* still carried on its activities, if in a more subdued and modified manner. In this respect, the organization's independence of action was of course severely limited. The changes in the name and sub-heading of its house-magazine faithfully reflected the changing predilections of the Ministry of Propaganda. Until August 1939 it was called *Contra Komintern*, the 'Organ of the Anti-Bolshevik World Movement';[32] in the following month it became *Die Aktion*, with an eccentric sub-heading a 'Newspaper against Plutocracy and National Incitement',[33] which was altered, in December of the following year to 'Newspaper for a New Europe'. In September 1941 the circle was completed when this newspaper appeared together with a supplement called *Contra Komintern, Kampforgan der antibolschewistischen Weltbewegung.*

Before the big anti-Communist campaign that was launched at the 1936 *Parteitag*,[34] the newly founded society concerned itself mainly with publishing or sponsoring the publication of books. *Bewaffneter Aufstand!* (Armed Uprising!) was written by the *Antikomintern*'s, chairman, Dr. Adolf Ehrt. In 1933, it was the society's most highly prized propaganda asset: by the end of the year, the fourth edition of the book—the fourth set of 50,000 copies—had been published; in the following year, an additional 75,000 copies were printed in German, and 160,000 in English, French, Swedish, Dutch, and Spanish. The book's sub-title was 'Revelations about the Communist Attempt at a *Coup d'État* on the Eve of the National Revolution'; it was based on a passage from Hitler's proclamation on 1 September 1933: 'There were weeks, at the beginning of the year, when we passed by, within a hair's breadth, the abyss of Bolshevik revolution.' This form of National Socialist propaganda was more vicious and gruesome than any other. The enemy was contemptible, and it had to be battered to death by the blows of words; photographs of stores of weapons, of degutted houses, of dead stormtroopers were distributed throughout the book with morbid regularity. In this respect, the second of the *Antikomintern*'s much advertised

---

[32] *Kampforgan der antibolschewistischen Weltbewegung.*
[33] *Kampfblatt gegen Plutokratie und Volkerverhetzung.*
[34] See page 92.

publications by Ehrt and Max Roden, entitled '*Terror—A Bloody Chronicle of Marxism in Germany*' (Berlin 1934) sank even lower. It set a new standard in atrocities propaganda. Page after page of revolting, detailed photographs of the stormtroopers who perished in street-fights were printed to prove that Marxism is evil.

These publications were intended for export rather than for the home market; in the introduction to *Terror*, the joint authors expressed the opinion that 'The international view of the new Germany still suffers because of an unusual misunderstanding. Nourished from contaminated sources, even the well-disposed press of other nations is guilty of an enormous distortion of history, which is keenly supported by the enemies of National Socialism and by the opponents of national honour and freedom.' The historical error, it was said, consisted of regarding the period of the Weimar régime as a time of freedom, whereas the truth was now declared to be that, in these years, the Marxists conducted a campaign of 'uninterrupted bloody terror against the German nation'.

A few months before the launching of the international anti-Communist drive, the *Antikomintern*'s activities were intensified, and they began to receive more attention in the German press. The *Berliner Börsen-Zeitung*—the equivalent of the *Financial Times*—obviously commanded a readership susceptible to anti-Communist propaganda, and it usually brought the most detailed reports on the *Antikomintern*'s activities. On 10 November 1935, it published a characteristic declaration by the *Antikomintern*. Its opening paragraph read:

'On 7 November the Soviet state celebrated the eighteenth anniversary of the Bolshevik revolution. The cannon-fodder of the Communist world revolution were driven across the Red Square. Tanks and bomber-aircraft were paraded. The Internationale was sung. In a telegram to Stalin from the official opening meeting, the expansion of Communism over the whole world was again stated to be the target.' After the juxtaposition of the plight of the Russians under the Soviet system with the jubilant, healthy Nazi Germany, the declaration concluded: 'The Soviet propaganda everywhere is trying to undermine the foundations of states, and to gather strength for new advances by employing the united-front slogans. As before, world revolution is the target. Today, the knowledge has started to dawn everywhere that Bolshevism is not a "Russian" affair, but that—because of its international character—it is resolved to interfere with the life of every nation. And everywhere, the forces of defence against the imperialist claims to power of the Third International are rallying. The struggle against the Comintern as the Bolshevik centre of subversion and murder has to summon all the forces that do not want to see their nations and states sold out to Communist chaos. The aim is a broad front against international Communism.'

At the same time, the *Antikomintern* began to extend its activities to broadcasting. On 16 October 1935, one of its chief executives, a Dr. Klein, wrote to Dr. Scheiner at the *Reichssendeleitung*, informing him of the activities of his organization up to date,[35] and adding: 'It is therefore essential that, apart from the press, exhibitions, lecture tours etc., broadcasting should be, before everything else, put at the service of this work.' Klein indicated that the *Antikomintern* should have, in November, some thirty topics ready for radio talks and plays; they included a play about mass deportations in the Soviet Union, a talk on the 'Kaganovich dynasty', another on 'race-pollution as a principle', and one on 'Trotsky, the eternal Jew'.

The *Reichssendeleitung* took up Klein's suggestion: in the following years the *Antikomintern* became the main supplier of this type of material to the German broadcasting system. It was constructed on the same lines as the *Antikomintern* publications; although it was of necessity repetitive it added a certain amount of colour to Nazi broadcasting. '*Bolschewismus*' was publicized as the main enemy of the human race, and the depths it had reached were contrasted with the achievements of National Socialism. Perhaps the best example of this type of broadcast was transmitted in the networked 'report on the week' on 31 July 1937. It was entitled 'At First They Were Seven!' (*Erst waren es Sieben!*—it referred to No. 7 party card carried by Hitler), the fourth *Antikomintern* broadcast in connexion with an exhibition, then touring German towns, called 'Bolshevism'. This is the beginning of the script:

[35] *RRK* papers at the Allied Document Centre, Berlin, File No. 11980

First voice: When you, dear listener, walk through the various rooms of '*Bolschewismus*'—

Second voice: —when you have seen the Italian section, and taken in the struggle of fascism against Bolshevism—

First: when in the Hungary room the rule of terror by one Bela Kun has come to life for you,

A female voice: when you have been through the days of horror of the Munich Soviet Republic—

First: ... and the atrocity of the Spanish civil war ...

Female: ... and the abominable suffering of the Russian nation itself—

First: when you have seen all these horrors, this poverty, this frightful blood sacrifice of Bolshevik terror all over the world—

Second: ... then you come to the end of your journey in a room that shows pictures of the Third Reich—

First: and the frightful nightmare lifts—as if you came out of a dark cellar again into the bright light and the sun—

Second: ... and then you go on and remain standing for a while in front of a picture of the Führer—

In the following months, from the beginning of October 1937 until the end of the year, the *Antikomintern* scriptwriters were busy. The *Deutschlandsender* transmitted seven of their broadcasts; Breslau and Königsberg five each, Berlin and Hamburg two each, and Leipzig, Stuttgart, Munich and Cologne one each.[36]

Since the campaign against *Gesamtmarxismus* was never far from the centre of Nazi propaganda—it was consistently used, inside Germany, to reinforce the loyalty of the Germans to Hitler's régime—the services of an organization like the *Antikomintern* were indispensable; there were, however, times when the campaign was given a special prominence. The *Reichsparteitag* in September 1936 was devoted to it. The National Socialist régime was more confident than at any other point in its three years' existence: the demilitarized zone in the Rhineland had been successfully occupied and a vote of confidence in the Nazi government had been passed in the *Reichstag* elections in March; the spectacle of the Olympic Games in Berlin had been brought to its impres-

[36] Cf. Dr. R. Kommass, report of 24 January 1938, *RRK*, File No. 11980.

sive conclusion. The hostilities in Spain had just been opened; the anti-Bolshevik campaign was unfolded against the background of the first moves in the civil war.

The campaign was launched a few days before the opening of the party rally. On 4 September the *Völkischer Beobachter* printed a front-page headline story, entitled: 'Soviet Officials as Railway Robbers'. The story was even slighter than its title: the Russians had placed the Japanese Olympic team, returning to Tokyo across Siberia, under strict supervision, and they impounded a portrait of Hitler and a *Hitlerjugend* dagger that had been presented, in Berlin, to one of the team's leaders. From then on the number of news items dealing with the Soviet Union increased; on 8 September, the first day of the party rally, an exhibition on the theme 'World Enemy No. 1—World Bolshevism' was opened in Nürnberg. In his address, the Deputy *Reichspropagandaleiter* set the tone for the anti-Soviet campaign: 'Today, Germany is the unshakable fortress of peace and order against Moscow'.[37]

The civil war in Spain provided Hitler with the peg for the anti-Communist campaign. In his proclamation—it was read to the rally, as usual, by *Gauleiter* Adolf Wagner—he described a situation in Spain that bore only a remote relation to reality. Franco, he declared, had not attempted a Fascist *coup* against the legal government; the Soviet Union had invaded the country.

'We see around us the signs of evil times. What we have preached about the greatest world danger of this second millenium of our Christian history . . . is becoming a frightful reality. Everywhere, the undermining activities of the Bolshevik string-pullers are beginning to take effect. At a time when bourgeois statesmen talk of non-interference, an international Jewish revolutionary centre in Moscow is attempting, through broadcasts and thousands of financial and agitation channels, to revolutionize this continent. Do not tell us that we, by continuously pointing out these facts, want to develop in Germany a psychosis of fear. Even today we are not afraid of a Bolshevik invasion of Germany, not because we do not believe in it, but because we are determined to make the nation so strong that it— as National Socialism has already done away with this world

[37] *VB*, 9 September 1936.

conspiracy internally—will defeat any attack from the outside with the most brutal determination.'[38]

In his speech on 10 September, Goebbels elaborated on Hitler's ideas in some detail. He laid special stress on the international aspects of the Bolshevik threat; its underlying thesis was that 'Bolshevism must be destroyed if Europe is to become sound again'.[39] He said at once that 'What we understand by ideals and *Weltanschauung* in general has nothing to do with what is usually referred to as Bolshevism. As far as that is concerned, it is a pathological, criminal nonsense, demonstrably thought up by the Jews and now, under Jewish leadership, it aims at the destruction of civilized European nations and the creation of an international Jewish world domination.'

Goebbels took pains to present Communist parties outside the Soviet Union as the 'foreign legions of the Comintern', and as the gravest threat to national life. They had—because Moscow was behind them—unlimited financial resources at their disposal; they used the same subtle propaganda techniques as Moscow. Indeed, countries that allowed strong Communist parties to operate on their territories were more or less 'under the dictate of Stalin'. The propaganda of these parties was international and aggressive; it was designed to mislead as to the true nature of Communism. It demanded 'maximal guarantees for peace' and yet, at the same time, the Soviet government indulged in an 'obviously imperialist arming'. It was impossible to come to an agreement with Bolshevism: although Goebbels said that National Socialism was not for export, only a country that adopted the 'social form of national organization' could fight Bolshevism successfully. Four days later, on 14 September, Hitler's concluding speech to the rally dealt with the Bolshevik threat again.

Indeed, the main aim of National Socialist propaganda at the time was to create an anti-Communist psychosis in Europe in the same way as it had created one inside Germany in the years 1932 and 1933. In 1936, the Nazi propagandists launched a powerful onslaught on the Soviet Union. It was designed to secure international support for Hitler, and it achieved some remarkable successes: it is likely that, without this preparatory move, the Nazi conquests of 1938 and 1939 would have been

[38] M. Domarus, op. cit., page 638. [39] *VB*, 11 September 1936.

94

difficult, or perhaps impossible, to accomplish. Nevertheless, the close connexion of the anti-Soviet campaign with the civil war in Spain was its most serious flaw. The insinuation that the Soviet Union had somehow invaded Spain and that the Communists were trying to overthrow the established order did not sound very convincing to the supporters of the legal Spanish government.

The force of the campaign continued unabated throughout 1936: the German–Japanese Anti-Comintern Pact was presented as an instrument for combating world Communism. Although, in the following year, the colonial question started being given more prominence than before, it was complementary, from the propaganda point of view, to the anti-Communist drive. On the one hand the Nazi régime showed itself as reasonable, and prepared to negotiate, even though it regarded its demands as fully justified; on the other, it was presented as an uncompromising enemy of Bolshevism, the perpetrator of chaos and unreason. At one point, the two aspects of Nazi propaganda were brought together. In October 1937 the directives issued to speakers by the *Reichspropagandaleitung*[40] included one on the 'Bolshevization of the Colonial Empires'. It stated that Bolshevism, apart from aiming at independent countries, was hard at work for a breakthrough for its ideas in colonial territories. Under the slogan of the liberation of the natives from imperialist exploitation it had begun to revolutionize the natives of the colonial possessions. According to the directives for Nazi speakers, the dissembling promises and instigations of Communism fell, especially in these areas, on fertile soil.

In the years before the Hitler–Stalin Pact of 1939, the anti-Communist propaganda conducted by the National Socialists pushed the hard facts of the diplomatic relations between Germany and Russia into the background. Rather than attempting to explain foreign policy on its own merits, the Nazi propagandists adopted the technique of creating popular images of foreign countries: they were made additionally inflexible by the admixture of National Socialist ideology. The Soviet Union received a

---

[40] *Aufklärungs und Redner-Informationsmaterial der Reichspropagandaleitung der NSDAP und des Propagandaamtes der Deutschen Arbeitsfront*, Lieferung 10 October 1937, Blatt 4/33.

great part of the propagandists' attention. Although this technique had the advantage of being easily intelligible, it was found lacking when sudden switches of foreign policy had to be publicized.

In 1939, Germany's relations with the Soviet Union strained the ingenuity of the *Promi*. Propaganda about the Soviet Union could no longer be regarded as a substitute for diplomacy: it had to follow closely diplomatic manœuvres. At the 18th Party Congress on 10 March 1939, Stalin made the first of the intricate moves that finally brought Germany and Russia together. Until late in May, Nazi propaganda with regard to the Soviet Union showed an unusual hesitation. On 12 May the *Reichspropagandaamt* asked the editors of German periodicals 'not to occupy themselves in any way—therefore not even in the form of quotations from the foreign press—with the foreign rumours of a *rapprochement* between Germany and Russia'.[41] Again, on 25 May, editors of German newspapers were advised that 'As long as the result of English–Russian negotiations is not known, a reserved attitude must prevail. Therefore no prophecies about their possible outcome! The press can, however, hint in the commentaries at the threat created by this alliance of England with Bolshevism.'[42]

By the end of May, the Germans appeared to be entirely exasperated with the Russians, and they made a determined effort to settle the issue one way or the other. They opened negotiations, with the Soviet Chargé d'Affaires in Berlin, on 30 May; at the same time, they instructed their agent in Moscow to resume discussions on economic matters.[43] On the same day, the *Reichspropagandaleitung* issued rather a pessimistic directive concerning the government's attitude towards the Soviet Union: 'For reasons already known the press controversy against the Soviet Union has recently been held back. This reserve can be— as soon as the situation is cleared up after the inclusion of the Soviet Union in the system of encirclement—again given up. Our supposition, that the Soviet Union wanted to gain as much as it could by its policy of procrastination, has been proved

[41] *RPA*, 12 May 1939.
[42] ibid., 25 May 1939.
[43] Cf. G. L. Weinberg, *Germany and the Soviet Union*, page 31. Leiden, 1954.

right. This directive does not, however, mean that a new campaign against Bolshevism should start in the German press in, so to speak, an apoplectic manner; it should be regarded as a basis for our attitude towards Soviet policy in the near future.'[44]

On the following day—31 May—the favourable Soviet reaction to the diplomatic initiative from Berlin removed the hesitant note from German propaganda. Newspaper editors were informed: 'It has already been announced that at the moment the time is not ripe for an anti-Soviet campaign. The press is therefore asked that, in connexion with reports on the "Condor Legion", animosity to Bolshevism, rather than to the Soviets, should be referred to: the ideological character of this fight should be stressed.'[45]

For more than ten weeks after the issue of this directive the Nazi propagandists had to maintain a reserved attitude towards the Soviet Union. In the meantime other pursuits began to occupy the propagandists. On 14 August, the first directive concerning German territorial demands on Poland was issued to the press. On the same day, negotiations were set in motion that finally led to the series of agreements concluded between Germany and Russia. In the evening of 23 August, the Non-Aggression Pact was signed in Moscow: the day before, the first of a number of detailed directives was released. Journalists were advised to comment on the significance of the Pact on the following lines: 'The news has acted like a bombshell all over the world. The decision represents a sensational turning point in the relations between the two countries, and it reaches back to the traditional community of German-Russian interests. The historical premises for such a formulation of policy have to be gone into deeply. . . . It can certainly be stressed that the announcement found a deep response in the nation. While the democracies talked, we and the Russians have acted.'[46] Further, the journalists were informed that the Pact was a natural outcome of the negotiations between the two countries on economic matters; while these were being discussed, the desire, on both sides, for an extension of the understanding to political affairs came to the foreground. The co-operation between the two states was also founded on their

[44] *RPA*, 30 May 1939.   [45] ibid., 31 May 1939.
[46] ibid., 22 August 1939.

97

respective economic structures: agricultural Russia was complementary to the highly industrialized Germany. At this point, the journalists were reminded not to touch on the ideological differences between the two states. They were also forbidden to speculate on the changes in the international situation, or on the future of the Anglo–French military mission in Moscow. In the routine instructions on 24 August the editors were again reminded that any speculation on the effect of the Non-Aggression Pact on other countries and on the Anti-Comintern Pact were to be scrupulously avoided. No quotations on the subject from the foreign press were to be used; 'favourable comments from friendly and neutral countries, on the other hand, can be naturally passed on in detail'.[47] Approved pictures of Ribbentrop and Molotov were, at last, released.

On the same day, however, the *Reichspropagandaleitung* issued a more detailed set of instructions. The triumphant tone was kept up. The Non-Aggression Pact, it was said, would become the cornerstone of the relations between the two countries. The speed with which the negotiations were concluded was pointed at as having been especially impressive; it was also a proof of the earnestness and openness with which the contracting parties approached the various problems. There were to be no more diplomatic 'by-ways' for the two partners; their path lay straight and narrow before them. 'The hopes that were still nourished yesterday in the foreign press', the directive announced, 'that the German–Russian negotiations would be endlessly protracted, whereas the English–French–Russian military negotiations might achieve a surprising conclusion, were completely destroyed by last night's events. At this point newspapers can certainly let a quiet malice [*Schadenfreude*] ring through, but it should not form the basis of the commentaries.' German newspapers were further to point out that consultations between the two partners were foreseen in the Pact, and they were to stress that the document was to remain valid for ten years in the first instance, becoming operative at once. It followed from the Pact, the directive pointed out rather ominously, that Germany and Russia would settle between them the outstanding problems in their spheres of influence in eastern Europe:

[47] *RPA*, 24 August 1939.

VII*a*. Respectable Hitler. Forty-four years old, Germany's Chancellor. 1933

I*b*. Austrian Nazis paint a *kenkreuz* on a rock face. 1934

VIII*a*. *SA* troopers and *Stürmer* posters. Party Rally, Nürnberg. 1935

VIII*b*. 'Jews are not wanted here.' 1935

the time was not, however, suitable for a deeper exploration, in the German press, of the various opportunities the situation offered. The deepening of the co-operation between Berlin and Moscow was to occasion an increasingly warmer tone in regard to the Soviet Union. The *DNB*—the official Nazi news agency—report that brought a quotation from *Pravda* concerning the ideological differences between the two régimes was not to be used by the journalists as the starting point for a polemic against the Russians.

A supplementary set of instructions filled in some interesting detail. Although the journalists were again strongly requested to make the tone of their observations on the improvement of German–Russian relations 'a degree warmer and more sympathetic'; they were advised, at the same time, to bear in mind the 'attitude of the German reading public up to date'. The public was bound to be puzzled by a flood of jubilant articles celebrating the newly-found friendship: this was why the theme should be entrusted only to the ablest members of the editorial staff. The 'warming up of the tone' had to be achieved delicately. The impression that the friendship between Germany and Russia was merely a tactical manœuvre was to be avoided by every means; the survival of the idea of co-operation between the two countries over the past hundred years was to be regarded with satisfaction.

The campaign to make the Pact acceptable to the German public was regulated to the smallest detail. Photographs from Moscow had to be approved by the *Hauptreferat Bildpresse* of the Propaganda Ministry before they were used; pictures could be released more freely only when the public was 'psychologically prepared'. There had also been many enquiries, to the press department of the *Reichspropagandaamt*, as to whether the new Russian policy meant that the publication of reminiscences of the battle of Tannenberg, on the occasion of its anniversary, were undesirable. The answer was that they could be published, as 'the treatment of the military and strategic achievement of the German military leadership and the soldierly qualities of the army can never spoil the relations between two brave nations'. There were therefore no objections to the publication of articles on the Tannenberg engagement: they had to be, however,

99

8

tactful.   No allusions were to be made to the basic causes of the conflict; terms like 'Cossack hordes' were entirely out of place.

The diplomatic negotiations with the Russians continued throughout the following month: on 28 September a treaty of friendship was signed by Ribbentrop and Molotov, who announced, on the same day, that the definitive settlement of the Polish question had created the basis for a lasting peace in eastern Europe.

By then Nazi propaganda had, however, changed gear. A few days before the German invasion of Poland on 1 September, the topic of German–Russian understanding was dropped, and the second-string campaign—it was concerned with Poland, Danzig and other related topics—began, at the end of August, to move into its place. Parts of Hitler's speech to the *Reichstag* on 1 September were still inspired by the sentiments of the Russian–German friendship campaign of the previous week; nevertheless, both the National Socialist leaders and the German public found it difficult to keep up such sentiments. The twenty months of friendship between the two countries formed a kind of propaganda interlude, without connecting links with the propaganda line before August 1939 or after June 1941. During this period the Russians annexed the Baltic States, marched into eastern Poland, and occupied Bessarabia and northern Bukovina: although they were acting in accordance with the agreements with Berlin, the public reactions in Germany to the Russian moves were highly unfavourable. Only the most careful direction of every means of political publicity kept these public attitudes under control.[48]

When this self-restraint was at last given up, a sigh of relief was clearly audible. It was sounded in the speech by Hitler on 22 June 1941, the day on which Germany invaded Russia; '. . . sentenced to a long silence lasting many months, the hour has at last come when I can speak openly. . . . You have all felt that this step' (i.e. the invasion of Russia) 'was a bitter and difficult one for me to take. The German nation has never harboured inimical feelings towards the peoples of Russia. The Jewish—Bolshevik rulers alone have endeavoured, from Moscow

[48] W. Hagemann, op. cit., page 272.

during the past two decades, to set on fire not only Germany, but the whole of Europe.'[49]

The all-clear signal had been given: later on the same day, the press was instructed, rather breathlessly, that 'One should remind the reader that the Pact with Russia was never for us a question of ideology. We have never admired Soviet institutions, and there can be no question of some internal vacillation. National Socialism has grown up in the struggle against Bolshevism. The agitation was stopped only during the period of truce, and now we are returning to our original precepts. Plutocracy and Bolshevism have a common Jewish origin, their ideas and aims are the same. One can reach back to the old programme of the Comintern, its role in 1918, its activity in Spain, etc. The true feelings of the German nation—which it had formerly entertained towards Bolshevism—must be once again set free. The methods used by Bolshevism today are the same as those [employed] against us in the internal political struggle. We must prove that the mean game played by Bolshevism has never altered, in regard to other nations as well, over the past twenty years. Formerly, we presented Bolshevism without its mask, and we can return to that [practice] today. Regardless of treachery, they wanted to deceive and betray us, there can be no doubt about that. Bolshevism has waited for its hour. We have proof that it would have stabbed us in the back.'[50]

Although no great enthusiasm for the war on Russia was evident—there existed a certain weariness and concern over the threat of war on two fronts—the hate campaign against the Soviet Union unleashed immediately after the invasion of Russia was quite unnecessary. The propaganda switch in the summer of 1941 was more acceptable to the German public than that performed some two years before.

The campaign against *Gesamtmarxismus* ran like a red thread through the texture of Nazi agitation. From humble beginnings —the back-street brawls in Munich in the early nineteen-twenties—it grew into the biggest operation mounted by the National Socialist propagandists. It became a drive mainly against Communism and the Soviet state; twice before the war it

[49] *VB*, 23 June 1941.
[50] W. Hagemann, op. cit., page 273.

101

was given a special prominence: on both occasions, the magnitude of the threat to Germany and to Europe was grossly exaggerated. The anti-Communist campaign brought returns, for the Nazis, beyond the dreams of avarice. In 1932, it helped Hitler to achieve power in Germany, and in the following year to establish and consolidate a National Socialist dictatorship. The campaign that was anti-Communist in theory, and as a propaganda effect, became anti-liberal in political practice. In 1933 it became a witch-hunt that aided the suppression of every kind of opposition to Hitler's rule and the establishment of a one-party state. It was used for diversionary purposes in a similar way as was the antisemitic campaign.

Indeed, the two propaganda themes were intended to reinforce each other: Hitler knew that it was necessary to focus the attention of the nation on a single enemy; it is possible that he thought of both the themes as equally effective. In practice, however, they had to be treated separately: the intensity of the antisemitic campaign could remain more even because its target was nebulous. The anti-Communist campaign, on the other hand, had to be suspended or modified according to the demands of the diplomatic relations with the Soviet Union. Outside Germany, the antisemitic campaign appears to have been less effective than the anti-Communist drive. The National Socialist propagandists did not possess sufficiently reliable information on the effectiveness of their propaganda abroad; anyway, they did not seem greatly concerned. They were content to export the themes of home propaganda, and they expected them to be just as effective abroad.

On the whole, the antisemitic drive disappointed the high claims Hitler had made for it. It was effective—but only in combination with a variety of other factors—in eastern Europe; elsewhere, it repelled rather than attracted. The international anti-Communist campaign, on the other hand, was more rewarding. It convinced many Europeans that Hitler's dictatorship was more acceptable than Stalin's and that Germany—'the bulwark against Bolshevism'—should be allowed to grow from strength to strength. Indeed, the same section of the European public came to see Continental politics exclusively in terms of a clash between Communism and National Socialism. The Nazis never bothered, however, to understand either the intricacy or the appeal of Marxist doctrine. Their anti-Communist agitation in Germany was marked by abuse and exaggeration and underscored with physical violence. It was brutal and unsubtle, but it was never meant to be anything else. It was intended to warn off non-Communists, inside and outside Germany, rather than to destroy Communism in Russia.

V. NAZI FOREIGN BROADCASTING

GOEBBELS found broadcasting a highly attractive medium of mass propaganda. It was more suited than the press for employment in an authoritarian state; it was easier to control centrally, it was not wasteful of manpower; it left no easily accessible record. Above all, it was immediate and it penetrated.[1] Apart from these advantages, broadcasting to foreign countries offered some additional ones. Broadcasters could not be controlled by governments abroad as easily as other agents of propaganda; indeed, wireless broke down the customary definition of international law concerning 'sovereignty of air space', and it enforced the formulation of the opposite principle of the 'freedom of the ether'.

When Hitler came to power, the National Socialists had a lot to learn about broadcasting: for some time, the writers on the subject were more active than the broadcasters themselves. Alfred Lau, for instance, the editor of the *Preussische Zeitung* who later became the head of the Königsberg station, suggested, soon after the National Socialists took over power, that an hour should be devoted daily to a broadcast to territories in the East inhabited by Germans. Problems of foreign policy were of course mentioned on German home transmissions, and radical solutions were suggested for them. But they were either inspired by over-confidence on the part of the new rulers of Germany, or they were intended to probe the mood abroad: on one occasion, such a broadcast elicited a protest from the Polish government. Indeed, in 1934, the Nazi leaders showed themselves willing to limit their freedom of action in foreign broadcasting. Following the treaty of friendship with Poland, signed in January, the official radio organizations in Warsaw and Berlin came to an

[1] See page 50.

agreement—on 13 October—that was to limit mutually hostile propaganda. The National Socialist broadcasters undertook, for instance, to omit all references to the oppression of the German minority by the Polish government. The order affected the German press as well, and it remained valid—and it was in fact enforced—until 1939.

The Germans in Poland received enough attention from the Nazi propagandists later, in the months that preceded the invasion of Poland on 1 September. There existed, however, *volksdeutsche* minorities elsewhere: they became the first, and they remained the most important, targets for German foreign broadcasts. The National Socialists were able to carry on the programming practices that had been established under the Weimar Republic, and designed to maintain contact with Germans abroad. But after 1933 the content of these broadcasts began to change. The Germans abroad had to be convinced of the merits of Hitler's state, they had to be drawn into organizations sponsored by the *NSDAP*; they had to be prepared to further, at a later date, concrete political demands.

The campaign took place under the sign of the misleading emotive slogan *Heimkehr ins Reich* (neither the Austrians nor the Sudeten Germans were in fact 'returning' to the Reich), and its intensity was indicated by the increasing numbers of long- and medium-wave broadcasts—the former from the *Deutschlandsender*, and the latter from Leipzig, Breslau, Königsberg and Munich stations—to the Germans on the other side of the frontier. The number of *volksdeutsche* broadcasts rose from 236 in 1933 to 924 in 1937 and then to 1,500 in the following year.[2] In an essay on the role of wireless in the creation of Great Germany[3] Hans Kriegler, the chief of the broadcasting department in the Ministry of Propaganda, wrote: '. . . the year 1938/39 must be regarded as the most active time of our broadcasting work. For long weeks and months of momentous political events, wireless was the centre of popular interest as never before. There were days, even weeks, when in the whole of Germany, as well as among the Germans on the other side of the

---

[2] H. Pohle, op. cit., page 399.
[3] *Der Anteil des Rundfunks an der Schaffung Grossdeutschlands, Handbuch des deutschen Rundfunks, 1939–40*, pages 5–10.

frontier . . . the wireless receivers were in almost continuous use'.

The first Nazi broadcasting onslaught was aimed against Austria: the famous 'radio war' developed in the summer of 1933, soon after Dollfuss banned the Austrian National Socialist Party. We shall have an opportunity to discuss Hitler's propaganda in Austria later;[4] at this point the second big broadcasting campaign—it preceded the Saar plebiscite—will be our main interest. Under the Versailles Peace Treaty, the future of the Saar territory was to be settled in 1935: the area had been receiving some attention from German broadcasters before Hitler came to power. In 1930 the Cologne station arranged a series entitled 'Saarland', and in August 1932 the 'Saarland Frontier Report' was broadcast, which contained an interview with the Chancellor, von Papen; in November 1932 all German stations transmitted a speech on the Saar problem that was made at the meeting on the theme 'German Frontiersmen in Distress'.[5]

During the first year in power, the National Socialists continued to produce similar broadcasts: their purpose was to remind the inhabitants of the Saar territory that they had not been forgotten by their mother country. Nevertheless, the broadcasts that originated from Cologne, Frankfurt or Stuttgart were never properly co-ordinated; sometimes the speeches by local party functionaries, with their exaggerated demands, were harmful to the foreign policy of the Berlin government.[6]

A systematic propaganda campaign to the Saarland was launched at the beginning of the year 1934. Early in January, Goebbels ordered the setting up of an office for the co-ordination of broadcasting to the Saar area. It was officially given the unrevealing name of *Westdeutsche Gemeinschaftsdienst*, and Adolf Raskin, who had worked in the Saarland as a journalist and who, immediately before his latest appointment, had looked after music and light entertainment for the West German broadcasting network, was appointed the head of the new office. Its function was to approve every broadcast relating to the Saar territory before transmission; Raskin himself enjoyed the full confidence of the Minister of Propaganda. Goebbels was content

[4] See Chapter VI.   [5] '*Deutsche Grenzvolk in Not*'.
[6] H. Pohle, op. cit., page 409.

to inform Raskin of his views on the situation at occasional meetings, otherwise leaving him to work on his own. At the same time, close co-operation between Raskin and *Gauleiter* Bürckel, the government plenipotentiary for the Saar, ensured that propaganda would remain in line with foreign policy.

From 25 April 1934, every Wednesday evening, the series 'Our Saar—The Way to Understanding is Clear'[7] was networked throughout Germany. A few days later, Raskin's organization demanded that 6 May should be set aside as the 'Day of the Saar', and that all German broadcasts on that day should be devoted purely to Saarland. *6 May* was a Sunday, and the programming relentlessly drove home the Saarland motif.

6 a.m.	'Reveille from the Saar.' Networked.
6.15–8.15	'Hamburg Harbour Concert with Guests from the Saar.' Networked.
9.00–9.30	Protestant Service from Saarbrücken. Transmitted by Cologne, Stuttgart, Frankfurt, and Munich.
9.30–9.35	Bell-chimes of all the Saarland churches. Networked.
10.15–10.45	Catholic Mass from Saarbrücken. Cologne, Stuttgart, Frankfurt, Munich.
10.50–12.00	Music. Short stories from the Saar.
12.00–1.00	A miners' brass band from Saarland. Frankfurt, Stuttgart, Cologne, Munich.
2.15–2.45	Children's hour: 'Kasperl visits the Saar children'. Frankfurt, Cologne, Stuttgart, Munich.
3.00–4.30	Transmission of the Zweibrücken meeting, with a speech by the Minister of Propaganda. Networked.
4.30–6.00	Marches of the former Saarland regiments, popular music, etc. Stuttgart, Frankfurt, Deutschlandsender.
6.00–6.20	'Foreigners speak about the Saar question.' Frankfurt, Stuttgart, Deutschlandsender.
8.45–10.00	'Jakob Johannes. A Story of the Saar.' A radio play by Willi Schaeferdiek (based on a true event). Networked.
10.45–12.00	An evening of entertainment with Saarland wit, anecdotes, jokes, etc. Stuttgart, Frankfurt.

Until the plebiscite in January 1935, the so-called 'National Hour'[8] as well as school and youth broadcasts were frequently

---

[7] '*Unsere Saar—Der Weg frei zur Verständigung*'.
[8] '*Stunde der Nation*'.

employed for Saar propaganda. In the last broadcasting hours of the year 1934 all German stations transmitted a programme entitled '1935—in thirteen days—the Saar Returns Home'. The final concentrated onslaught on the ears of the German listeners was made on the first Sunday of the new year. The composition of the programme ran on similar lines to those of 6 May: the morning masses were celebrated by high Saarland ecclesiastics; bands from the Saar provided the music; the day culminated in a transmission from a mass meeting at the Berlin Sportpalast.

The National Socialist propagandists left nothing to chance. They had provided the programmes; they were determined to see that there should be enough listeners. Compared with the territory of the Reich, where there were 77 listeners to every 1,000 inhabitants at the time, the density in the Saarland was considerably lower at 24 to 1,000.[9] The local National Socialist circle of listeners[10] looked after the supply of the *Volksempfänger*, cheap receivers produced in Germany;[11] in the months between January 1934 and April 1935 some 4,000 sets were distributed in the Saarland, and the number of listeners went up from 28,000 to 40,000. In addition, the National Socialist listeners' associations organized community listening to transmissions of important party events; about fifty such meetings were organized during the Saar campaign, and the total number of listeners attending meetings throughout the area often exceeded 100,000. In conformity with broadcasting practice inside Germany, the National Socialists preferred community to individual or family listening in the Saarland; a group of people was more receptive to propaganda effects produced, say, by Hitler's speech.

There can be no doubt that broadcasting played the decisive role in the success of the National Socialist campaign. The Germans were of course unlikely to lose in the plebiscite: but they would never have won by such an overwhelming margin without an effective propaganda campaign.[12] It must be borne in mind that the task of the National Socialists in the Saarland was not a simple one. Before 1933, the Catholic Centre, the Social Democrats,

---

[9] H. Pohle, op. cit., page 412.   [10] *Rundfunkhörerverband.*
[11] See page 51.
[12] Of the votes cast, 90·76 per cent were for the return of the Saar to Germany, 9 per cent for the retention of the *status quo*, and only 0·24 per cent for the transfer of the area to France.

and the Communists had run the biggest organizations: in January 1935 the voters in the plebiscite had to decide the return of their province to a National Socialist Germany. There were, however, certain circumstances that favoured National Socialist propagandists. The French made only a belated attempt to counter German broadcasting to the Saar. When the Strasbourg station began to be employed, it could not hope to affect the hold over the Saarland audiences already gained by the Nazi broadcasters. They did not, however, concentrate on the Saar alone. The aim of their technique was to create a *Saar-atmosphere* in Germany as well: a feeling of national community of interests that transcended former party divisions. The National Socialist leaders were of course aware of the important role broadcasting had played in the Saar campaign, and especially in creating the link between the Reich and its former province; they were to use the same technique on a number of occasions before the outbreak of the war. Soon after the conclusion of the campaign Goebbels wrote: 'German broadcasting in particular put its far-reaching powers at the disposal of the successfully concluded Saar struggle. In about fifty large networked broadcasts and over 1,000 individual broadcasts the living connexion between the Reich and the Saarland, which was still detached at the time, was maintained, and the basis was laid for the great plebiscite victory on 13 January.'[13]

The following big broadcasting campaign—it was connected with the 1936 Olympic Games in Berlin—was of an entirely different type. The Saar campaign had been arranged for the purpose of national expansion; the Olympic Games for that of national representation. Before the arrival of the foreign guests in Berlin, the Nazis had to undertake an extensive 'Potemkin village' operation. All such notices as 'Jews not admitted' were taken away from the entrances to hotels and restaurants; Streicher's newspaper *Stürmer* could not be bought in the streets, and many other aggressive Nazi propaganda devices either disappeared or were toned down.

Nevertheless, the effort was successful. The Olympic Games were an ideal vehicle for propaganda, and the transmissions

[13] J. Goebbels, *Nationalsozialistischer Rundfunk*, pages 12–13. Munich, 1935.

from Berlin made an indelible impression on foreign audiences many times larger than those in attendance at the capital. At the previous Olympic Games—at Amsterdam in 1928 and at Los Angeles four years later—no arrangements were provided for simultaneous reporting; in 1936 the Germans took great pains to make available as many facilities as possible. Indeed, the technical achievements alone of the planners were impressive.

A special allowance of 2,000,000 marks for broadcasting was made: 450 additional wireless workers were ordered to Berlin in the summer of 1936. Three hundred microphones, 220 amplifiers, 20 transmitting vans were put at the disposal of foreign broadcasters. The arrangements for broadcasting the Olympic Games—they started being made early in the year 1935—first came to test during the ten days' winter sports events at Garmisch-Partenkirchen, when some 300 reports and commentaries were broadcast to 19 countries.[14] This output was supplemented by the productions of the German short-wave network.

Some time before the beginning of the summer Games, language courses in German were transmitted on the short waves; the Berlin station, on the other hand, ran courses in English, French, Italian, and Swedish for the benefit of German hotel-keepers and other interested people. Foreign broadcasts also contained detailed advice on travel in Germany, on excursions in the environs of Berlin and other topics of interest; the periodical *Olympia Dienst* was printed in four languages, and it enlightened foreign journalists on the arrangements made for broadcasting and its employment at the Olympic Games.

The facilities provided in the summer of 1936 were used by 19 European and 13 overseas countries; 92 foreign reporters described races and other competitions, while provisions were made to record 62 reports simultaneously. About as many German as foreign reporters were at work, and of these 17 were on the staff of the German short-wave transmitter. During the 16 days of the Olympic Games 2,500 reports were broadcast in 28 languages. The effort and the accomplishment of the German broadcasters was indeed impressive, and they did not go unnoticed. The majority of the foreign radio representatives sent telegrams

[14] H. Pohle, op. cit., pages 416 and 417.

to Goebbels, full of admiration for the achievements of the German broadcasters; a director of the American NBC said in his concluding report from Berlin that 'the work done by the *Reichsrundfunk* remains without precedent in the history of broadcasting'.[15]

The short-wave system which the National Socialists used during the Olympic Games, both to supplement the reports of foreign broadcasters and to enlighten those countries that did not send their own reporters, had first gone into operation in 1926. On Christmas Day that year the first musical programme was exchanged between the United States and Germany; in February 1930 Solf, Germany's former Ambassador to Japan, spoke on the problems of disarmament, and his speech was transmitted to America and networked by NBC in a coast-to-coast broadcast. The short-wave programmes transmitted by the authorities of the Weimar Republic were, however, largely non-political; anyway more people heard of the technical achievements at second hand, through the press, than heard the broadcasts themselves.

The National Socialists regarded 1 April 1933 as the birthday of the German short-wave broadcasting. At first, they concentrated on the United States and on the countries of Central America; the programmes transmitted during the day were selected from suitable home broadcasts: the night programmes, on the other hand, bore the characteristics of National Socialist short-wave broadcasting from the very beginning. The new rulers of Germany needed political credit as well as markets for their goods. Apart from these tasks, the short-wave transmitter never neglected the Germans abroad. The broadcasts were used to instruct members of the Nazi *Auslandsorganisation*, to strengthen them in their faith, and to bring new members into the organization. The National Socialist broadcasters soon learned the rules of this type of work, and they made a considerable contribution to perfecting the short-wave technique. Only a few sets were equipped with short-wave bands at the time; 'fading' made reception usually unsatisfactory. There were no mass audiences: an average listener could not be expected to put up with all the disadvantages and difficulties; the

15 H. Pohle, op. cit., page 418.

111

usual type of listener to short-wave broadcasts was one with some special technical or political interests.

When the National Socialists came to power, they inherited from the Weimar Republic only one short-wave transmitter that beamed broadcasts to America. The enterprise was run by seven employees who had neither an official chief, offices, nor studios they could call their own. In the middle of April, Kurt von Böckmann—he had run the Bavarian network for eight years—was appointed the head of short-wave broadcasting; in June the second newscast in English was started, and soon afterwards news was broadcast for the first time to Central and South America in Spanish. The Christmas message in 1933 was read by Hess; it was broadcast by three new transmitters. The world was divided into four zones—North America, Africa, Asia and Australia, and South America; the first broadcasts to the three new zones went out on the first three days of February. The National Socialist authorities succeeded in getting diplomats from the various zones to send messages to their own countries. The network of German short-wave broadcasts was completed early in 1935, when a transmitter for South Asia and another for Central America went into operation. At the time of the Olympic Games eight stations were in working order, and they were serviced by more than a hundred men. At this point the Germans overtook the overseas services of the BBC, and they continued to improve their position until the outbreak of the war. In 1939 ten transmitters were looked after by some 250 people, who produced more than seventy hours of programmes every day (see table on page 113).

With the increase in broadcasting time, the number of languages that were employed also went up: English was used for North America, Spanish for Central and South America and, from 1937, Portuguese for special regional purposes; English, Portuguese, and Afrikaans in Africa, as well as Arabic for the Mediterranean regions within the reach of this transmitter; English, and from 1937 Dutch, were used for broadcasts to Asia and Australia. German was of course employed in all the four zones; broadcasting became the most important means of keeping in touch with the Germans overseas.

More time was allotted to music than to any other feature of

	1933	1934	1935	1936	1937	1938	November 1939
United States	2.00*	5.15*	5.45*	5.55*	6.55*	7.00*	11.55*
Africa	—	4.45	4.30	6.55	7.50	7.45	8.10
East Asia	—	4.45	7.00	10.15	10.55	10.55	11.10
South America	—	4.00	4.15	7.55	7.55	7.50	9.15
Special area—Brazil	—	—	—	—	—	—	4.10
South Asia—Australia	—	—	7.00	10.15	10.55	10.55	11.10
Central America	—	—	5.45	6.55	6.55	7.00	2.50
Europe	—	—	—	—	—	—	11.00
Special broadcasts in Arabic—	—	—	—	—	—	—	1.50
Total hours and minutes	2.00	18.45	34.15	48.10	51.25	51.25	71.30[16]

* All times shown are hours and minutes broadcast daily.

[16] Heinz Pohle, op. cit., page 428.

113

the programmes; it bound together the news, political commentaries and economic reports, in which special attention was given to European prices for the main overseas export products. Plays and serials—many of them on famous men from the age of discoveries, colonization, or of the wars of liberation—were quite popular with the planners of programmes in Berlin. A special stress was laid on the pioneering work done by the Germans; the achievements of the National Socialist régime were also extolled. But an attempt was made to exclude the more obvious forms of propaganda; a good deal of care was devoted to the 'German Study Circle', a series of programmes on a variety of academic subjects.

We have already seen that short-wave broadcasts could not be designed for mass audiences; the individualism of this kind of broadcasting could, however, be used for the creation of the closest possible personal contact between the broadcaster and his listeners. The aim was to produce an 'atmosphere of friendship and confidence' that was different in kind from the emotive relationship between the speaker and his mass audience. It was a process that took a long time, but the German broadcasters thought the results justified the expenditure, especially in the case of their compatriots abroad. In the first year of its operations under National Socialist direction, short-wave broadcasting devoted special attention to the national festivities of the various countries: they often asked their diplomatic representatives to the broadcasting house in Berlin; at the same time, the country in question was asked to make arrangements to transmit the broadcasts on its own network. Nevertheless, addressing a particular country was too broadly based an operation: very often a particular town, school or a wireless club was singled out and addressed by Berlin. Greetings to individual listeners became very popular, and a special period of five to ten minutes daily was made available for them; the same intimate contact was also maintained by reading the listeners' letters, answering their enquiries and organizing discussions of topics selected by the listeners.

The speakers also did their best to maintain a high level of cosy chumminess. They addressed their listeners as their good friends, they told them of their private joys and sorrows. An

114

announcer, for instance, broke off while making a joke to go and shut the window—he, of course, described this action—because there was a dog barking outside the studio, and he did not want it to interfere with the reception of the programme in some remote part of the Brazilian forest. Indeed, one of the listeners in Brazil wrote to the broadcasting house in Berlin: 'I believe that one must live in a primeval forest in order to learn to appreciate the wireless.'[17]

Nevertheless, the spoken word would have been soon forgotten without support from the printed word, and the National Socialist broadcasters developed the 'zone service' which was designed to inform the listeners of forthcoming programmes and to remind them of past ones. Every month 75,000 copies of bilingual programme sheets were distributed to various clubs, listeners' groups and to individuals; some 3,000 matrices were also sent out to interested newspapers abroad. All these services were provided on request, free of charge. Until America's declaration of war on Germany, the programmes of the German short-wave transmitter were published in all specialized radio magazines in the United States as well as in some of the daily newspapers; the 150 German-language papers often published detailed reports on the content of the broadcasts.

The attempt to establish an intimate personal contact with the listener was by no means a revolutionary innovation in broadcasting: American radio-commercials had been trying to do precisely the same thing for many years. Nevertheless, the National Socialists employed the technique, for the first time, for political rather than commercial purposes. It later spread from short- to medium- and long-wave bands; during the war, the personal touch was indispensable to broadcasters who ran the various military stations as well as those designed to maintain the links between soldiers and their relatives and friends at home.

There can be no doubt that the German short-wave broadcasts achieved some remarkable successes. The listeners' letters to Berlin bore witness to this: although their contents were questionable, the fact that they arrived in large numbers at least showed that the broadcasts had aroused interest. The Americans were especially sensitive to this form of propaganda: the

[17] H. Pohle, op. cit., page 432.

115

Institute for Propaganda Analysis—the only institute of its kind—was founded in New York in 1938 partly as a countermeasure to German broadcasts. In the same year, an American radio commentator described the short-wave transmissions from Germany as the 'biggest and most powerful propaganda machinery in the world', and as 'the most frightening institution for the spread of political doctrine'.[18] The success was due, to some extent, to the element of technical surprise; many listeners were attracted by the technical accomplishments and by the novelty of the broadcasts. Nevertheless, some of the credit must go to the planners of the short-wave transmissions. Only on this channel of propaganda the National Socialists used a 'soft-sell' technique. The political contents of short-wave transmissions remained moderate even when other forms of Nazi propaganda began to assume an aggressive tone; at no time did the broadcasts contain a high charge of offensive agitation.

A difference in kind between the contents of the short-wave broadcasts—indeed, this was true of National Socialist broadcasting as a whole—and the general tone of Nazi propaganda certainly existed, and it was made possible by a conspicuously autonomous development of broadcasting under Goebbels. There were some purely administrative reasons for this: the Minister of Propaganda was in sole and undisputed charge, his collaborators were hand-picked, and they were more easily controllable than, say, the journalists. The new broadcasting techniques had to be developed empirically, and they sometimes did not correspond to the broader phases of Nazi propaganda. At a time when Hitler's régime was mainly concerned with the achievement of recognition and respectability abroad, the broadcasters indulged in an aggressive radio war against Austria[19] and, soon afterwards, in the expansive Saarland campaign. Nor were the powerful anti-Soviet blasts of 1936 adequately echoed in the short-wave transmissions; the Nazi broadcasters were also trying hard to make their régime internationally palatable during the Olympic Games in the summer of 1936, at a time when the broader campaign for international acceptance was being quietly superseded by other pursuits.

[18] C. Searchinger, *Voice of Europe*, page 383. London, 1938.
[19] See page 128 et seq.

Although broadcasting was sometimes used in an independent manner, it cannot be said to have run counter—perhaps with the exception of the Austrian radio war—to the general aims of Nazi propaganda. Indeed, there were certain idiosyncracies of National Socialist publicity that were fully shared by broadcasting. The Nazis employed foreign languages on the short-wave bands only; but even here, news and other spoken programmes were usually bilingual, using German plus the regional language. On the medium- and short-wave bands—best suited for short-distance transmission in Europe—the National Socialists did not develop a foreign-language service before the war. During the Czechoslovak crisis in 1938 and 1939, for instance, they did not even bother to set up a Czech-language service. On the whole, broadcasting, like other expressions of National Socialist propaganda, was circumscribed by the view that the German nation was the most suitable vehicle for the Nazi revolution.

In certain circumstances, however, this weakness could be converted into strength. In the Saarland campaign, the greatest achievement of the National Socialist broadcasters was the complete identification of National Socialism with German nationalism. The former party structure in the Saar territory was ignored and obliterated; the aims of the Germans in the Saar and those of Hitler's government were presented as being identical. The creation of the *Saar-atmosphere* inside Germany on the one hand, and on the other of a feeling in the Saarland that the whole nation stood united behind the demand for reunification, was a propaganda technique that came to be employed by other media as well, and that was used on several fateful occasions before the outbreak of the war.

VI. AUSTRIA: AN APPEAL TO COMPATRIOTS

In the National Socialist view, the Austrian nation did not exist as a separate entity; in terms of Nazi propaganda it was a 'halluci-nation'. Since February 1920—when the party programme was published for the first and the last time—the *Anschluss* of Austria was regarded as a political and economic necessity; in 1928, the *NSDAP* leaders declared again that they were not prepared to neglect a single German in the 'colony of the League of Nations, Austria'.[1] Indeed, to try and create a distinct form of Austrian patriotism was, from the Nazi point of view, nothing but treason against the German *Volk*.

For this message, a potentially receptive audience existed in Austria. The Austrian problem was created in 1918, when the Habsburg Empire fell apart. From one of the dominant peoples of the Empire, the Germans of Austria became the citizens of a small, insignificant state. They tried hard to break out of the impasse. On 12 November 1918 the provisional National Assembly in Vienna declared Austria a part of the German Republic; the same programme was formulated by the Constituent Assembly on 12 March in the following year. The demand of course followed the spirit of President Wilson's principle of self-determination, but it threatened to upset the new order for Europe that was being planned, at the time, by the victorious Powers. Germany would have gained some six and a half million inhabitants and the new state of Czechoslovakia would have become largely encircled by a strong Germany. The peace treaty signed by Germany on 28 June 1919 outlawed the *Anschluss*; it contained an article recognizing the independence

[1] Ulrich Eichstädt, *Von Dollfuss zu Hitler*, page 22. Wiesbaden, 1955.

of Austria, as well as binding Germany unconditionally to observe this provision.

There existed, in Austria, resentments similar to those in Germany, and they cut across the divisions between political parties. The grudge against the 'dictated' conditions of peace was reinforced by a feeling that the Western Allies had wilfully broken up the Habsburg Empire, and thus deprived the Austrian Germans of their former prominence. At the same time, some kind of Danubian federation was impracticable: the rift between those successor states of the Habsburg Empire that benefited by the outcome of the war—Czechoslovakia, Poland, Yugoslavia, Rumania—and those that suffered—Austria and Hungary—was too deep, and the way to restoring harmony would have been arduous and long. Nor was the creation of a genuine Austrian patriotism a task that could be accomplished swiftly and, anyway, it would have hardly done away with the reality and the feeling, among the Austrian Germans, of political impotence.

Apart from the ties of nationality, the similarity between the post-war political background in Austria and Germany, and the fact that Hitler himself was an Austrian, many of the roots of National Socialism itself could be traced to Austrian soil. Indeed, a professor at Vienna University remarked with a good deal of justification that 'National Socialism is that movement which puts the Prussian sword at the disposal of Austrian lunacy.'[2]

An extreme form of nationalism developed in Austria–Hungary during the last three or four decades of the state's existence; its growth was expressed in the formation of political parties that recognized no loyalties other than the purely national. A few of them were named 'national-socialist': the first organization of that name was in fact founded in 1897, by the Czechs. It was intensely chauvinist; although it never developed racial or anti-parliamentary doctrines, its Panslav, pro-Russian policy was not entirely innocent of certain racialist features, and it implied approval of the Tsarist autocracy. It was founded with the explicit intention of counteracting Marxism among the

---

[2] 'Der Nationalsozialismus ist jene Bewegung, die das preussische Schwert der Österreichischen Narretei zur Verfügung gestellt hat.' W. Daim, Der Mann der Hitler die Ideen gab., page 15.

working classes. Seven years later—in 1904—the Germans in Bohemia founded the *Deutsche Arbeiterpartei Österreichs* at Trutnov (Trautenau). Its leader, Walter Riehl, intended—like his Czech forerunners—that his party should attempt a conversion of the working class to nationalism; it exploited the economic and political animosities between the Czechs and the Germans in the ethnically mixed borderlands of Bohemia and Moravia. After the break-up of the Habsburg Empire the organization split into an Austrian and a Sudetenland branch: the Czechoslovak Republic, and not Austria, inherited the largest share of the National Socialists from the defunct Empire. Of the four leading- figures of the old *Deutsche Arbeiterpartei*— Walter Riehl, Rudolf Jung, Hans Krebs, and Hans Knirsch— the last three men continued their political activities on the territory of the Czechoslovak Republic, while only Riehl carried on his work in Vienna. But even Riehl's political attitudes had been determined by his early experience of the national struggle in Liberec (Reichenberg).[3]

Riehl was one of the few men who was on intimate—*du* (thou) —terms with Hitler; their first meeting took place at the small inter-state party rally in August 1920 in Salzburg; a few weeks later—from 29 September until 11 October—Hitler travelled in Austria and, for the first time in his political career, he spoke at Innsbruck, Salzburg, St. Poelten, and Vienna. After the failure of the Munich *putsch*, several prominent Nazis—Hermann Göring among them—fled to Austria, where they were looked after by their party friends. The exiles laid the foundation for a closer co-operation between the Austrian and the German movements: in 1926 the Austrian party was reorganized under the name of *NSDAP Österreichs (Hitler-Bewegung)*, and incorporated into the Reich organization; Austria became a *Gau* in the German party. In 1928 it began to receive financial subsidies from Munich; its membership then stood at 7,000 divided among 130 *Ortsgrupen*.[4]

Nevertheless, the National Socialists did not begin to make an impression on Austria's political life before the beginning of the

[3] Heinrich Benedikt (Editor), *Geschichte der Republik Österreich*, Vienna, 1954. An essay by Adam Wandruszka, "Österreichs politische Struktur", page 406.
[4] *Beiträge zur Vorgeschichte und Geschichte der Julirevolte*, page 4. An official publication, Vienna, 1934.

subsequent decade. Until then, they had remained the minority party within the 'national' group which, in its turn, was uncomfortably wedged between the Christian-Socialist and the Social-Democrat movements. A negative attitude towards the state was deeply rooted in the programme of the national camp: under the Habsburgs, Schönerer's party looked towards Berlin, rather than Vienna, for support for the Austrian Germans; Schönerer's successors disapproved of the Austrian Republic more than he had done of the Habsburg Empire. In this respect, the National Socialists remained within the tradition of the national group of parties; they were, however, more extreme and vocal in their demands, and they had valuable connexions in Germany. Indeed, the successes of the Austrian Nazis followed closely those of their party comrades across the frontier.

In the Austrian parliamentary elections in November 1930, the National Socialists polled 110,000 votes without winning a single seat. But two years later, in 1932, the local elections in Vienna, Lower Austria, and Salzburg in April, the Vorarlberg elections in November, and the Innsbruck municipal ballot, brought considerable successes to the National Socialists. They were also helped by the economic crisis and the fast-rising numbers of the unemployed; the plan of the Austrian government for a customs union with Germany—it had to be abandoned by the Austrians in September 1931 because of international opposition —also contributed to the radicalization of the political life of the Republic.

At the same time—in the summer of 1931—the German National Socialist leadership began taking a keener interest in the political situation across the frontier. The leadership of the Austrian party was rather weak, and it doubtless needed an injection of outside talent; in the same way, a tighter control of the Austrian movement from Munich could be ensured. Theodor Habicht, a small businessman from Wiesbaden, who had at first worked as a rather undistinguished journalist and later as a provincial functionary for the party in the Rhineland, was sent over to supervise the activities of the Austrian organization. He chose Linz for his headquarters: although he arrived unburdened by any knowledge of the complexity of the local politics, he succeeded in strengthening and extending the party organization.

Habicht received every help from the Munich leadership. Financial subsidies began to arrive regularly from the Brown House, and the National Socialists were able to unfold a full-scale propaganda campaign. The lessons they had learned in Germany were applied in Austria. Nazi agitation was especially aimed at the unemployed: the first *SA* units were recruited from their ranks. (Rudimentary *SS* units had made their first appearance in Austria early in 1930.) Towards the end of 1931, the National Socialists acquired a house in Hirschengasse in Vienna for 150,000 Austrian schillings, and it became the first permanent party headquarters.[5] New party offices and homes for the *SA* were opened in every Austrian province, and the various auxiliary organizations were set up on the Reich pattern: the *Hitlerjugend*, the students' union, the press club, the artists' club.

The summer of 1932 witnessed an intensified National Socialist propaganda campaign. First of all, the party became more militant: terror and intimidation were employed in Austria in the same way and for the same purpose as in Germany.[6] On 30 June the *SA* mounted its first major operation: they raided a country club in the Lainzer Zoo, and severely injured several guests. During the Austrian party rally in September heavy street fights developed between the Nazis and the Social Democrats in Vienna; the first photographs of injured *SA* troopers were taken and published in the Nazi press. Shortly before the party rally, Goebbels himself arrived in Vienna, and spoke at a public meeting at the Sportplatz Engelmann. Judged by the standards of Nazi meetings in Germany, the stage management at the Viennese Sportplatz left a lot to be desired. Nevertheless, the slogan on the only banner displayed—'Citizens of Vienna awake! Give power to Hitler!'[7]—could leave no one in doubt as to the intentions of the Nazis.

As a sequel to the summer campaign, a 'two-months plan' for propaganda was put into operation in the autumn. Some 300 public meetings were organized; the antisemitic drive came to the foreground, and a number of raids on Jewish shops in Vienna and elsewhere took place. At the same time, an ever-growing number of party members from the Reich spoke or appeared at

[5] *Beiträge zur Vorgeschichte und Geschichte der Julirevolte*, page 4.
[6] See page 16.   [7] '*Wiener erwacht, gebt Hitler die Macht!*'

public meetings—Robert Ley, Erich Koch, Walter Spahn were among them—while others—Erich Berger, Fritz Steinert, Gerhard Weyh and Walter Graeschke—joined Habicht at his Linz headquarters.

All this work made possible the National Socialist successes in the local elections in 1932: the election landslide made a profound impression on Dollfuss and his cabinet. The opponents of National Socialism became concerned at the possibility that their adversaries might come to power by parliamentary means.

In October 1932, Dollfuss issued the first of his emergency laws. It was an unnecessary step that broke up the structure of Austrian party organizations. It opened the road for a clerical-fascist, and later for a National Socialist dictatorship. Although the Christian Socialists—Dollfuss's party—had suffered heavy losses, especially in Vienna, the Nazi election victories were achieved at the cost of other parties belonging to the 'national' camp: the *Grossdeutsche* party, the *Landbund*, and the national group inside the *Heimwehr*. Nevertheless, the core of the electors belonging to the two main political movements, the Christian Socialist peasantry and the Social Democrat workers, remained largely immune to the attractions of National Socialism.[8]

In the meantime, the official relations between Berlin and Vienna were friendly: after January 1933, the situation radically changed. Until that date none of the Austrian parties was averse to the idea of the *Anschluss*. But when it became the official—if undeclared—policy of the German government after January 1933, the leading parties in Austria came to delete the demand from their programmes. In March, both the Christian Socialists and the Social Democrats renounced incorporation into the Reich as a part of their programme.[9] At the same time, the government of Dollfuss began taking sharper measures against the National Socialist movement. On 4 March, the Chancellor suspended Austria's democratic constitution; on 15 May Hans Frank, the Nazi Minister of Justice, was expelled from the country; on 19 June the Austrian National Socialist party was banned.

[8] Cf. A. Wandruszka, op. cit., page 409.
[9] U. Eichstädt, op. cit., page 24.

The wisdom of forcing the National Socialist movement to operate underground was, of course, questionable: in this way, it acquired its martyrs as well as new adherents. Above all, it became more difficult to control. Documents, lists of members and a part of the finances of the Nazi organization were placed in the care of undercover party members; meetings took place in an inconspicuous manner at private houses, and news and orders were transmitted by word of mouth. The organization, run on the same principle as Communist party cells, was resilient enough to take the strain of illegal work. Eventually, lists of members were destroyed and replaced by code names; security precautions, especially where contacts with the Reich leadership were concerned, were stringent. Propaganda material continued to be produced: one cell in Vienna distributed some 50,000 leaflets in three months.[10] The aim of Nazi agitation was to undermine, by every means, confidence in the state. One of the techniques employed—it had been first used by the Russian Social Democrats during the 1905 revolution—consisted in urging the citizens to withdraw all their deposits from Austrian banks.

The National Socialists devoted particular care to the setting up of an intelligence network in Austria, which supplied the party headquarters in Munich with regular reports. Information gathered by the Nazis was evaluated in Munich by an intelligence centre especially instituted for this purpose and by the *Propagandaleitung*. Some of the information that was pouring out of Austria was then used for broadcasts on the Munich transmitter.[11]

The para-military organizations—the *SA* and the *SS*—also remained active after the ban on the party. At first, their members continued to meet in the attics and cellars of private houses; after several police raids, this method was abandoned. Later, small meetings were organized in the streets, where the possibilities of fast dispersal were better. The troopers arrived at the appointed place singly or in pairs, to report and to obtain orders from their commander. Military training on a larger scale usually took place on Sunday outings. Illegal activity demanded a new division of

[10] *Beiträge zur Vorgeschichte und Geschichte der Julirevolte*, page 9.
[11] See page 129.

the troopers: they were divided into specialized units for recruitment, propaganda, and terrorist purposes.

After the acts of terror in June that led to the ban on the party, the Nazi agitation continued unabated. The *Hakenkreuz* insignia were painted on houses, trees, and rock-faces; the appearance of Nazi leaflets was commonplace in Austrian towns. In October, the National Socialists went to much trouble to place their flags, rolled up, on public buildings; they were provided with an intricate clockwork mechanism, that made them unfurl at a particular time. But again, propaganda had to be reinforced by terror. At the beginning of October, the first tear-gas attacks occurred in cinemas, shops, and other public places: although they caused some confusion, they were not effective enough. At the end of the month, the first 'paper bombs'—forerunners of the *bombes plastiques*—were exploded. They were made from a mixture of pasteboard and black gunpowder, with a primitive ignition mechanism; they looked like litter, and could be left lying about in the streets.

The Austrian police were soon able to collect enough evidence to prove that a large part of the terrorist equipment came from Germany. The first transport of explosives and of printed propaganda material was impounded on 19 October 1933 at the frontier near Salzburg; one of the largest consignments was confiscated on 24 December at Anthiesenhofen in Upper Austria.[12] A number of Austrian Nazi party members were employed by the German frontier police; their task was to run the underground connexions with Austria. In this way the newspapers printed in Germany—*Der rote Adler, Die Alpenwacht, Die Volkstimme,* and the *Mitteilungsblatt des Kampfringes der Deutschösterreicher im Reich*—were made available to the Austrian National Socialists. Apart from newspapers, leaflets and pamphlets, copies of a forged declaration by the government in Vienna, inviting the Austrians to support the *Winterhilfe*, the Nazi relief action for the poor, were found among the contraband propaganda material.

After the ban on the party and the deportation of Habicht from Austria (in May, Hitler's government had unsuccessfully attempted to provide Habicht with diplomatic immunity by

[12] *Beiträge zur Vorgeschichte und Geschichte der Julirevolte*, page 11.

appointing him Press Attaché at the Embassy in Vienna; on 12 June, Habicht and several other Reich functionaries of the party were arrested and expelled) the headquarters of the Austrian Nazis were transferred to Germany. With the help of his Austrian party comrades—*Landesleiter* Proksch, Biegler, the leader of the *SS*, and Reschny, the leader of the *SA*, were among them—who fled the country when Dollfuss began to take strong measures against the party, Habicht built up a new leadership for Austria. The illegal organization continued as an integral part of the *NSDAP*, and it was therefore directly controlled by the party leadership, and ultimately by Hitler himself.

While the exiled party leaders relied on the underground organization to generate a certain amount of indigenous agitation, most of the propaganda activity against the Austrian government in fact originated from Munich. Habicht was the official publisher and editor of the *Österreichische Pressedienst* which was printed by the Munich publisher M. Müller and Son; it was designed to supply the German and foreign press with news from Austria. And at the end of May 1933, Goebbels himself began to take an interest in the treatment of the Austrian question in the German press. Indeed, the campaign became a testcase of the direction of the German press by the *Promi*: newspapers were to be used, for the first time, to support a major propaganda drive.

In a sharp memorandum on 15 June, German journalists were reminded that Hitler's cabinet expected to receive every support from them, and that they must unconditionally toe the line.[13] A few weeks later Otto Dietrich, the head of the Press Department in the Ministry of Propaganda, summoned a special press conference; he told the journalists that their main task was to enlighten every German as to the reasons why the struggle for Austria had to be waged. For the first time, an 'atmosphere' had to be created: a topic was to be brought, and maintained, before the public; it was a trial run before the Saarland campaign.[14]

In the following months, the German press was ruthlessly exploited in the drive against Dollfuss's government. The press had

<hr />

[13] Ralf Richard Koerner, *So haben sie es damals gemacht; Die Propagandavorbereitungen zum Österreichanschluss durch das Hitlerregime 1933–1938*, page 43. Vienna, 1958.
[14] See page 106.

to confine itself to discussion of the internal situation in the Republic: its foreign relations were hardly ever touched upon. When Dollfuss met Mussolini in August 1933, for instance, the journalists were advised to make no comment and to publish a few selected opinions of the foreign press.[15] This reserve was partly occasioned by the fact that Austria's foreign affairs—especially as far as her relations with Italy were concerned—were a highly sensitive topic; more important, however, was the endeavour of Hitler's government to keep its relations with Austria as a family affair, which admitted no outside interference.

Although the propaganda directives supplied the press with a consistent common denominator, and although all the German newspapers were committed to publicize basically the same ideas, there existed some variations in the forms they employed. On the whole, the official party newspapers enjoyed a greater freedom of expression than the rest of the German press.[16] They of course used this freedom only to handle the Austrian problem in a more aggressive manner than was officially required: their treatment of the subject simply intensified the party line. The official Nazi press, because of the connexions between its editors and the party leadership, was also used for the treatment of certain special questions, which fell outside the sphere of competence of the generally distributed directives.

Of the two editions of the *Völkischer Beobachter* published in Berlin and in Munich, the south-German edition devoted more space to the Austrian problem than that printed in Berlin; it went into greater detail and appeared to have entertained more caustic views on the subject. Before the July *putsch* in Vienna, both editions carried a situation report on Austria almost every day; the Munich edition stood, however, in a closer contact with the local *Reichspropagandaleitung* and with Habicht, whose articles it often printed. The attitude of the newspapers that were not run by the party was more restrained towards the friend— the Nazi movement in Austria—as well as towards the foe—the Austrian state. Indeed, before Goebbels achieved a complete centralization of the German press, there appeared some interesting deviations.

In this respect, the case of the *Deutsche Allgemeine Zeitung* and

[15] R. R. Koerner, op. cit., page 44.   [16] ibid., page 25.

its editor, Fritz Klein, is the most illuminating. One of the most distinguished of the German dailies, Klein had run it, since 1925, on national, *grossdeutsch* lines. The Austrian question was of particular interest to the newspaper, which dealt with it, before and after January 1933, in great detail. Although Klein was a nationalist he was not a Nazi. For four months after Hitler came to power, Klein was highly critical of the National Socialist policy towards Austria. In a leader on 30 May, the editor of *DAZ* again demanded a 'sensible policy towards Austria', and he accused the members of Hitler's cabinet of lacking in 'civil courage'. All the copies of the newspaper were impounded that day, it was banned for three months, and Klein was forced to resign as its editor. When it reappeared, the *Deutsche Allgemeine Zeitung* followed the party line.

Although the offences committed by Klein did not appear particularly striking, they stand out against the background of uniformity of the German press. On superficial consideration, it might appear that the south-German newspapers took a more active part in the Austrian campaign than the press of north Germany—this was true for a short time of the two editions of the *Völkischer Beobachter*—but, in fact, the central direction of the non-party press was fast becoming more efficient, and the regional differences in their attitudes towards Austria soon disappeared. Yet the newspapers without any direct connexion with the party served an important purpose, in selling the National Socialist attitude towards Austria to the German public.

Whereas the main task of the press was to create a suitable climate of opinion inside Germany, broadcasting was employed to forge a link between the two countries. The National Socialist broadcasters were faced with a difficult task. They had to demonstrate, in the first place, that the views of the Nazi government and the German public on the Austrian problem were identical; they had to attack the Vienna government and prove that its very existence, rather than its policies, was contrary to the wishes of the Austrian public.

In March 1933 the Bavarian network, with its powerful Munich transmitter, began to be used for the purposes of the Austrian propaganda campaign. On 18 March Hans Frank, the Nazi Minister of Justice, addressed the 'oppressed party comrades in Austria' from the studios in Munich. The passage in Frank's speech in which he warned Dollfuss's government not to do anything that might force the German National Socialists to come to the rescue of their Austrian party comrades was especially offensive: the Austrian Minister in Berlin handed in the first of many official protests. The German reply promised to examine the text of the speech; when it was found that the text was not available, Hitler simply told the Austrian Minister that he was unable to 'run after every speaker'.[17]

Soon after his arrival in Munich in the summer of 1933, Habicht came to play the leading role in the Austrian broadcasting campaign. Of the eighty-four propaganda lectures on and for Austria, broadcast from Munich between July 1933 and February 1934, Habicht delivered twenty-one; they called for the end of Dollfuss's régime, they incited the population to resistance to the government, and they advised the Austrians to boycott the products of the state monopolies. The evening transmissions contained short situation reports that specialized in descriptions of the poverty of the population and of the persecution of the National Socialists. The suppression of most of the political parties in February 1934 gave a new impetus to Nazi propaganda: the government was presented as the enemy of political freedom. A large number of local reports from Austria—they were always related to the wider context of *Grossdeutsch* history—were transmitted, such as the programme on 'Graz, the Town of the German *Südmark*' on 10 January 1934; historical serials and plays also played down the differences between the Austrians and the Germans. Two radio plays—Alfons von Czibulka's *The Reich Saves Vienna* and Reimesch's *The Town in Arms*—dealt, in ridiculously imprecise terms, with the subject of the siege of Vienna by the Turks in 1683; they were transmitted by the majority of the German stations in August and September 1933. Within the framework of the 'Hour of the Nation' series, there was broadcast a play by A. Weinberger entitled *The Flight Home*, which described the flight of the persecuted National Socialists from Austria to Germany.[18]

Although the Vienna government repeatedly protested against

[17] Konrad Heiden, *Adolf Hitler*, vol. 2, page 16. Zürich, 1937.
[18] H. Pohle, op. cit., page 404.

the concentrated broadcasting onslaught, its representations produced no results. The Austrians had no effective means at their disposal for countering Nazi radio propaganda. The transmissions from Munich could be heard all over Austria, and in some regions better than the local stations; the technical broadcasting arrangements in Austria played into the hands of the Germans. The geographical shape of the Republic—its disproportionate length from the east to the west compared with its width, and the fact that Vienna, with its large concentration of population, lay in the easternmost part of the state—made a consistent radio coverage of the area difficult. The capital city alone disposed of a powerful transmitter; farther west, the stations at Linz, Innsbruck, and Salzburg were seriously underpowered.

The transmissions from Munich were keenly listened to in Austria, and their aggressive tone doubtless attracted new sympathizers for the Nazi cause. The deterioration of the political situation—the conflict between Dollfuss's government and the Social Democrats that culminated in the siege and shelling of the workers' quarters in Vienna in February 1934—contributed to the success of the Nazi broadcasting campaign. In its early stages, it was reinforced by the leaflet-raids over the territory of the Republic by German planes: the leaflets contained information on the times and wavelengths of the Munich broadcasts. The first violation of Austria's air-space occurred on 14 July 1933: the raids were continued until August, when a protest by the Great Powers in Berlin was successful in putting a stop to them.

The agitation that radiated from Bavaria had to be, according to the basic precepts of Nazi propaganda, reinforced by a physical threat. This was done through the institution of the 'Austrian Legion'. It consisted of some 15,000 men, mostly refugee *SA* or *SS* troopers from Austria. They were trained by German Nazis, equipped with *Reichswehr* arms, and stationed at a number of camps in Bavaria. The government in Vienna was well informed about the Legion: from the middle of September 1933, it had at its disposal a large number of reports from 're-defectors'. Again, the Austrian representations were without avail: in a note of 21 September, the *Auswärtiges Amt* explained that Austrian refugees were assembled in labour camps 'in the interests of

IX*a*. Funeral orator. Dr Goebbels. 1936

IX*b*. Goebbels at the Exhibition, 'Ten Years' Fight for Berlin'. 1936

X*a*. Austrian plebiscite posters. 1938

X*b*. The first Nazi poster in Poland. 'England! This is your work!' 1939

public order and on charitable grounds'.[19] Nevertheless, the existence of the Austrian Legion caused deep concern to successive governments in Vienna. A few months after its foundation, the *Kampfring der Österreicher*, its civilian sister organization, was set up in Germany. It embraced the Austrians living in the Reich, and it publicized among them Nazi views on the solution of the Austrian problem.

Finally on 12 July 1934, a directive to the press advised that the campaign should be somewhat cut back: at that time, the Nazi propagandists regarded public opinion in Germany as thoroughly prepared for the Austrian *putsch*. The tactics of the revolutionaries were partly moulded by the propaganda situation: the capture of the studios of the Vienna broadcasting station—the only dangerous adversary of Munich—was one of the main aims of the rebels. While a detachment of *SS* troops, wearing the grey uniforms of the Austrian army, occupied the Chancellery and shot Dollfuss dead, another *SS* group forced their entry into the broadcasting studios, where they made the announcer read, at pistol point, the sentence: 'The Dollfuss government has resigned. Dr. Rintelen has taken over the business of government.'

The abortive *putsch* in Vienna marked the culmination and the end of the first phase of the Nazi propaganda campaign in Austria. The Austrian party leadership badly overestimated their resources and strength: they doubtless did so in order to keep their allies in the Reich interested. For a short time after the events of 25 July, Theo Habicht and his friends continued to feed the propaganda machinery in Germany with their own material. The first enthusiastic reports on the *putsch* that were supplied, on 25 July, by Habicht to *DNB*, the official news agency, had to be suppressed; two days later, Hitler's government officially regarded the events in Austria as a purely internal Austrian affair. Anyway, by 27 July, Habicht had been relieved of all his party functions.

The failure of the July plot taught the Nazi leaders a lesson of first-rate importance: they would never again embark on an adventure as ill-prepared as that in Austria. They had forgotten that they were no longer running a party without any

[19] U. Eichstädt, op. cit., page 35.

131

responsibility; when confronted with the stark facts of the situation, they were not ready to commit the full resources of the state to the advancement of their movement. Although Hitler had made an attempt to enlist Mussolini's support for a change of the Austrian régime, he did not, however, make certain that the Duce would approve of the kind of change Habicht was planning.[20] Indeed, the Nazi leaders had no cause for surprise when, immediately after the *putsch*, Mussolini declared that he would protect Austria's independence. In the evening of 25 July, four Italian divisions began to move towards the Austrian frontier.

Hitler tried to deceive Mussolini when he said that the annexation of Austria was of no interest to him; he was, in turn, misled by Habicht as to the degree of support the National Socialists commanded in Austria.[21] The support Hitler had given Habicht was inspired by emotion rather than by clear-sighted political calculation; the Austrian adventure resulted in a setback for the broader Nazi propaganda pursuit abroad—the attempt to inspire confidence in their régime. But even in a more technical sense, the efforts of Habicht's organization were not properly integrated into the National Socialist propaganda effort. When Habicht interfered, for instance, in Austria's civil war in a broadcast from Munich on 19 February 1934, German newspapers received the following strictly confidential directive: 'Emphatic advice has come from a high official source [the Chancellery] that yesterday's radio talk by Habicht does not, as far as the German press is concerned, exist. In no circumstances should notice be taken of the broadcast. . . .'[22] Later, in the summer of 1934, it became clear that Habicht was entirely out of touch with Goebbels and the Ministry of Propaganda. The Ministry knew nothing of the *putsch* plans: the treatment of the revolt, and

[20] The meeting between Hitler and Mussolini had taken place some six weeks before the *putsch*, on 14 and 15 June 1934. Hitler told Mussolini that it was impossible for him to come to terms with Dollfuss; at the same time, however, he informed the Italian dictator that the question of the *Anschluss* was of no interest to him because it was not internationally feasible. He went on to say that he had no particular person in mind as a replacement for Dollfuss, but that the future Chancellor would have to proclaim an election as soon as possible, and that the National Socialists would have to be taken into the government. *Docs. Ger. For. Pol.*, series C, vol. 3, page 10.

[21] *IMT*, vol. IX, page 294.

[22] R. R. Koerner, op. cit., page 47.

especially of its early stages, in the German press, was extremely uneven; a carefully prepared and centrally directed campaign was conspicuous by its absence.

For one day and two nights, the dilemma that the *putsch* had placed before Hitler's government remained unresolved. The *Reichsleitung* of the party in Munich was unable to disown the Austrian *Landesleitung*, its integral part, and the headquarters of the rebels. At 3 a.m. on 26 July, the Austrian frontier guards at Kollerschlag arrested a Reich German. He was carrying detailed instructions for the Austrian National Socialists on the measures to be taken after the demise of Dollfuss's government, as well as the key to the code that was to be used for the transmission of messages to Germany.[23] The Austrian Legion was drawn up alongside the frontier; during the two nights following the *putsch*, a number of illegal crossings from Germany into Austria took place. The *Kampfring der Österreicher* had been mobilized a few days before 25 July, and all its members able to perform military duty were alerted.

Habicht and his Austrian *Landesleitung* remained hopeful longer than the Nazi leaders in Berlin. On 26 July Hitler wrote to von Papen asking him to head a special mission to Vienna and to replace the German Minister, who had—in view of the failure of the revolt in the capital—acted unwisely. In the letter to von Papen, Hitler expounded the new party line in regard to Austria: 'The attack on the Austrian Federal Chancellor, which the Reich government most sharply condemn and regret, has aggravated, through no fault of ours, the already unstable situation in Europe. It is accordingly my wish to contribute to a relaxation of the tension in the general situation and particularly to see the relations with the German–Austrian State, which have long been troubled, led back once more into normal and friendly paths.'[24]

In the letter to von Papen, Hitler adopted the views of his Foreign Ministry. The diplomats had known even less about Habicht's activities than Goebbels, and they had advocated caution all along the line. In a communication to the Ministry of the Interior on 25 July, Bülow set out all the dangers connected with an aggressive Nazi action in Austria. He added that 'The

[23] U. Eichstädt, op. cit., page 56.
[24] *Docs. Ger. For. Pol.*, series C, vol. 3, page 252.

latest attacks on Germany, however, which are growing steadily more severe and which, according to reports at hand, must be expected to be taken up by other foreign countries in the near future, make it urgently advisable for all authorities here to realize the increasing gravity of the situation and the international dangers arising from it.'[25]

The penalties of failure came down swiftly upon Habicht's head. The Austrian *Landesleitung* was disbanded, and Habicht himself was divested of all his party functions. Two days after the *putsch*, the National Socialist leaders were united in condemnation of Habicht's work in Austria: even Steinacher, the head of the *Volksbund für das Deutschtum in Ausland*, chipped in with a sharp criticism of the manner in which the revolt had been conducted.[26] While the Munich headquarters of the Austrian Nazis fell into oblivion, the Ministry of Propaganda and the Foreign Ministry regained their rightful places in the Nazi counsels in regard to Austria. Indeed, the prompt diplomatic action and its backing by propaganda did away with much of the discredit Hitler's régime had incurred through its activities in Austria.

Goebbels's press directive on 27 July announced that 'Austrian questions should be treated with a cool reserve, and polemic or even invective should be avoided.'[27] The order concluded the militant campaign of the German press against the Austrian government, and it initiated the second phase that was to last for two years, and that was dominated by the attitude of 'cool reserve'. At the same time, the National Socialist leaders were obliged to tighten up the propaganda apparatus: they realized that extremist trends inside their own party could be as dangerous as opposition outside it. In order to avoid aberrations of the Habicht type in the future, Hitler informed Goebbels, Hess, von Papen, and the Office of the Secret State Police on 8 August that 'In order to ensure the uniform policy which I wish to see pursued in future, I hereby order that neither party authorities nor anyone else may discuss, either on the wireless or in the press, questions concerning German–Austrian policy, unless agreement has previously been reached between the Reich

[25] *Docs. Ger. For. Pol.*, series C, vol. 3, page 240.   [26] ibid., page 283.
[27] R. R. Koerner, op. cit., page 54.

Propaganda Minister and the present Minister in Vienna, Herr von Papen. In particular I forbid party authorities to discuss such questions on the wireless on their own initiative.'[28]

In the summer of 1934 the Austrian problem was demoted from the first rank in the Nazi scheme of foreign propaganda: its place was taken by questions that appeared easier of solution: the Saarland, the Rhineland, and armament parity. This did not of course mean that Austria entirely disappeared from Nazi publicity. The intensive pre-25 July campaign had to be tapered off slowly; from 17 August reporting on the subject was to be undertaken on the following lines: 'All reports have to be founded in the spirit of conciliation. News of abuses that have been recently perpetrated in Austria should be published only when they are absolutely reliable.'[29] Although the word 'conciliation' meant little more than the absence of virulent attacks on the Austrian government, the new party line was strictly enforced until the next major event in the relations between the two countries.

This was the German–Austrian treaty, signed on 11 July 1936. There was no need for special propaganda preparations for the treaty and, anyway, the negotiations for it had been conducted in secret. It is quite likely that Goebbels had known nothing about the negotiations. On the evening of 11 July Goebbels arranged a special press conference at his Ministry; he did not appear very enthusiastic about the agreement between Vienna and Berlin. He said that the task of the German press was to create the impression that the treaty would contribute to the pacification of Europe;[30] according to a reliable eye-witness he answered an enquiry as to what the pact was really about by saying that 'it is the prelude to an Austrian 30 January 1933'.[31] Neither in the years before nor after the conclusion of the Austrian–German friendship treaty did the National Socialists actually give up hope for the creation of a *Grossdeutsche* Reich. In diplomatic terms, their 'conciliatory' attitude meant that the international situation ruled out any other move in regard to Austria; in terms of propaganda it implied that the vitriolic

[28] *Docs. Ger. For. Pol.*, series C, vol. 3, page 299.
[29] R. R. Koerner, op. cit., page 56.
[30] ibid., page 62.
[31] *Der Hochverratsprozess gegen Dr. Guido Schmidt*, page 487. Vienna, 1947.

tone, used from the spring of 1933 until July 1934, was no longer admissible.

Meanwhile, the Nazi party in Austria was going through a critical period of its illegal existence. From the end of July 1934 it was entirely on its own: all its relations with the Reich organization were broken off. The para-military organizations had suffered considerable losses; many party functionaries fled to Germany and some to Yugoslavia, while others were arrested and sentenced to death (thirteen capital sentences were pronounced by the Austrian courts after the July rising) or to long terms of imprisonment. For a short time, the party disappeared from Austria's political life.

It did not take long to recover. In the spring of 1936 another police action had to be taken against the Austrian National Socialists, and a new wave of arrests swept across the country. A comprehensive police report on the state of the Nazi movement, which was drafted on 4 April 1936, pointed out that 'despite three years' fight against it by the security authorities, the illegal apparatus still possesses a striking power that should not be underestimated'.[32] No significant changes had occurred, according to the report, in the social composition of the movement since 1933. The leadership still consisted largely of the unemployed intelligentsia; the para-military organizations still attracted the down-and-out ex-service men; the ideas of the movement were applauded by the lower-middle classes, the dispossessed bourgeoisie, and by Austrian youth. Although Nazi propaganda had made little impression on the working classes, it had achieved success, by 1936, among the peasants. Again, Nazi ideas fared better among the economically depressed sections of the peasantry in the frontier districts and especially in the mountains. Indeed many foreign visitors gained the impression that in Austria, 'the Third Reich begins at the height of 3,000 feet'.[33] There were illegal Nazi newspapers in circulation among the peasants, which described conditions in the Reich in a simple and laudatory manner; the peasants with Nazi sympathies were convinced that in the Reich, the National Socialist state imposed no taxes on the farmers.[34]

[32] Guido Schmidt Prozess, page 468.   [33] A. Wandruszka, op. cit., page 410.
[34] Guido Schmidt Prozess, page 469.

In 1936, Nazi pamphlets could still be found in Austria, *Hakenkreuz* flags were still being unfurled from public buildings, swastika signs were painted in conspicuous places. Although the Austrian Nazis continued to regard the Reich as their lodestar and though they continued to be impressed by the achievements of Hitler's régime, hints as to their connexions with the Reich movement disappeared from their propaganda. It concentrated on internal Austrian matters: the demand for elections and for economic improvement. The strained political relations with Germany were equated with the depressed state of Austria's economy; and the campaign was reinforced by intensive anti-semitic agitation. The staple technique of Nazi propaganda—the identification of National Socialism with the nation—was exploited to the full. Every measure by the state against the National Socialists was treated as another move towards the oppression of the German nation.

Although terrorist activities were in abeyance at the time, the Austrian security authorities expected them to come into play again. Indeed, the Republic's high officials took a pessimistic view of the future. Apart from terrorism, they thought the Nazis might intensify their agitation among the workers; they knew that their own ranks were weakened by the presence of Nazi sympathizers. Although the view was put forward that the Nazi movement had to be combated in an uncompromising manner, nobody expected the effort to be rewarded by success. In the spring of 1936, Austrian officials were convinced that a strong National Socialist movement would exist in Austria as long as Hitler's régime remained in power in the Reich. They saw no immediate prospect of a political change in Germany.[35]

The situation remained unresolved until March 1938. The attempts of Schuschnigg's government in the previous year to gain support from the moderate wing of the Nazi movement came to nothing; early in 1938, the Austrian authorities discovered yet another Nazi plan for a *coup d'état*. Finally, on 12 February, a meeting took place between Hitler and Schuschnigg at Berchtesgaden. Here, under massive threats of military intervention, Austria's Chancellor was forced to come to an agreement with Hitler that set off the events of the following

[35] *Guido Schmidt Prozess*, page 471. Report of 4 April 1936.

weeks. Seyss-Inquart, the Viennese lawyer and a Nazi sympathizer, became the Minister for Security; the public activities of the Austrian National Socialists took place, from now on, undisturbed. On 9 March, Schuschnigg's government announced that a plebiscite would take place on 13 March; after two days of hectic plotting and counter-plotting, the Chancellor showed himself willing to rescind the order. But the German troops were already massed on the other side of the frontier; Schuschnigg resigned and, in the evening of the same day—11 March—a government under Seyss-Inquart was formed. On 13 March it issued a decree on the annexation of Austria to the Reich. On the following day, Hitler gave the 'grand account on things accomplished' on all German and Austrian transmitters. He said: 'As the Führer and Reich Chancellor of the German nation and of the Reich I report to history the entry of my home country into the German Reich.'[36]

Against the background of fast-moving political developments, the effectiveness of Nazi propaganda depended on its elasticity. During the first stage of the preparations for the *Anschluss*, in the early weeks of 1938, it had to pursue two distinct and somewhat contradictory aims: it had to avoid giving the impression that the Reich Nazis had begun to interfere in Austria's internal affairs, while making it clear that the relations between the two countries could no longer be regulated by the treaty of July 1936. After the Berchtesgaden agreement of 12 February, Nazi publicity set out to prove that the Austrian problem could be solved only on National Socialist terms, that the agreement had left no margin for other solutions.[37]

Every reference to the fact that another *coup d'état* was being mounted in Austria was scrupulously avoided. When the government in Vienna released the news of the discovery of the plans by Leo Tavs for a Nazi *putsch*, the German press at first ignored the reports, and then a few newspapers simply denied their authenticity. No propaganda preparations were made before the Berchtesgaden meeting; immediately after its conclusion, the German press was advised that 'Only the *DNB* communiqué is to be printed about the talks between the Führer and Dr.

[36] M. Domarus, *Hitler, Reden und Proklamationen*, vol. 1, page 824.
[37] R. R. Koerner, op. cit., page 69.

Schuschnigg. No comments are to be made.'[38] The order for silence was lifted only four days later, on 16 February, when the German press received a detailed directive on the treatment of the Austrian situation.

The reorganization of Schuschnigg's cabinet and the political amnesty were to be regarded not as the final 'pacification' of Austria, but only as a basis for its achievement. People of National Socialist convictions were to be granted the same freedoms as the members of other movements: all this was to happen, however, within the framework of the Austrian constitution. The journalists were forbidden to quibble (no petty criticism), or to turn their minds to the past. The international angle on the situation was that Hitler was trying to do away with the causes of world tension, and that at Berchtesgaden he had achieved a remarkable success. It had to be acknowledged, however, that the Austrian statesmen met him half way. Quotations from the foreign press, including indications that the first steps towards the annexation of Austria had been taken, could be used; speculations on the *Anschluss* were, however, in no way to be emphasized. It would be quite wrong, the directive pointed out further, even to hint that Schuschnigg had given way under pressure.[39]

The Nazi publicity maintained the line given in this directive until two days before the *Anschluss*. The news of Schuschnigg's speech of 9 March on the plebiscite, for instance, was not published till some twenty-four hours later. Indeed, the arguments used shortly before and during the *Anschluss*—that the annexation was taking place on Austrian initiative—could have been employed only after a singularly restrained propaganda campaign in Germany. It entered its last phase on 11 March. At the morning press conference, editors of evening newspapers were invited to pay more attention to the events in Austria. Any semblance of uniformity was, however, to be avoided; tabloid newspapers were to use prominent headlines, while the more serious dailies were to devote two front-page columns to Austria. Later on, at night, more detailed directives were transmitted to the press. The allegations against Germany which Schuschnigg had made in his farewell speech were to be sharply denied. The

[38] R. R. Koerner, op. cit., page 70.   [39] ibid., page 72.

ultimatum—the Chancellor's resignation or occupation of
Austria by German troops—was to be presented as having come
from Schuschnigg's colleagues, and not from Berlin. The Austrian
side of the picture was to be filled in by reports on the unrest
among workers that had broken out in several towns; the
German attitude of non-interference underlined by stressing that
Hitler had not demanded the reorganization of the Austrian
government. At the same time, the contents of the declaration
broadcast by Seyss-Inquart were released: the journalists
were told that Seyss-Inquart, as the only Minister remaining in
office, was acting in place of the government, and that he had
sent a telegram asking the Reich cabinet for troops to restore
order in Austria. Directives for various types of commentaries
were also issued: the impression of spontaneity was to be achieved
through careful management.[40]

Although one day before the *Anschluss* the aim of Nazi
propaganda was to create the appropriate 'annexation mood'—
in this sense it anticipated events—on 13 March it was toned down
to produce the right background for the fast-changing political
situation. The 'liberation' and the 'return home' of Austria
were celebrated; the development had to be presented, however,
as having had a 'peaceful character'. The reports suggesting that
a panic situation prevailed in Austria disappeared from the German press; the word 'war' had to be carefully avoided, and the
process of annexation described as completely orderly. At the
same time, only 'positive' foreign reports—especially English
and Italian—were to be quoted; two days later, newspaper editors
were asked sharply to deny all negative foreign opinions.[41] The
annexation campaign was concluded on 16 March, the day of
Hitler's arrival in Vienna. The event was treated as the most
important centre-piece of the day's news: Hitler was hailed as the
liberator of Austria.

Compared with the first groping steps in 1933 and 1934, the
second Austrian campaign was executed smoothly and efficiently.
In 1938, Goebbels conducted the propaganda orchestra with a
supreme mastery: there was no discordant note. First the
simulated dissociation from the Austrian events, then a detached
kind of interest, the shifting emphasis in the treatment of news,

[40] R. R. Koerner, op. cit., page 79.   [41] ibid., pages 79–81.

the guidance as to comments and quotations, were all carefully calculated to produce the desired effects. The 'annexation mood' in Germany, a seemingly spontaneous phenomenon, was in fact carefully engineered. Above all, the propagandists had accepted that they were a part of the overall state machinery. They had to follow the manœuvres of the National Socialist foreign policy: the presence, in the background, of the German armed forces made a considerable contribution to the ultimate success of the Austrian campaign.

In comparison, the abortive *putsch*, run for the party by Theo Habicht, four years earlier, appears amateur, and doomed to failure. The National Socialists regarded Austria as a part of Germany: it was, after all, another *Gau* in the party organization. And party attitudes and arrangements blinded them to the international implications of their actions. Until 1933, the overspill of the Nazi organization from the Reich into Austria had been tiresome for the Austrian officials, but it had not created an explosive international situation. Yet the party carried on its policy in regard to Austria even after Hitler acquired his official residence in Berlin. The National Socialists were slow to realize that their new responsibilities committed them to a new kind of behaviour; that, in order to achieve their aims in Austria, they could no longer rely on the twin instruments of party organization and propaganda only: that there was a big difference between supporting a sympathetic cause abroad and committing the full resources of the state to this support. In addition, Habicht made the customary mistake of conspirators with powerful outside supporters. He misled his allies in the Reich as to the strength of the Nazi movement in Austria: the failure of the *putsch* in July 1934 was his ultimate penalty. The Nazi leaders benefited by the Austrian lesson, and they never made the same mistake. They never again regarded the state as a mere extension of the party: propaganda had to be guided by cool calculation rather than by emotion, and it had to fall into line with the foreign policy of the Reich.

VII. BRITAIN AND SUBVERSION

In the years between 1933 and 1939, it is impossible to detect a long-term and coherent strategy behind National Socialist propaganda abroad. The appearance of consistency was created by certain persistent and recurrent themes in Nazi agitation, and by the fact that there existed a strong connexion between propaganda at home and abroad.[1] On their way to power, the National Socialists had seen Europe in terms of a hostile constellation of states that was preventing Germany from achieving her justified aims. After 1933, they had to withdraw this negative image from circulation: it stood in the way of achieving their main aim at the time. First of all, they had to try and make their régime acceptable abroad. Hitler's famous 'peace speech' on 17 May 1933 launched this campaign, and it set the pattern for many similar pronouncements that followed. For the first time, Hitler used the *Reichstag* as a platform for speeches that were brought to the attention of the whole world. He pointed out how faithfully Germany had fulfilled disarmament obligations imposed on her by the Versailles Treaty;[2] he intimated that Germany was prepared to co-operate with all European countries on the basis of trust and equal rights. The 'acceptance' theme kept recurring, in a number of variations, in propaganda designed for foreign consumption, until the last weeks before the outbreak of the war.

The Nazi propagandists never wearied of pointing out that a strong leadership was now making decisions in Berlin on behalf of Germany, that the country was no longer a burden to anyone else, and that other European governments should therefore be grateful to the National Socialists for assuming the responsibility. The argument that Hitler's party had defeated Communism in

[1] See page 76 et seq.
[2] M. Domarus, *Hitler, Reden und Proklamationen*, vol. 1, pages 269 et seq.

142

economic achievements

the heart of Europe was of course often used in the drive for acceptance; during the implementation of the four-year plan—announced at the party rally in 1936—the economic motif came to the foreground of Nazi propaganda. It consisted of an account of Germany's achievements in the economic field, and it was often accompanied by offers of trade treaties, especially to the agrarian countries in south-eastern Europe.

Nevertheless, concurrently with the propaganda campaign for acceptance, the campaigns for the subversion of the established order in Europe were developed. Superficially, the two broad pursuits of National Socialist propaganda appeared incompatible; they were not so in fact. From the abortive *putsch* in Austria in the summer of 1934, to the occupation of post-Munich Czechoslovakia in March 1939, subversive propaganda campaigns were confined to Central Europe; the drive for acceptance was largely aimed at the European Powers that were seen as the main pillars of the *status quo*.

The secret circular sent out to all its missions abroad by the Foreign Ministry on 26 April 1933, and entitled 'Propaganda Against Germany and Counter-propaganda'[3] clearly regarded France as Germany's main adversary. In the field of international propaganda, the French activities were the most suspect; the Germans regarded the French as the main architects of the postwar order in Europe; among all the Great Powers, France had the greatest interest in the preservation of the *status quo*. But in the National Socialist perspective, France was not a dangerous adversary at all. A long time before, Hitler had detected the trend that France was becoming 'more and more negroid',[4] and that its population was on the decline, an artificial decline at that. In the long-term Nazi view, the French were the extreme example of a 'dying nation': a charming, lovable, perhaps a fortunate people, but at the end of its political tether. Apart from its rather base political manœuvres, it had no higher aims, and it was therefore without consequence. It had become, or was becoming, a small nation with a crushingly large spiritual heritage.[5]

[3] *AA* Presseabteilung, 86774/E60698383–4.
[4] *Mein Kampf*, page 525.
[5] H. Rauschning, *Die Revolution des Nihilismus*, pages 363–4. Zürich, 1938.

Indeed, by the time Hitler came to power, Britain had taken over from France the political leadership of Europe: the situation remained unchanged until the outbreak of the war. A week after Hitler's appointment as the Chancellor of the Republic, the German Ambassador reported from London that 'A comparison between the French hegemony under Laval in the autumn of 1931, with England in a state of almost total financial impotence and greatly impaired political activity, and the present situation, which shows England to be active and France in an increasingly defensive position, provides clear proof of the change-over that has taken place.'[6] It further stimulated the attention the new rulers of Germany lavished on Great Britain: when they made statements intended for general consumption abroad, they had London, rather than Paris, in their minds.

It was a recurrent theme in *Mein Kampf* that Great Britain was Germany's natural ally against Russia, and that without her backing Germany could make no move in the East; Hitler also believed that British and French diplomacy were bound to come into a sharp clash on the Continent, from which Germany could only benefit. The Nazi leaders spared no effort to make an impression in Great Britain: the effects they aimed to achieve ranged from persuading the British to accept the new order in Germany to influencing the decisions of their government. Although the *Promi* found it difficult to create a sharp image of Great Britain for the home market, the country always loomed large in the calculations of the National Socialist leaders. For them, Britain's friendship was indispensable for the achievement of their aims on the Continent, and especially in its eastern territories; in the two years before the war, British acquiescence became essential for the completion of Hitler's piecemeal conquest of central Europe.

In their relations with Great Britain, the National Socialist leaders usually lacked self-confidence, and they were highly sensitive to criticism. Soon after they assumed the responsibility of government, a striking example of the way in which they mismanaged this relationship became available. Alfred Rosenberg visited London early in May 1933; he said that his object in visiting England was to 'clear up certain misconceptions which

[6] *Docs. Ger. For. Pol.*, series C, vol. 1, page 26.

existed abroad in regard to recent events in Germany'.[7] It is
very likely that Rosenberg had consulted Hitler before he left for
London, and that he went with the Führer's blessing. It was
neither a secret diplomatic mission nor a propaganda trip. In
both respects the journey was a dismal failure. The leading Nazi
ideologist made a very bad impression in London. The reasons for
his visit as well as his status were vague, and he arrived without
any official credentials: a situation that would hardly recommend
itself to the Foreign Office. It was not clear from his behaviour
whether he was offering or expecting some kind of political
advantage; he gave the impression of confusing propaganda with
diplomacy, and of believing his own side's propaganda. Vansittart
later described his visitor as a 'Balt who looked like a cold cod'.[8]
When faced with the civil servants, Rosenberg tended to behave
like an unscrupulous agitator; at his press conference, he gave the
impression of distance and inscrutability. He got a very bad
press: only the *Sunday Graphic* gave him an opportunity to
enlighten its readers with an account of what the Nazis stood
for. In the end, he wisely decided to cut his visit short and leave
London as unobtrusively as he could.

The failure of Rosenberg's visit to London had far-reaching
consequences. It resulted in a sharp decline of his prestige in the
party, and it extinguished the hopes he had placed on his private
foreign ministry.[9] More important, the Nazi leaders, in their
attempts to influence the British, gave up the direct and personal
approach: from now on they relied almost exclusively on their
diplomatic representation.

Indeed, in regard to Great Britain, National Socialist propaganda commanded none of the advantages offered by the direct
connexions of the party with the Germans in, say, Austria or
Czechoslovakia. The Nazi leaders could afford to disregard the
views of the German Minister to Vienna because they possessed
alternative sources of information and other instruments for
conducting their policy towards Austria. This was not the case in
Britain. Here, the suggestions of the diplomats carried some
weight. They were based on an intimate knowledge of local

<hr />

[7] *Docs. Brit. For. Pol.*, Second series, vol. V, page 204.
[8] Lord Vansittart, *The Mist Procession*, page 475. London, 1958.
[9] See pages 60–62.

conditions, and they were usually expressed in a convincing manner.

In his detailed report on British–German relations, dispatched on 16 August 1933, Hoesch, the Ambassador to London, pointed out that the idea of a 'systematic and organized campaign of propaganda should from the start be discarded as erroneous'.[10] He went on to say that, since the end of the First World War, the British had lost their taste for propaganda because they 'were forced to experience too strongly the anguish of the modern art of propaganda, when it meant, at the time, bringing to boiling point and infecting with war mania a people who were in themselves entirely averse to the war, and in no way prepared for it. Neither a propaganda campaign in the press, however ingeniously prepared—if such a campaign could be carried out here at all— nor a swamping of England with pamphlets in which the German point of view is explained, nor finally the dispatching of more or less official publicity agents seemed to me suitable means for the winning of public opinion here. Everything tempestuous, vehement, and blatant must be avoided, and it would be better to reckon with the possibility of only a slow change for the better than the possibility of failure through over-hasty attempts.'

Among the appropriate methods for influencing British public opinion, Hoesch listed trips by prominent Englishmen to Germany and, he wrote, 'gracious reception and attentive treatment of these travellers in Germany seem to me desirable'. The suggestion was taken up by Nazi authorities: in the six years of peace, thousands of officially sponsored visits to Germany took place. Some of them produced interesting results. In May 1934 Sir Arnold Wilson, a Tory M.P., was invited to visit Germany by the *Deutsch-Europaeischer Kulturbund*, a Nazi-sponsored organization. In that and in the following year he travelled in Italy, Belgium, and France as well as Germany. In May 1936, the first edition of his book, *Walks and Talks Abroad*, was published; the second edition followed in October, and the third in April 1939. Sir Arnold described his own political outlook as similar to that of Lord Milner—'national rather than international'[11]—he also detested the 'anti-Christian basis of Communism'. Although

[10] *Docs. Ger. For. Pol.*, series C, vol. 1, page 761.
[11] Third edition, page 1.

XI*a*. 'Check to the King!' 1940

XI*b*. Churchill, a sniper. 1941

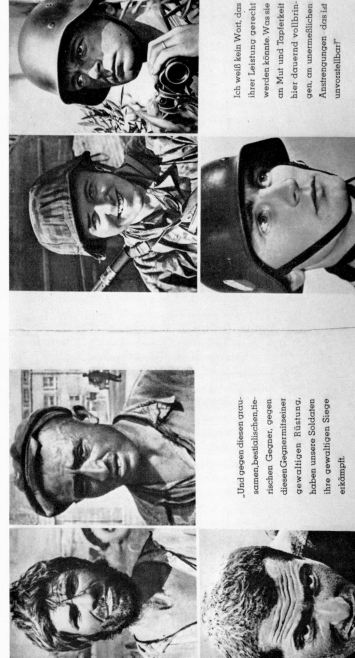

"Und gegen diesen grausamen, bestialischen, tierischen Gegner, gegen diesen Gegner mit seiner gewaltigen Rüstung, haben unsere Soldaten ihre gewaltigen Siege erkämpft.

Ich weiß kein Wort, das ihrer Leistung gerecht werden könnte. Was sie an Mut und Tapferkeit hier dauernd vollbringen, an unermeßlichen Anstrengungen - das ist unvorstellbar!"

XII. The Soviet *Untermenschen* contrasted with the defenders of European civilization. 1941

prop. made people
see Germany
wrong

he abhorred the persecution of the Jews in Germany and the
Nazi racial doctrines, he wrote that 'I cannot refuse to recognize
that the Nazi government has in the past three years achieved
much and secured and maintained, in face of great difficulties, a
far more ample measure of public acceptance and approval than
any of its predecessors. Judged by whatever internal standard—
of national health, of employment, of public amenities, of internal
development of the standard of living of the masses—the recovery
of Germany has been without parallel in Europe, though at a
heavy cost, not to be measured in cash.'[12] Although Germany's
attitude towards the Jews, Sir Arnold wrote, increased the
country's difficulties in many, but not all, foreign markets, he
was confident that the present régime would survive; he believed
that the structure of the Nazi state would grow in strength and
would endure because it had 'the passionate support of many,
and the assent of the great majority of Germans at home and
abroad'.[13]

Sir Arnold was convinced that Britain could learn a lot
from the totalitarian countries—Germany, Italy, and perhaps
even Russia—how to look after her own citizens better, how to
improve social services, even how to breed a better type of child.
He quoted, with approval, Hegel's dictum about the state as
being 'the product of reason, endowing every individual with
new forms of liberty in return for the surrender of some selfish
privileges'.[14] The enforced surrender of selfish privileges in
concentration camps was also witnessed by Wilson on his travels;
he went to see Dachau, and he reported that 'this is nothing new'.[15]
The traveller saw many places, talked to many people, and
the tale he brought back with him was not very enlighten-
ing. He accepted the suppression of minority opinions as something inevitable, and anyway, he was not interested in them. The
views he faithfully reported were Nazi; when he described a
situation as odious or unintelligible to the English mind, he
usually produced the Nazi point of view in order to explain it to
his fellow-countrymen. He was plainly impressed by Germany,
and he was out to impress his readers.

A variety of similar books appeared before and even after the

---

[12] *Walks and Talks Abroad*, 3rd edition, page ix.   [13] ibid., page xi.
[14] ibid., page xvi.   [15] ibid., page 83.

11

outbreak of the war.[16] Some of their authors—notably Sir Arnold Wilson—later changed their views as to the nature of Hitler's régime. When they wrote their books, however, they all believed that they were making a contribution to the cause of understanding between Britain and Germany, which they regarded as essential for the preservation of peace in Europe. The books sympathetic to Hitler's Germany were, in comparison with the amount of anti-Nazi literature, in the minority: their authors were trying to present the views of the 'other side'. But in the process, they made use of Nazi propaganda material, and they contributed to the effort of making Hitler's régime acceptable to the British public. Their books were the outcome of innocuous public relations work, recommended by the German Ambassador to London. They were not dishonest insofar as their authors did not intentionally mislead their readers: they were misleading because they leaned over backwards to present the case for the 'other side'.

The German diplomats in London also made a determined effort to influence the British press. The Embassy became the fountainhead and controlling agency for these activities. From the spring of 1933 it had on its staff a young man called Sigismund-Sisso FitzRandolf, who ran its press department. He had had no diplomatic experience; he was responsible to the *Promi* direct rather than to the Foreign Ministry. In the spring of 1933, the Ministry approved of the principle that propaganda material should flow through British, rather than German, channels: the principle was formulated in connexion with an offer from a British journalist to put a newly-founded agency at the disposal of the German government.[17] But the offer was not taken up by Berlin, and the principle was abandoned.

FitzRandolf was assisted by a large contingent of 'correspondents': as the number of the newspapers published in Germany was decreasing, the number of the German correspondents in Britain grew. By the beginning of 1938 there were sixty of them in London, and a year later eighty. Most of them were engaged in propaganda and espionage activities. Their influence

---

[16] Arthur Bryant's book *Unfinished Victory* belonged to this category; it was published in January 1940.
[17] *AA*, K2113/K582609–616 and K528623.

on the press was negligible; Nazi propaganda in Britain was vulnerable because it could easily be traced to its sources; it could be, in the last instance, curbed by administrative measures. The first German journalist in London to receive a deportation order, as early as November 1935, was Dr. Thost of the *Völkischer Beobachter*; in August 1937, the Home Office refused three journalists renewal of their permits to stay; more expulsions followed in 1939.

One of the most thorough attempts to influence the press in favour of Hitler was made, in the first half of July 1936, by Freiherr von Rheinbaben. He was a retired diplomat, who had served with the German delegation to Geneva in the years between 1926 and 1933; he had also held the post of Secretary of State in the Reich Chancellery. He was, at the time of his visit to London, an active and well-known publicist. He undertook the mission at the instigation of Dr. Johannsen, the head of the *Aufklärungs-ausschuss* in Hamburg, a propaganda organization closely connected with the Foreign Ministry; its main purpose was to find out which newspapers would be prepared to print articles by Rheinbaben.[18]

As far as the national newspapers were concerned, Rheinbaben drew a blank; he was more successful in the field of the serious periodicals of opinion. Sir Arnold Wilson, the editor of *The Nineteenth Century and After*, promised to take an article of 4,000 words on a topic of foreign policy; Professor Gooch, the editor of the *Contemporary Review* undertook to publish 3,500 words by Rheinbaben on German foreign policy; Vernon Bartlett, the editor of the *World Review* was prepared to accept a longer article on Germany's attitude to the reform of the League of Nations. It was prominently featured in the September number, under the title 'German Views on League Reform'. The article called 'German Foreign Policy' appeared in the October issue of the *Contemporary Review*: it presented the well-worn themes of Nazi propaganda. Hitler's Germany was 'unthinkable without the peace treaty', the most deplorable agreement in the annals of European history; Nazi Germany was a powerful bulwark against the 'bolshevization' of Europe. The article concluded on an ominous, yet hopeful, note: 'To prevent war by a wise policy

18 *AA*, 5918H/E435115–132.

before it is too late is a thousand times better than to prepare for it and organize it by a hundred pacts.'

Although Rheinbaben was perhaps more effective than any other German in exerting direct influence on the British press, he was by no means optimistic about the Nazi effort in this field. Summing up his experiences after the trip to Britain, he wrote: 'it is a rare exception when the placing of whole German articles in the English press actually succeeds. I was told on two occasions that, on the whole, the material sent to Britain by the various organizations in Germany was not suitable for publication. The English press refuses everything that looks like "propaganda". Although there existed the wish, in this country, for 'some kind of understanding with Germany', it ran against the 'powerful forces that continually influence the public against Germany'. And Rheinbaben concluded: 'The forces working against us in England by the printed word must at least be "contained" by us in the same field, that is by the printed word.'

National Socialist propaganda was unsuccessful in achieving the objective set out by Rheinbaben at any point before the war. Most of the papers that upheld the editorial policy of an understanding with Germany after 1933—*The Times* was one of them—had done so before Hitler's coming to power. Although Barrington-Ward, a member of *The Times* editorial staff, maintained connexions with the German Embassy before and after 1933, *The Times* policy cannot be said to have been directly influenced. Its sharply defined distinction between news and comment made the printing of news unfavourable to Hitler's Germany possible. This confused the Nazi propagandists: they were quite unable to see the point.

Indeed, they were unsuccessful in making a lasting impression on any of the available means of mass communication in Britain. Reporting on Nazi Germany in the national press remained consistently hostile, even when the paper's editorial policy was based on a desire for an understanding with Germany. According to Rheinbaben the BBC, in its choice of lectures, excerpts from the press, etc., also had 'little understanding of Germany'.[19] Nazi propagandists had to be content when they succeeded in influencing media with a much more confined

[19] See footnote, page 149.

reach, such as low-circulation books, pamphlets, magazines, and the pro-German societies.

The organizations fostering Anglo-German friendship became, from the point of view of Berlin, one of the most important instruments of Nazi propaganda to Britain. Early in 1935—when the way for the naval agreement was being prepared—the initiative for the foundation of a 'German institute' in London came from a Mr. Kitson. He was a friend and collaborator of Colonel Fleischhauer, the publisher of the antisemitic magazine the *Weltdienst*, and he wrote to Fleischhauer about the project. Rosenberg was also interested, and recommended it to Göring's attention.[20] A month later, Prince Bismarck reported from London that the idea of a German institute was by no means new. There already existed the *Deutsche Akademische Austauschdienst*, the activities of which could be broadened.[21] In the following years, this organization came to be employed for the purposes of cultural propaganda; it operated mainly in academic circles and organized exchange visits for approved students and teachers, German language courses, discussions and lectures.

On the British side, public opinion followed government action. Three months after the conclusion of the Anglo-German naval agreement, in October 1935, a society called 'The Anglo-German Fellowship' was founded. It was set up to 'promote good understanding between England and Germany'; it was non-political, and its membership 'does not necessarily imply approval of National Socialism'.[22] The Germans, for their own part, were not slow in reciprocating the interest the Fellowship showed in them. A sister organization—the *Deutsch-Englische Gesellschaft*—was established in Berlin; the Duke of Saxe-Coburg-Gotha became its President, and it was housed in an imposing building in Bendlerstrasse, between the Zoo and the American Embassy. It was formally opened in January 1936, and some twenty members of the Fellowship accepted the invitation to the opening in Berlin. In comparison with the official Nazi munificence showered upon the *Gesellschaft*, the Fellowship was seriously under-capitalized. It had received one donation of

[20] A letter from the press-section of the *Reichsleitung* of the *NSDAP*, 15 March 1935, to Dr. Gritzbach, Göring's personal assistant, *AA*, 5849H2/E428056–057.
[21] *AA*, 5849H2/E428058.
[22] From a pamphlet published by the Fellowship in 1936.

£500 from a British firm, and a number of smaller sums from business and private sources; its secretary, Elwin Wright, was to be found in rooms at the unprepossessing Hotel Metropole in Northumberland Avenue, London, W.C.2.

A similar organization called 'The Link' was established in July 1937. Two years after its foundation, the society was running some thirty-five active branches, the largest of which in Birmingham, had more than 4,000 members. Whereas the Fellowship specialized in improving understanding between the two countries through personal contacts, 'The Link' operated on a lower social level than the Fellowship; it organized lectures and meetings that were often addressed by German nationals; its functions were more blatantly propagandist.

A member of the council of 'The Link' was Mr. C. E. Carroll, who edited the *Anglo-German Review*. This was a monthly magazine that appeared for the first time in November 1936; it was expensively produced and sold at 1s until June 1937, when the price was halved because, it was said, of the great success it had scored. Early in 1939, the *Review* claimed a readership of 12,000. It is likely that the *Review* received subsidies from Berlin via 'The Link': although it had started as an independent magazine, it became closely associated with the pro-Nazi organization. 'The Link' was tainted by Fascism more obviously than the Fellowship. In August 1940, Charles Lines, the secretary of its Birmingham branch and a former member of the BUF, was detained under Section 18b of the Defence Regulations.

The friendship societies were regarded as more effective, for propaganda purposes, than the political organizations of the local Fascists. The National Socialists did not attempt to organize, before the war, a right-wing international movement on the lines of the Comintern. Apart from Nazi parties in German territories outside the Reich, they neither trusted nor used any other national organizations. The British Fascists were in fact neglected by Hitler's government. Laudatory articles on Sir Oswald Mosley and his movement of course appeared in glossy propaganda publications such as *Europa will leben*,[23] and large uniformed delegations of the British Union of Fascists made

[23] By Werner Haas, Berlin 1936.

inevitable appearances at party rallies in Nürnberg. Symptomatically, there was no mention of the Union of Fascists in the memorandum for Hitler that Rosenberg produced some months after his ill-starred visit to London in 1933.[24] The reports of the Embassy concerning the Fascist movement were detailed and quite frequent: they were not, however, calculated to arouse the interest of the leading Nazis.[25]

Although the Fellowship was set up with the blessings of the Foreign Office,[26] it became a sitting target for Nazi propaganda. Its members were well-meaning people who desired an improvement in Anglo-German relations: their error lay in their failure to understand the true nature of Hitler's régime. The prominent men who sat on the committees of both the Fellowship and 'The Link' were not as blameless. Instead of warning the nation of the dangers that lay ahead, they used their influence only to confuse the judgement of grave political issues.

Nevertheless it is impossible to account for the powerful movement, in this country, for an understanding with Hitler's Germany by the operation of Nazi propaganda. The men who upheld such a policy acted largely for reasons of indigenous British origin, and many of them carried on a policy that had been initiated before 1933. The desire for an understanding was also strengthened by the anti-Communist and anti-Soviet attitudes current among certain influential right-wing circles: such attitudes can usually be traced to Lord Milner and his set. Milner opposed the terms of the peace treaties while they were still in the making: for him, Germany was fast fading out as Britain's most dangerous adversary, and it was being replaced by the rising menace of Bolshevik Russia. In comparison, Nazi antisemitism struck no responsive chord in Britain; on the contrary, it repelled rather than attracted.[27]

Although the direct influence exercised by Nazi propaganda in Great Britain was only marginal, indirectly the National Socialists were more successful. In the course of Goebbels's foreign campaigns—in the Saarland and the Rhineland, in

[24] Das politische Tagebuch Alfred Rosenbergs, pages 129–36.
[25] Cf. for instance, Prince Bismarck's report in June 1934; AA, 5849H2/427978–982.
[26] A letter from Sir Leonard Lyle to the News Chronicle, 9 July 1940.
[27] See page 79.

Austria and in Czechoslovakia—the reactions in London were of the greatest interest to Hitler's government, and they were closely followed. The impression they produced was, from the point of view of the *Promi*, quite satisfactory. The artificial nature of 'popular enthusiasm' among the Germans inside and outside Germany remained hidden from the view of the British politicians: many of them saw German nationalism as a spontaneous force that had to be satisfied.

By the spring of 1938 the National Socialist propaganda machinery had reached its peak performance. It was a formidable instrument, impressive to observe in action. It was completely integrated into the diplomatic and military manœuvres of the Reich government. The beginning of the last phase of the *Anschluss* campaign[28] coincided with the launching of the propaganda drive against Czechoslovakia. On 20 February 1938 Adolf Hitler spoke to the *Reichstag* deputies; the speech was transmitted by all the German and, for the first time, the Austrian broadcasting stations. (The Austrian broadcast was made possible by the agreement between the Führer and Schuschnigg at Berchtesgaden eight days before.) At the same time, Berlin cinemas showed a closed-circuit television transmission of Hitler's performance. He spoke of 'ten million Germans' isolated in two neighbouring states: it is likely that many of his listeners did not, at first, understand, and that they thought of Danzig and Poland. But in February 1938 all was still well in Danzig, as far as Hitler was concerned; the improvement of Germany's relations with Poland had been facilitated because the country was not run by 'western parliamentarianism, but a Polish Marshal'.[29] The 'ten million Germans' Hitler had in mind lived in Austria and Czechoslovakia.

The *Volksdeutsch* revolution that had been inaugurated in central Europe in January 1933 was now being brought to its concluding stages. The subversion of the established order, Hitler knew, could be accomplished by the Germans living in this area. After Austria, Czechoslovakia became the main target of the *Promi*. The campaign which led to the conclusion of the Munich agreement in September 1938 was conducted in a highly flexible manner, employing different permutations of the basic

[28] See page 138. [29] M. Domarus, op. cit., page 802.

propaganda themes according to the needs of the day, even of the hour. There were no traces of such disastrous experiments as those that had confounded the initial onslaught against Austria. For the first time the Foreign Ministry—now under Ribbentrop's direction—came to play an important and integrated role in a subversive propaganda drive. It was at its most effective when supporting Henlein and his *Sudetendeutsch* party. This policy had been inaugurated as early as the spring of 1935, when Henlein received a subsidy of 331,711 marks for propaganda purposes during the campaign preceding the general elections in May.[30]

Apart from supporting the propaganda generated by the Sudeten German party, the Reich backing gave the Germans in Czechoslovakia the self-confidence they needed to challenge the authority of the government in Prague. They were never left for long to work independently of Berlin, even when the aim of Nazi propaganda was to create the impression that the conflict concerned exclusively the Czechs and the Germans of Czechoslovakia. As in the preceding foreign campaigns, the propagandists made a determined and successful effort to create a 'Sudeten atmosphere' in Germany herself. The link between the Sudeten Germans had to be forged, a 'spontaneous' mood had to be created. Finally, powerful offshoots of the Sudeten propaganda were intended to reach London and Paris.

Indeed, while the relentless war of nerves between Berlin and Prague was conducted, both parties closely followed the reactions in the western capitals. Hitler's aims were diametrically opposed to those of Beneš: the President of Czechoslovakia strove to draw the attention of the Western Powers to the threat to peace and the *status quo* in central Europe; Hitler, on the other hand, wanted to lull any suspicions that might have existed in these countries. The fact that their respective pursuits put the two men into false positions was of course exploited by the *Promi*. It was easy for the propagandists to present Beneš as an intransigent warmonger, and Hitler as the defender of peace.

The occupation of Prague marked the last stage of Hitler's easy, piecemeal conquests as well as of the smooth efficient

[30] *Docs. Ger. For. Pol.*, series C, vol. 3, pages 908 and 969, note 3.

operation of Nazi propaganda. In the Austrian and the Sudeten campaigns, the propagandists had played a prominent role. Although they kept a wary eye on the reactions abroad—a considerable part of their activities was directed at influencing foreign public opinion, and a special foreign press section was set up at the Ministry of Propaganda—they were pursuing limited objectives, where concentrated effort was both necessary and possible. The situation began to change in March 1939. The British guarantee to Poland was followed by minor and badly co-ordinated campaigns against the governments in London, Paris, and Washington; soon, there was the preliminary work to be done on behalf of the German–Soviet pact.[31] The preparatory work for the attack on Poland was therefore comparatively short, and it had to be fitted in among all the other pursuits of Nazi publicity.

Indeed, in the last months before the war, Nazi propaganda was skipping a good deal from one subject to another rather than developing one major theme gradually; from having been concentrated, it was becoming diffuse. Goebbels had not yet emerged from the crisis that occurred at the end of 1938;[32] at the same time, military problems were fast becoming the centre of Hitler's interests. In a way, when they launched their publicity campaign on behalf of the army,[33] the propagandists began to dig their own graves. There also exist numerous indications that, for reasons of security, officials of *Promi* and of allied agencies were now worse informed than before. Until 25 August 1939, for instance, the press was not allowed to report on the activities of the *Wehrmacht*, and it was officially told of the military preparations only the following day.[34] On a higher level, Fritzsche, a close collaborator of Goebbels and well-known broadcaster, was unaware of the true background to the alleged Polish attack on the Gleiwitz broadcasting station.[35] The sham attack on the *Gleiwitzsender* was in fact carried out by one of Himmler's *Einsatzgruppen*,

[31] See page 96.
[32] In his autobiography, Hans Fritzsche—*Hier spricht Hans Fritzsche*, page 18. Zürich, 1948—points to the political reasons for the decline in the influence of Goebbels; in their biography of Goebbels, Manvell and Fraenkel deal with the Minister's personal entanglements at the time.
[33] See page 159.
[34] *RPA*, 25 and 26 August 1939.
[35] H. Fritzsche, op. cit., page 178.

commando units which were usually employed for secret acts of a provocative nature. They had been first employed in the Sudetenland, and they were now fast coming into their own. The former balance of terror and propaganda was being upset to the disadvantage of propaganda.

VIII. PROPAGANDA IN THE WAR

No military engagement was considered by Hitler in connexion with the occupation of Austria. On 14 February 1938 he approved General Keitel's suggestion that neither the army nor the air-force were to make any preparations. Only 'false but credible information' was to be spread and manœuvres near the frontier executed, creating the impression that military preparations against Austria were being undertaken.[1] On the day of Austria's occupation the War Ministry had no reports of military moves by other European states.[2]

In the course of the Sudeten propaganda campaign, however, the Führer was ready to consider the possibility of a cold war becoming a hot war. On 21 April 1938 at a meeting between Hitler and General Keitel, the basic directives for Operation Green—an armed assault on Czechoslovakia—were laid down.[3] The idea of an unprovoked attack 'out of the blue' and without any obvious justification was turned down, because of 'hostile world opinion which might lead to a serious situation'. Military action, the two men agreed, could be taken 'after a period of diplomatic discussion which would gradually lead to a crisis and to war'. A lightning action against Czechoslovakia could, however, be based on an incident, such as the murder of the German Minister in the course of an anti-German demonstration. After some de-tailed tactical instructions, a short section C of the memorandum was entitled 'Propaganda'. It contained only two rough-and-ready directives: (1) Leaflets for the conduct of the Germans in 'Green' territory; (2) Leaflets with threats to intimidate 'Greens'. The actual occupation of the Sudetenland in October 1938 was

[1] *Docs. Ger. For. Pol.*, series D, vol. 1, editor's note, page 520.
[2] ibid., page 588.
[3] ibid., vol. 2, pages 239–40.

officially regarded as a military operation, and all reporting of it came under the censorship of the Supreme Command of the *Wehrmacht* (*OKW*). Although the *Promi* and the *OKW* were in constant touch during the campaign, and there was an army press officer attached to the Ministry, this meant a departure from the usual practices of Goebbels. He was inclined to rely on a tight control of the propaganda apparatus based on detailed directives, rather than on the censorship of independently produced material.[4] It was not until 10 p.m. on 15 October that the *Promi* resumed its former position as the sole controlling agency of the press.

But soon, the propagandists themselves were instructed to foster the prestige of the army. Four days after the co-operation between the *OKW* and the *Promi* was terminated, the *Reichspropagandaamt* issued an order to the press on 'making the army popular.'[5] The German press was congratulated on the role it had played in the Sudeten crisis, and then requested to proceed to a no less important internal campaign. 'Through a longer and uninterrupted pressure by the German press, in word and in picture, in individual reports, in comments and in leading articles, the self-confidence of the German nation in its own strength and its military power should be reinforced.' It should be pointed out, the directive went on, that the great successes of Germany's foreign policy had been made possible by absolute military preparedness. In the last analysis—and this *motif* was to be stressed again and again—the whole German nation had been prepared to fight for the 'right to live' of its 3,500,000 Sudeten compatriots.

Goebbels disapproved of the war: he knew that it would affect his own and his Ministry's position. He remarked that Hitler would 'soon listen to his generals only, and it will be very difficult for me.'[6] Hitler of course saw the necessity of retaining the services of his leading propagandist and of the apparatus Goebbels had built up over the years. On 8 September 1939—a week after the invasion of Poland—the Führer dictated a 'command' concerning propaganda.[7] It pointed out that 'Propaganda is an

---

[4] See page 45.   [5] *RPA*, 19 October 1938.
[6] Helmut Heiber, *Goebbels*, page 286. Berlin, 1962.
[7] *Docs. Ger. For. Pol.*, series D, vol. 8, page 30.

important instrument of the Leadership for forwarding and strengthening the will to victory and for destroying the enemies' morale and will to victory.' The *Promi* remained the 'central agency for the practical application of propaganda. Breaking it up during the war would be comparable to breaking up certain components of the *Wehrmacht*.'

Nevertheless, Goebbels's fears were justified: from the first, the war severely circumscribed the competence of his Ministry. From the beginning of the war, directives for publicity came from three different sources: the *Promi*, the Foreign Ministry, and the department of *Wehrmachtspropaganda* in the Supreme Command of the Armed Forces (*OKW*). Goebbels was unsuccessful in establishing a clear supremacy for his Ministry. The co-ordination of the directives took place at daily meetings; from December 1940, the deputy Reich press director Sündermann was in the chair, and the heads of the press departments in the agencies concerned took part in the meetings. At the same time, Otto Dietrich, the Reich press director and Sündermann's immediate superior, was in the anomalous position of being, on the one hand, one of Hitler's most trusted collaborators and, on the other, an Under Secretary of State in the *Promi*.[8] He spent most of his time in the Führer's personal entourage, and his directives often came into conflict with those of the Minister of Propaganda. The co-ordination of the directives to the press was not very effective: often the contradictions had to be ultimately resolved on the editorial desks.[9]

In addition, the key reports on the war situation were published in the form of the communiqués of the Supreme Command of the *Wehrmacht*. They were put together on the basis of information which flowed from diverse sources and through a variety of controlling agencies—a process in which the Ministry of Propaganda played only a small part. The original information came from one of the three operational headquarters: the army, the navy and the air-force dispatched their daily reports to the *Abteilung Wehrmachtpropaganda* at the Supreme Command. Here, the three reports were collated and then passed on, as drafts of the '*Wehrmacht* sphere of competence' (*Wehrmachtbereich*) to

[8] Louis P. Lochner, *The Goebbels Diaries*, page 235, London. 1948.
[9] Cf. W. Hagemann, op. cit., page 440.

the Führer's Headquarters. The draft reports concerning the 'home sphere of competence' (*Heimatbereich*)—insofar as they did not relate to the air-force as a part of the armed forces—originated at the *Promi*: their importance increased later in the war, with the growing intensity of the Allied air raids. The two drafts were again collated at the Führer's HQ, and put before Hitler. Only after his approval, the *Promi* received the final communiqué for publication through the official news agency, the *DNB*, and through the broadcasting network.

Such a process was of course a long one, and it became longer as the war went on: on many later occasions the communiqués were two days old. Nevertheless, the *Wehrmacht* enjoyed a good deal of prestige in the nation, and the reports published under its auspices became the most important instrument of war-time publicity. They were generally regarded as more trustworthy than information derived from civilian sources.[10]

As the importance of the Ministry of Propaganda declined, and its work became technically simpler, the Minister's activities grew more and more hectic. During the first, victorious phase of the war, Goebbels looked after everything. He toured armament factories in the Ruhr and the wharves in Hamburg; he was seen in the capitals of the occupied countries shortly after the arrival there of the military; he received Japanese youth leaders, Spanish publishers, Dutch poets. Everything interested him, from the price of potatoes to the sexual needs of the foreign workers in Germany. He planned a vast new building for his Ministry, which was to be erected soon after the fast-approaching end of the war.[11] He also devoted a lot of care to keeping himself in the eyes of the German public: he wrote and broadcast more then ever before. He of course remained loyal to Hitler, and he helped where he could. The *Promi* produced anonymous letters for employment in France during the military attack; Goebbels instructed his assistants, Gutterer and Raskin, to publish a diary recording the pornographic experiences of a British soldier in Paris for distribution in France.[12] Churchill fast became the Minister's main enemy, and Goebbels poured scorn and abuse upon his head. Apart from one exception, the Minister of

[10] W. Hagemann, op. cit., pages 412 et seq.
[11] H. Heiber, op. cit. page 292.　　　　　　　　　[12] ibid., page 290.

Propaganda never ran out of commentary for important occasions during the war. After Hess's unexpected descent, by
parachute, on Scotland, Goebbels disappeared from Berlin.
When he was informed of the party line—it had been worked out
by Dietrich and Bormann, and approved by Hitler—that Hess
was 'mentally sick', he strongly disapproved.[13]

Nevertheless, the victories of the armed forces opened fresh
vistas before the propagandists. The experience and technical
knowledge they had gained in manipulating public opinion in
Germany could now be put to use in the occupied as well as the
'allied' countries. Under the guidance of *Promi*, the *Gleichschaltung* of the means of mass communication was swiftly
carried out. New Nazi newspapers began to appear; new controllers were installed at the broadcasting stations; occupied
Europe became a monopoly market for Goebbels's films and
travelling exhibitions. At the same time, an attempt was made to
work out and publicize a plan for the reorganization of Europe.
As the Hitler–Stalin pact was still operative, it was impossible
for National Socialist propaganda to stake any claims to defending Europe from Bolshevism. For the time being, the Reich and
the European themes had to be employed: in this respect, there
existed some tenuous connexions with pre-war propaganda.

At the party rally in 1938, a new ideological opening had been
tentatively explored: ideas connected with the Holy Roman
Empire were briefly paraded before the party members. Seyss-
Inquart had brought with him the Imperial insignia from Vienna,
and they were ceremonially handed over to the Mayor of
Nürnberg. Germany was presented as the leading power in
central and eastern Europe, an area to which Britain and
France were 'alien', and as a power which was able to impose
here a *Pax Germanica*. Hitler's first aggressive moves had taken
place under the slogan *Ein Volk, ein Reich, ein Führer;* in March
1939, the Czechs were taken 'under the protection of the Reich'
at their own request.

As the offensive against France was drawing to its close, the
first number of the weekly *Das Reich* appeared in Berlin on 26
May 1940. Under Goebbels's sponsorship, the newspaper became
the most representative example of Nazi war-time journalism or,

[13] H. Heiber, op. cit., page 296.

more precisely, of the first phase of the military engagement. The ideas publicized in *Das Reich* were firmly based in the sense of Germany's military supremacy. The concept of the 'Reich' took precedence over that of '*Europa*'; although the Empire was not proclaimed 'holy', it was to be 'eternal'. It was unique and German, indisputably at the head of the non-German states. It was a vague concept, containing the racial, authoritarian, and hieratic ideas of the Nazis, as well as embracing a variety of historical notions. The Germanic Empire was to hold sway in northern Europe; in the south, an accommodation had to be made for the Roman Empire of Mussolini. The geographical extent of the 'new order' was left undefined; political commitments were also usually avoided. It was assumed that political reconstruction would be carried out on the basis of the National Socialist pattern. Europe was to be built up as a self-contained economic unit, capable of resisting blockade and of breaking the international economic supremacy of Great Britain.[14]

Although a broadly-based plan for Europe was bound to remain incomplete without France, the National Socialists found it by no means easy to assimilate her into their schemes. Quite apart from concrete political difficulties, the work of conciliation was retarded by various ideological predilections on the part of the National Socialists. The victory over France represented for them a victory over the 'worn-out' ideals of the French revolution. Germany's military triumph was seen as the ultimate proof of the superiority of Nazi ideals, which were diametrically opposed to those of 1789. The National Socialist leaders were never quite able to take seriously the attempts to carry out a 'national revolution' in Vichy France. In addition, Nazi publicity tended to regard the victory over France as the defeat of the Versailles 'system'. British and French supremacy which had lasted for two decades disappeared without a trace, as did all the parliamentary systems and some of the small states established by the peace treaties.[15]

Against the background of distrust of the Vichy régime as well

[14] Cf. *Survey of International Affairs, 1939–46, Hitler's Europe*, page 47.
[15] Cf. Paul Kluke, *Nationalsozialistische Europaideologie, Vierteljahreshefte für Zeitgeschichte*, 1955, pages 253 et seq.

as the feeling of superiority on the part of the National Socialists, the 'soft-sell' propaganda which was employed in regard to France often lacked conviction. During the military assault, the small secret transmitter *Humanité* had been run on super-patriotic lines: after the conclusion of the treaty of armistice, appeals to French patriotism and self-interest continued to be made. Indeed, every sign of successful political co-operation with Pétain and Laval was accompanied by an effusion of propaganda of good will. It aimed at antagonizing the French public against the politicians who had driven the country into the war on Germany; it pointed to Berlin's magnanimous treatment of defeated France. She was allowed to keep her fleet and sovereignty in her colonial Empire; many of the prisoners-of-war were set free; permission was even granted to France to build up a new army. It was a pity, the agitation was later continued, that the agreement of Montoire of October 1940 had been sabotaged, that the French officers had broken their word, and that the Toulon mutiny had forced the Reich to employ severe repressive measures. Most of these arguments were restated, with some bitterness occasioned by retrospection, in Hitler's letter to Pétain of 27 November 1942.[16]

Until the summer of 1941, the National Socialist publicity pursued an elusive ideal in regard to Europe. Hostility to Britain and her exclusion from the affairs of the Continent were the only constant points of Nazi propaganda at the time. A variety of plans for the partitioning of France were publicized and dropped; the *Grossraum* projects concerning the Mediterranean and Africa got bogged down in the uncertainties in south Europe: France was unreliable, and Spain remained neutral. At the same time, Hitler remained immersed in military problems, and he would enter into no commitments which might restrict his freedom of action in the military field. Although some striking technical successes were achieved in the field of *Gleichschaltung* of the means of mass communication in occupied and 'allied' Europe, the construction of *Festung Europa* was far from complete at the time of the attack on the Soviet Union.

The German Army crossed the frontier of the Soviet Union at 3 a.m. on 22 June 1941. Hitler now embarked on, in his view, the

[16] *Das Archiv*, edited by Alfred-Ingemar Berndt, page 735. Berlin, 1942.

decisive stage of the war. In contrast with the detailed military planning of the 'Barbarossa' operation, very little propaganda preparation had been made. The demands of military secrecy ruled out, of course, a propaganda drive on the pre-war pattern; the Nazi–Soviet pact was still in force, and anyway, the campaign was expected to be one of short duration. At first, the propagandists themselves appeared to have been taken by surprise: they confined themselves to reiterating Hitler's arguments concerning the absolute necessity of the action against the Soviet Union. The decision of the Führer, it was explained, had been occasioned by a British–Bolshevik conspiracy against Germany.[17] The first instructions to the newspaper editors issued on 22 June were unusually hesitant: 'Unfortunately we had been unable to prepare the German nation, as on previous occasions, for the forthcoming decisions; this must now be done by the press. It must provide intelligible reasons, because it is politically educated, and the nation is not. We must make it clear that this [i.e. the attack on Russia] does not represent a change. Reporting on Russia was banned for months, so that the press should be spared difficulties during the necessary switch [of policy]. Now at last we can speak freely of the hypocrisy, by which the Soviets tried to deceive us for many years. The true feelings which the German nation instinctively entertains towards Bolshevism must be freed again. Bolshevism has waited for its hour. We have proofs that it would have stabbed us in the back at a suitable moment.'[18]

But soon the campaign in the east, as well as the broad European perspectives, were brought into a sharper focus. A week later the German press was instructed that 'Reports from the whole world make it apparent that a rising of the whole of Europe against Bolshevism can be noted, as it could not have been observed until now. Europe marches against the common enemy in a unique solidarity, and it rises, as it were, against the oppressor of all human culture and civilization. This hour of birth of the new Europe is being accomplished without any demand or pressure from the German side. On the contrary, it is

[17] See Hitler's declaration to the German nation on 22 June 1941, *Das Archiv*, volumes 85–87, pages 250–5.
[18] W. Hagemann, op. cit., page 251.

clear that even the small and the smallest states have understood the common European task, since they have called up their sons to make a blood sacrifice for the common idea. For this reason we do not want to speak of a crusade. Newspapers are faced here with the immense task, as it is essential, especially in regard to America, that the unity of Europe in the fight against Bolshevism is made clear to the new world as well. The great hour has also come for the settling of accounts with the English phrases and thesis that Adolf Hitler is a dictator, who rushes restlessly from country to country like a modern Genghis Khan, because one aggression forces him to other, further, and new [aggressions]. Adolf Hitler has proved himself to be the military leader of Europe on behalf of the common culture and civilization, and is recognized as such by the whole European world.[19]'

Almost all European nations took some military part in the Russian campaign: Finnish, Hungarian, Slovak, Italian, and Rumanian units were later joined by volunteers from Spain, Belgium, France, Holland, and Norway. However insignificant the participation of these allies was in fact, the whole of Europe could now be presented as defending itself against the threat of *Judeo-Bolschewismus* (the Jews were, incidentally, later described as the 'cement' of the alliance between Soviet Russia and the Western Powers), a threat which was compared with the earlier 'perils from the east'—Hun, Mongol, but not Turk—and the whole of Europe was to benefit from Germany's victory. Hitler himself took up the theme: on 11 December 1941 he asked the *Reichstag*: 'What then, my deputies, is Europe? There exists no geographic definition of our Continent, but only an ethnic and cultural one. The Urals are not the border of this Continent, but [the border has been] always the line which divides the Western from the eastern way of life [*Lebensbild*]'[20] In private, Hitler was more explicit: discussing the frontiers between Europe and Asia he said that: 'The real frontier is the one that separates the Germanic world from the Slav world'; the Slavs were peoples who 'are not destined to live a cleanly life. They know it, and we would be wrong to persuade them to the

[19] *Vertrauliche Information R. Spr. Nr. 317, Infr. Nr. 49,* of 30 June 1941; quoted in a footnote of Paul Kluke's article *Nationalsozialistische Europaideologie, Vierteljahreshefte für Zeitgeschichte,* 1955, page 259.
[20] *Das Archiv,* volumes 91–93, page 790.

contrary. . . . It's better not to teach them to read. They won't love us for tormenting them with schools. Even to give them a locomotive to drive would be a mistake . . .'[21] Indeed, the campaign in the east added a new dimension to the Nazi European propaganda drive. It implied that there existed two sharply defined civilizations in Europe, one of which was vastly superior; it foreshadowed not only the widely divergent treatment of the inhabitants of the occupied territories in the west and in the east of Europe, but also the *Untermensch* propaganda against the Slavs, the robot-like sub-human creatures from the east.[22]

Nevertheless, the National Socialist propagandists faced, in the summer of 1941, completely new tasks. Although a good deal of their activities before the summer of 1939 had concerned the Soviet Union, they had no experience of propaganda to the Soviets.[23] In this respect there lay two broad choices before them. They could identify the Soviet régime with the peoples over which it ruled, and declare a ruthless fight on them. They could work, on the other hand, for the creation of a system of selective alliances with certain social groups and nationalities, and devote their energies to driving a wedge between Stalin's régime and the people of Russia.

A month after the invasion of the Soviet Union, Goebbels set up a secret station that specialized in broadcasting to Russia. It was run by Torgler, a former Communist deputy to the *Reichstag*, and by Albrecht, a Russian of German extraction who had reached the office of Vice-Commissar for Forestry before fleeing to Germany during the Moscow purges in 1936. The station ran three political subdivisions: one of them was based on a general opposition programme, another expounded a Trotskyist line, and another, possibly the most important of the three, conducted a 'national Bolshevik' policy. It maintained that 'Stalin, the slave of the capitalists, had sold the socialist fatherland to the plutocrats'.[24]

There also exists evidence that the *Abteilung Wehrmacht-*

[21] *Hitler's Table Talk*, pages 37 and 34. London, 1953.
[22] See page 169.
[23] See page 103.
[24] Rudolf Semmler, *Goebbels—the man next to Hitler*, pages 47–49. London, 1947.

propaganda was prepared to use the technique of driving a wedge between the Soviet régime and the inhabitants of the occupied territories. A circular from the *OKW* to the armed forces stated that: 'The enemies of Germany are not the peoples of the Soviet Union, but exclusively the Jewish-Bolshevik Soviet government with its functionaries and the Communist Party, which is working for a world revolution.' The German army did not come as an enemy of the local population, it came to free it from the 'tyranny of the Soviets'. Although hints that the Soviet Union would break up into a number of individual states were to be avoided, German propaganda was to employ the appropriate languages in the occupied territories. Expressions like 'Russia', the 'Russians' and the 'Russian army' were to be discarded, and replaced by 'Soviet Union', the 'nations of the Soviet Union', and the 'Red Army'.[25] In practice, however, the army propagandists had to proceed with caution. In their leaflets to the Red Army—some 400 million of them were dropped over the Russian lines before the end of 1941—the Germans were simply described as liberators and the Soviet troops were invited to surrender. Yet, in spite of suggestions from the field and from the army propaganda experts that more positive slogans on such topics as self-government or private ownership of the land should be employed, no changes were allowed.[26]

Until the end of September 1941 the official statements on Germany's military achievements had been rather factual and guarded. But Hitler's estimate of Germany's military superiority at that stage of the war, and his stance as the conqueror of the east, profoundly affected the tone of Nazi propaganda. On 3 October, caution was abandoned and a high note of triumph was sounded. Hitler, who had made no public speech for five months, said on that day: 'I am saying this today for the first time, because I can say it today, that this enemy [in the east] has been struck down and will never rise again.'[27] Six days later, Dietrich released a special announcement to the press and the

[25] *Trial of the Major War Criminals*, col. XXXIV, document 026-C, pages 191–95. *Weisungen für die Handhabung der Propaganda in Falle 'Barbarossa'*, June, 1941.
[26] Cf. A. Dallin, *German Rule in Russia*, page 66. London, 1957.
[27] *Das Archiv*, vols. 91–93, page 579.

broadcasting system to the effect that 'with the formations already encircled, Timoshenko has sacrificed the last remaining armies of full fighting strength of the total Soviet front.' On the same day, in a broadcast on the *Deutschlandsender*, Hans Fritzsche said 'It is certainly possible that a régime of criminals with nothing else to lose will continue to drive their people to resist the advancing German front: that the seed of hatred of Germany and the fear of Bolshevik commissars will provoke further acts of senseless resistance.' But, Fritzsche claimed, further Russian resistance was futile.[28] Goebbels regarded such announcements as the biggest propaganda blunder of the war. They were, in his view, entirely irresponsible;[29] they certainly encouraged dangerous illusions.

In Hitler's opinion the military superiority of Germany had been proved, and the foundations of an eastern Empire had been laid. The Germans were now in a position to rule in the east, and they could do so without the aid of a calculated appeal to the Soviet peoples. Indeed, from the beginning of October, all discussion of the future of the occupied territories in the east was to be kept out of propaganda to the Soviets; no political commitments in regard to the local population were to be made.[30] Such confidence resulted in a ruthless attitude. In his 'order of the day' on 2 October Hitler said that 'this enemy does not consist of soldiers but to a large degree only of beasts'.[31] The theme concerning the subhumanity of the enemy—of the Slav *Unter-mensch*—thus received an official sanction from the highest place. Photographs of Red Army prisoners-of-war began to appear in German newspapers in ever-increasing numbers. These men were described as culturally and spiritually inferior; they were, in terms of Nazi propaganda, a mixture of the low and lowest humanity, truly subhuman. It was a theme which suitably complemented the 'European' campaign: the threat to Europe was depicted in the darkest colours.

The *Untermensch* propaganda made an especially strong appeal to the *Waffen SS*: it was bound to affect the treatment of the population in the eastern territories, of the prisoners-of-war, and

28 WL., Exhibit USA 723, 3064 PS, A09584.
29 R. Semmler, op. cit., pages 54–55.
30 A. Dallin, op. cit., page 66.
31 *Das Archiv*, vols. 91–93, page 562.

of the labour imported to Germany.[32] It could be ultimately traced to Hitler's crudely indiscriminating attitude to the peoples of the Soviet Union. There had existed an ambiguity in his view of Russia long before the war: when he thought of the 'Jewish-Bolshevik ruling clique' he was quite prepared to make a distinction between it and the 'Russian people'; when he turned, however, to the plans for Germany's expansion in the east, the distinction disappeared, and its place was taken by contempt for the people who lived there.[33] And in 1941 Hitler did not set out to destroy Bolshevism in Russia, but to build up a German Empire in the east.

Alfred Rosenberg, the leading Nazi expert on the east, did not subscribe to this policy. The Great Russians were his main enemy: the peoples of the Ukraine and White Russia, of the Baltic states and of the Caucasus could be, in his view, set up in states dependent on the Reich, but enjoying a certain degree of autonomy. As the Minister responsible for civil administration in the occupied territories in the east—he was appointed to the newly-established *Ostministerium* in the middle of July—Rosenberg attempted to put his ideas into practice. He received little help from the Ministry of Propaganda. After a brief flirtation with the *Untermensch* line at the height of Germany's military triumph, Goebbels appeared ready, by the end of 1941, to return to more flexible methods of political warfare: although there existed, in this respect, no fundamental political differences between Rosenberg and Goebbels, their conflict developed into one of the bitterest inter-departmental rows of the war. Co-operation between the two Ministries, even of the most technical nature, proved impossible. Rosenberg jealously guarded the jurisdiction of his Ministry in propaganda matters: it possessed neither the experience and personnel, nor the equipment. When the *Promi*, for instance, offered Rosenberg broadcasting equipment, and although it declared itself ready to let the *Ostministerium* control the actual contents of the broadcasts, Rosenberg repeatedly turned the offers down. Attempts to produce anti-partisan propaganda films also failed; the cinemas in the occupied territories suffered seriously from shortage of material. Hundreds of

[32] Cf. A. Dallin, op. cit., especially pages 70 and 410.
[33] See page 85.

older German films could not be shown because they contained an actor, even an extra, who was a Jew.[34] Although Goebbels tried hard to establish a foothold in the territories administered by the *Ostministerium*, the eastern section of the *Promi* at first operated only among the prisoners-of-war and the imported labour in the Reich. Goebbels finally made a break-through in August 1943, when his Ministry was authorized to set up shop in the east. Rosenberg retained only the control of the press; broadcasting and film passed under the control of the Ministry of Propaganda.

Apart from Goebbels, Rosenberg was faced with a formidable opposition. Most of the Nazi leaders—Himmler, Göring, and Ribbentrop—acquired an interest in the 'eastern problem', and they all pursued their own, often contradictory, eastern policies. In addition to being responsible for special tasks, such as liquidation and segregation of the prisoners-of-war, Himmler and the *SS* took care of police and security matters in the territories administered by the *Ostministerium*, and Himmler was empowered to direct Rosenberg's subordinates in matters of security. Rosenberg, a singularly incompetent organizer, made a number of inept choices when selecting top personnel for his Ministry. Some officials were also forced on him; others, whose services Rosenberg wanted to secure, would not leave the army or the Foreign Ministry. The *Ostministerium* attracted failures and time-servers who cared little for Rosenberg's plans for the east. Finally, when the Ministry was reorganized in 1943, the influence of the *SS* within it considerably increased.[35]

Alfred Rosenberg's views on Russia received comparatively little publicity either in Germany or in the eastern territories. It was impossible to develop a unitary propaganda in the east against the background of administrative anarchy and incompetence, and continual inter-departmental squabbles that were caused more often by personal than by political differences. In face of the breakdown of indigenous administration, the formulation of a consistent policy and of a suitable propaganda to support it should have appeared a task of first-rate importance.

[34] Otto Bräutigam, *Überblick über die besetzten Ostgebiete während des 2. Weltkrieges*, pages 83 and 84. A publication of the Institut für Besatzungsfragen, Tübingen, January 1954.
[35] A. Dallin, op. cit., page 86.

It was not seen as such by Hitler. Ultimately, the exploitation of the economic and human resources in the occupied territories overrode all other considerations, and there was always the 'tough' line, for the soldiers and administrators alike, to fall back on. Only Himmler's *SS* units appear to have been consistent throughout. They had little use for propaganda, and their actions were enough to cancel any amount of mellifluous agitation generated from diverse quarters.

At the end of 1941, there was neither a clear-cut victory for the German armed forces in Russia, nor a consistent programme developed by the Nazi leaders for the future of the occupied territories. At first, there seemed no need for a determined effort to influence the Soviet peoples in Germany's favour. Indeed, in the first phase of the war, the swift succession of military victories was Hitler's best propaganda. But this phase was fast approaching its end. Early in December, the Red Army counter-attack halted the German advance in the suburbs of Moscow; a few days later, Germany and Italy declared war on the United States. The Anglo–Soviet–American partnership was then consolidated by the Washington and London treaties in February and May of the following year. At the beginning of 1942, Goebbels acquired an interest in defeatism in high military places: Hitler apparently had asked him to write a report on the subject.[36] It seemed as if Goebbels had sensed that he, and the instrument he represented, would again come into their own when the generals proved themselves inadequate to their task.

On 27 April 1942 Hitler spoke to the *Reichstag*; out of concern for the Führer's health, Goebbels had no spotlights installed in the chamber. After Hitler's speech, Göring introduced a new bill giving the Führer plenary executive, legislative, and judiciary powers: it was passed unanimously. Although Goebbels was at first quite pleased with the speech, reports on the reactions of the public which were passed on to the *Promi* were not favourable. The Germans were asking why the Führer had been given plenary powers, and why he had criticized conditions at home so sharply; there was also concern with the military situation. Hitler had spoken of a second winter campaign: there were no more promises

[36] Entry for 21 January 1942, *The Goebbels Diaries*, edited by L. P. Lochner.

of a speedy conclusion of the Russian war during the coming summer.[37]

Was it possible that Hitler was losing his touch as a speaker? After a cautious start, he had allowed the hopes of the nation to be driven sky-high in October 1941; after the first winter in Russia, the inevitable disappointment was setting in. The public image of the Führer had been that of a harbinger of success and of military glory. When there were no victories to announce, his powers as a speaker began to fail him. Unable to confine himself to factual statement, however unpalatable, the flights of his imagination and of his megalomania were being deprived of their foundations. He turned to criticism of the conditions in Germany, which neither convinced nor attracted; he may have been seeking a scapegoat, and he chose the wrong one. Goebbels must have felt some disillusionment when he wrote in his diary on 28 April 1942 that 'the Führer's speech represents, as it were, the cry of a drowning man'. And Hitler himself may have sensed the chill of approaching disaster. After a long silence, he made a determined effort at a come-back as a speaker on 30 September at the Sportpalast, and then again on 8 November in the Hofbraukeller in Munich. But the spell had been broken: in the future, his public appearances would be very rare indeed.

Hitler's decline as the leading speaker of the party created a gap which Goebbels did his best to fill. He chose a technique different from that of the Führer. From the end of 1942, Goebbels began to conduct a propaganda of pessimism—it was modelled on Churchill's example—that could serve as the driving force behind the total mobilization of Germany's resources. At a conference of the departmental heads of his Ministry on 4 January 1943, he said: 'I myself want to see disappear from my mind and from the mind of the Ministry the idea that we cannot lose the war. Of course we can lose the war. The war can be lost by people who will not exert themselves; it will be won by those who try hardest. We must not believe fatalistically in certain victory; we must take a positive view.'[38] And total war required a total exploitation of his audience. He switched over to a tone of 'steely factuality', but, above that, he appealed to the deepest

[37] Entry for 29 April 1942, *The Goebbels Diaries.*
[38] R. Semmler, op. cit., page 63.

173

defensive instincts of the nation: to hate and fear, to the need for self-assertion. On 18 November 1942 he declared, for instance, that: 'We want our nation to be filled not only with a deep love for its community, but also with an infernal hate of all the men and of all the forces who attack this community and who want to destroy it. When somebody objects that this is un-German, then I have to say: an exaggerated objectivity is a fault of the German character.'[39]

Hitler went on giving most of his attention to the eastern front, where, at the end of the summer, the struggle for Stalingrad entered its opening stage. The propagandists were to make yet another fatal blunder in regard to the eastern front. On 24 August 1942, the Supreme Command of the *Wehrmacht* made an urgent request to the press not to write about the forthcoming fall of Stalingrad, but simply about the beginning of the battle. On 3 September, newspaper editors were asked to prepare material about the enormous importance of this fortress of Communism and industrial centre; on 17 September, the newspapers were informed that the struggle for Stalingrad was nearing its victorious conclusion, and that a special report was to be expected within forty-eight hours. But five days later, on 22 September, an *OKW* spokesman told the journalists that their presentation of the Stalingrad battle had created an impression—against the wishes of the Supreme Command—that the capture of the town was imminent. Finally, the directive for the press for 16 October read: 'The important military successes in the northern part of Stalingrad take the first place in today's newspapers. Caution in make-up and comment is recommended, so that the reader may not gain the impression that an event, which he had awaited for weeks, was about to occur.'[40]

Stalingrad did not provide the propagandists with the victory they needed so badly. The hopes they had raised during the first phase of the campaign were dashed to the ground, and a psychological crisis accompanied the military defeat. In the last instance, the disaster had to be used for exhortations, to the nation, to a still greater war effort. Although the Stalingrad battle was held in the centre of public attention for many

[39] *VB*, 19 November 1942.
[40] W. Hagemann, op. cit., pages 261–2.

weeks, there were other disasters to be reported at the same time. At the end of October, Montgomery's Eighth Army broke through the German lines at El Alamein; on 8 November, Allied troops landed in North Africa; the intensity of the air-raids on the German towns was growing. But other, less tangible signs pointed to the fact that the Nazi domination of the air-space over Europe was highly vulnerable. The absolute monopoly of information the *Promi* strove for in Europe proved easy to break from the outside. The broadcasting war was also reaching the point from where the effectiveness of Nazi propaganda would begin to decline.

In the autumn of 1942, Nazi broadcasting policies had to be reviewed in accordance with Goebbels's drive for a total war effort. Early in November, the Minister of Propaganda appointed Hans Fritzsche to a new job. He became the political controller of German broadcasting, and also replaced Wolfgang Diewerge as the director of the broadcasting department in the *Promi*. In Fritzsche's view—and it can be assumed to have coincided with that of Goebbels—the main task of German wireless in the fourth year of the war was to create a bridge between the front and the hinterland. Broadcasting had to be made the most popular means of mass communication: 'it must speak to all, or it will reach none'.[41] Fritzsche also promised a better news service, brief, clear, and to the point. In addition, general military and political talks were to be broadcast more frequently and regularly during the peak hour, between 7.45 and 8 p.m. The speakers—soldiers and journalists, scientists and politicians—were to appear regularly, so that they would have an 'opportunity of establishing close contact with the listeners'. They were to use the method of 'candour towards the present, which distinguishes so conspicuously the articles published by Dr. Goebbels in *Das Reich*'. At the same time, these talks were to be modelled on the principle of an 'intellectual convoy'. This meant, Fritzsche explained, that just as in a convoy the speed of all ships was determined by that of the slowest vessel, such talks, addressed to the people, had to be based on the capacity of the masses.

Especially in regard to his news policy, Fritzsche had obviously

[41] Exhibit USA 723, 3064PS, A095849–58.

learned a lot from the BBC; from now on, broadcasting was to be more tightly controlled, on the lines laid down by Goebbels. Certain technical deficiencies were also becoming visible: spare parts for wireless receivers were hard to come by; families who had lost their sets in air-raids were to be issued with special vouchers. But, most important, broadcasting was to bind together the nation, which had become dispersed by the war. There had occurred a German diaspora—troops, civil administrators, members of the security and of the technical services, were working in the Balkans, in the Caucasus, in France, and in Norway. They came in contact with a variety of new impressions and influences; they were exposed to enemy propaganda. They had in fact broken out of the ring where monopoly of information was highly organized; they were moving on its periphery. Broadcasting was regarded, by the *Promi*, as the most suitable means for remedying the situation. But, even on the home front, there existed grounds for concern. Since the spring of 1942 Goebbels was apprehensive lest enemy propaganda succeeded in driving a wedge between the Nazi leadership and the nation. On 8 April the press was instructed to take absolutely no notice of the American argument that the war was conducted not against the German nation but against the National Socialists.[42]

The Nazi monopoly of information was now in danger and the threat came from enemy broadcasting. Even some time before the war, the *Volksempfänger*, the cheap popular wireless set[43] had been constructed in a manner that made the reception of foreign broadcasts difficult. After the outbreak of the war, listening to all stations not under German control was forbidden by a special law.[44] The ban included broadcasting from allied and neutral countries, and every part of their programmes, including music and entertainment. In addition, the rumour was spread that it was technically feasible to establish, by the use of a special detection equipment, the wave-lengths to which private sets were tuned in at any given time. Goebbels argued that listening to foreign broadcasts was the spiritual equivalent of a physical

[42] W. Hagemann, op. cit.,'page 257.
[43] See page 51.
[44] *Reichsgesetzblatt*, 'Verordnung über ausserordentliche Rundfunkmassnahmen', September 1939, page 1683.

self-mutilation by a soldier. It was known in Germany that no such ban on listening to foreign broadcasts existed in Britain: to this, Goebbels replied that 'first of all we do not cheat as much as the English, and secondly, we want to win the war'.[45] Special permits for the monitoring of foreign broadcasts were at first available to all the Ministries and other high party and state offices: Goebbels soon had many of them cancelled. It was explained, for instance, to Bernard Rust's Ministry of Science and Education that listening to foreign broadcasts was an unhealthy occupation, and that there had been a number of cases of nervous breakdown in the monitoring section of the *Promi*.[46] Although Goebbels was convinced that it did untold harm in spreading defeatism in high official quarters, he could do nothing about the Foreign Ministry's monitoring service, which distributed a daily news-letter.[47]

The achievements of the army had in a way protected the monopoly position of the Nazi propaganda in the first phase of the war. But as soon as the flow of announcements of military victories abated, and when the first reversals were cautiously announced, growing numbers of listeners began to turn to foreign broadcasts. Not only were there individual 'black listeners' (*Schwarzhörer*), but there existed whole groups, especially in the armed forces. The armed forces possessed the necessary technical equipment, and listening to foreign broadcasts became an accepted habit.[48] The legal and technical counter-measures proved ineffectual. They ranged from withdrawing permits from high officials to run their own monitoring services, to death sentences in occupied Europe; from the construction of the *Volksempfänger* to the confiscation of private wireless sets or at least of their short-wave bands. The confiscation of all private wireless sets was contemplated on several occasions with regard to a number of occupied countries and then, except in Holland in May 1943, decided against, on the grounds that it would have severely circumscribed the reach of Nazi propaganda itself. In addition, the *Promi* did not command sufficient technical resources to instal a satisfactory network of public loudspeakers,

[45] *Das Reich*, 12 October 1941.
[46] H. Heiber, op. cit., page 302.
[47] Entry for 24 January 1942, *The Goebbels Diaries*.
[48] Cf. W. Hagemann, op. cit., page 302.

on the Soviet pattern, either in the Reich or in the occupied territories. By the spring of 1943, Goebbels was well aware that the Nazi monopoly of information was seriously threatened. On 25 May he recorded in his diary: 'There are reports . . . that many people are again listening to foreign radio stations. The reason for this, of course, is our completely obscure news policy which no longer gives people any insight into the war situation. Also, our reticence regarding Stalingrad and the fate of our missing soldiers there naturally leads the families to listen to Bolshevik radio stations, as these always broadcast the names of German soldiers reported as prisoners.'

As the war situation began to take an adverse turn for the National Socialists, there appeared signs of the need for a discussion of first principles of National Socialism. And in such a discussion, propaganda was certain to occupy a central place. Some time in 1943, a detailed memorandum concerning the party and the state was circulated among the high Nazi leadership; although it was unsigned, Martin Bormann, the last man to have arrived at a position of power by making himself indispensable to the Führer, was very likely its author.[49]

Propaganda was, it was argued in the memorandum, the original function of the party: 'from the beginnings of the movement, propaganda was linked with it most closely'. Its direction should, therefore, return to the party; the author of the memorandum was frankly amazed at the manner in which propaganda had been allowed to pass under the control of the state. The memorandum was largely retrospective, it concerned itself with administrative detail, and it was an undisguised attack on Goebbels. Nevertheless, the basic principles of propaganda, its effectiveness, its content, remained unquestioned. If the leading Nazis had doubts on any of these points—there is no evidence that they did—they certainly never expressed them, even among themselves. The author of the memorandum was simply moved by a sentimental hankering for the heroic age of the Nazi movement. Propaganda was to become again what it used to be in the *Kampfzeit*.

In a way it did. Faced with a hostile world, Nazi propaganda

[49] Undated and unsigned memorandum, National Archives, USA, Microcopy No. T81, Roll No. R–7, Serial 17/14491–14773.

had to abandon its former megalomaniac pursuits and to concentrate, once again, on the German masses. In this crisis, Hitler gave Goebbels no help. Despite unrelenting pressure from the Minister of Propaganda, the Führer addressed his public only three times during the last ten months of the war, and then only over the wireless: the last two speeches by Hitler were read by Goebbels. But instead of acquainting the nation with the true facts of the crisis, Goebbels opted for a policy of 'frankness'. It meant that the fears of the nation had to be exploited for the sake of its dependence on the régime. And, of necessity, the meaning of 'frankness' had changed between 1943 and 1945. It meant more and more lies, a lengthening distance between grim reality and propaganda, more incitement to fanaticism. If we lose the war, the argument ran, then everything is lost; the enemy will impose a super-Versailles on Germany.

Nevertheless, in the midst of military disaster, Goebbels achieved a striking victory. In the concluding stages of hostilities, there appeared signs that the man who had faced political ruin shortly before the war, and the instrument that had been either discarded or neglected, would be restored to their former places of prominence. As the blows of the Allied war effort fell more and more heavily upon the Reich, Goebbels, an exception among the Nazi leaders, showed himself tough enough to stand up to them. He had managed to keep himself in public view early in the war; he gave a resolute backing to the policy of total war effort; he was to reap a belated reward for his exertions. After the attempt on Hitler's life in July 1944, he became the Reich Trustee for Total War; in April of the following year, Hitler appointed him the new Chancellor of the German Reich. Alone among the leading Nazis, he was to remain with the Führer until the bitter end.

179

IX. EPILOGUE

THE last conference of the Ministry of Propaganda took place on the morning of 21 April 1945. Twenty to thirty men, their faces haggard with lack of sleep, assembled in the film room of Goebbels's house in the Hermann Göring Strasse. It was dusty and dark there; the window-panes had long before been replaced by planks of wood; a few candles gave a sparse light. As always, Goebbels was slightly late; as always, he was dapper, elegantly dressed in a dark suit, his hair neatly plastered down to his skull. He began speaking before he sat down. He talked to the small, ghostly assembly as if he was addressing a monster-meeting at the Sportpalast: his theme was the treason committed by the old officers' clique against Hitler's Germany.[1] It is immaterial what was said at the conference. The means of communication had broken down in the beleaguered city; even if decisions had been taken, there existed no way of transmitting them to the few newspaper editors and broadcasters who were still carrying out their duties. Indeed, at the end of April 1945, the horizons of the Minister of Propaganda narrowed to the confines of the city of Berlin. Goebbels, who liked regarding himself as the man who won the capital of Germany from the Communists, was now defending it against the Red Army. There was an ironic continuity in his actions.

It was, however, too late in the day when Goebbels, and the skills he represented, began their return to favour. Total war and the fanatic defence of Hitler's Germany doubtless bore witness to the power Nazi propaganda exercised, in the concluding stages of the hostilities, on members of the Hitler Youth or on the aged veterans who were not fit to wage another war. The fact that these wretches were made to go on fighting for a worth-

[1] *Hier spricht Hans Fritzsche*, pages 27-28.

180

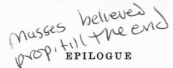

masses believed
prop. till the end

less, evil cause, in which Hitler himself no longer believed, was the last achievement of Nazi propaganda. At this time, when the distance between reality and propaganda (the National Socialists had always been rather careless about that) widened into a gaping abyss, Goebbels, alone among the Nazi leaders, grimly carried on his duties. The process that Hitler had set into motion could not be reversed. The decline of the material and military power of Germany could not be arrested by propaganda, however skilful. The wish that propaganda should become again what it had been in the 'period of struggle' could have been inspired only by sentiment, or by a complete failure to grasp the changing place of propaganda in the Nazi scheme of things. In National Socialist theory, its place never changed: in fact it went through three distinct phases.

In the *Kampfzeit*—until 1933—its task was to create a situation in which Hitler could, by capturing the 'masses', make a bid for power in the state. He was not compelled to use the technique of conspiracy; Nazi agitation took place in full view of the public. The National Socialists ran a *Sammelpartei*, a party of national integration, which drew on the whole community—with the exception, of course, of the Jews—regardless of class, occupation, or sex. It was a nationalist much more than a socialist party, and its nationalism was of a particular kind. It was the vicious and intolerant kind that had begun to develop, at the turn of the century, alongside the ethnic frontiers between the Germans and Czechs in the Habsburg monarchy. To this tradition of nationalism Hitler was the proper heir: his supreme vice as a politician was that he thought in its terms, and that he wished it upon the rest of the German nation.

At first, however, the technical equipment at the disposal of the Nazis was slight: the totalitarian parties, the Bolsheviks and the National Socialists alike, achieved power mostly unaided by the means of mass communication available at the time. Regarded from this point of view, Hitler travelled light: he was an effective public speaker, but he had to rely, for many years, on the carrying power of his voice alone; throughout the nineteen-twenties, the party press could lay no claim to mass-circulation figures. In addition, the full flavour of Nazi propaganda translated badly into the terms of the printed word: much of its

181

emotive quality was lost in the process. Public meetings, party rallies, and all the other activities generated by the party and its manifold offshoots, were regarded as more suitable vehicles for agitation than the press; physical violence was used with icy deliberation, as a propaganda asset.

Despite the effort they spent on propaganda, the Nazis did not create, unaided, the situation in which Hitler could grasp for power in the state. Their opportunity came with the slump in 1929. They had appealed to the discontented sections of the population, and they had cast the net of their organization over Germany: now they benefited hugely from the deepening economic crisis.

At this time, the National Socialist agitation proved especially aggressive: the physical struggle against the 'Marxists', accompanied by the generation of anti-Communist psychosis by Nazi propaganda, considerably sharpened political differences in the Weimar Republic. The National Socialist party proved more attractive to the unemployed than it had done to the employed workers; the anti-Communist drive appealed to the employers. At the time when there existed large numbers of potential recruits for the movement, its leaders were in a position to improve the methods of recruitment. They had their first taste of the new means of mass communication during Hitler's brief alliance with Hugenberg: nevertheless, after its break-up, the industrialists made it financially possible for the *NSDAP* to conduct propaganda on a massive scale. By the end of 1932, Hitler was running the largest political organization in Germany: it is impossible to think of such expansion of the movement without propaganda.

The anti-Communist campaign was carried on, and the Communists were outlawed and imprisoned after January 1933. Propaganda was still employed to secure maximum popular support for Hitler's régime, but, when it could be reinforced by other means of persuasion offered by the state, it lost some of its former value. It became one of the instruments for the maintenance of political power, rather than the most effective instrument for its achievement. Goebbels became the Minister of Popular Enlightenment and Propaganda; the heavy equipment —broadcasting, the film industry, mass-circulation press—

passed under his control. The Minister ruthlessly exploited the opportunities offered him by the rise of his party to power. He interfered with the lives of the people to an extent unparalleled in history. The news and even the comments in their papers were centrally supplied; a dissenting opinion could never take the form of the legally printed word. The films they saw and the broadcasts they listened to, all carried an indelible Nazi stamp. The party took care of their leisure time, their travel, their social activities; it presented newly married couples with copies of *Mein Kampf*.

Against this onslaught, the Germans were on the whole defence-less. At the last parliamentary elections, not quite a half of the electorate voted for the National Socialists; soon after January 1933, the majority of the Germans disposed of neither the organization nor of the means for expressing anti-Nazi views. Goebbels's propaganda took great care to identify Germany with National Socialism: the campaign was highly successful, and it did untold harm to the nation. Although the Nazi propagandists often treated facts and political realities with disdain, they regarded it as their professional duty to keep in close touch with the mood, the shifts of public opinion, in Germany. The information on the various non-Nazi ways of looking at things, and on the reactions to the official propaganda drives passed, in the opposite direction, through the same channels—the propaganda departments in the party hierarchy—as the directives that were handed down to the last propaganda cell. The Nazis in fact conducted quite a precise 'audience research', and they were able to attack the remaining knots of resistance, or fill in the various propaganda gaps, as the situation required. The pre-war achievements of Hitler's régime at home and abroad, and their skilful exploitation by propaganda, doubtless gained Hitler new adherents. In the six years of peace, the cumulative impact of Nazi propaganda on the Germans was tremendous; it is of course difficult to judge how divided, or undivided, Hitler's Germany embarked on the war. Be that as it may, the impression of unity, of the degree of Germany's identification with National Socialism, achieved by 1939, was indeed striking. Henceforth it would be difficult not to let the evil in National Socialism eclipse all that was good in Germany: it would be difficult for any judge of the National Socialist era, however detached, to regard the Germans and their system of government at the time as two quite distinct things.

After January 1933, new horizons opened before the Nazi propagandists. Their activities abroad suffered, however, from severe limitations. National Socialist ideology basically lacked international appeal; the leadership of the movement was also singularly short of men who possessed international vision or connexions. Goebbels thought of propaganda abroad as a mere extension of propaganda at home: this meant that the contents and the eccentricities of Nazi agitation in Germany were translated, indiscriminately, on to the international plane. The antisemitic charge in National Socialist propaganda abroad remained as high as that contained in the propaganda output intended for home consumption. At the same time, anti-Communism remained closely linked with antisemitism: whereas anti-Communism may have proved attractive to large sections of Europeans, antisemitism did not find a receptive audience abroad. The antisemitic content of Nazi propaganda repelled rather than attracted potential sympathizers.

Although they were short of men with knowledge of the foreign scene, the National Socialist leaders, like the Bolsheviks, distrusted the diplomats: their relations with the outside world could not somehow be contained in traditional diplomatic channels. The clash between propaganda and diplomacy was reflected in the perennial conflicts between the *Promi* and the Foreign Ministry, which did not cease even after a party member— Ribbentrop—took over the direction of Germany's foreign policy. Propaganda and the most intimate relations between the two party organizations replaced diplomacy in the relations of Hitler's Germany with Austria, until the summer of 1934; propaganda also played an important role in the relations with the Soviet Union until the spring of 1939. And then, of course, propaganda had to make Hitler's Germany acceptable to the outside world, and especially to the Great Powers (here the *Promi* was helped by the fact that the large majority of German diplomats remained at their posts after January 1933), and it had to prepare the way for Germany's conquests before the outbreak of the war.

lesson

The unsuccessful *putsch* in Vienna in July 1934 taught the Nazi leaders that they could no longer behave irresponsibly: that they could not promise more than they could deliver, and that aggressive propaganda should, in the last instance, be backed up by the full might of the state. During the Saarland campaign, Goebbels experimented, very successfully, with broadcasting. It created a 'bridge'—a feeling of community— that ignored both the frontier as it existed at the time, as well as the former political complexion in the Saarland. In the second Austrian campaign, and then in the drive against Czechoslovakia, Nazi propaganda achieved the peak of its efficiency. It was fully integrated in Germany's diplomatic and military manœuvres, it helped Hitler to achieve his objectives without any wastage of troops or ammunition. Indeed, the intensive generation of a 'Saarland' or an 'Austrian', or a 'Sudetenland' atmosphere, and its effect abroad, may be described as the most notable achievements of the Ministry of Propaganda. Although the popular enthusiasm that accompanied these campaigns was in fact artificially contrived, German nationalism, seen from abroad, appeared as a spontaneous force. To this view of German nationalism Hitler owed most of his pre-war successes in the field of foreign policy.

They were confined to central Europe. Here, the National Socialists were prepared to use their connexions with the Nazi parties run by their compatriots. Their propaganda of course remained intensely nationalistic when it was aimed at the *Volksdeutsche*. This predominantly German orientation of Nazi propaganda was its strength as well as its weakness. It was highly suitable for the subversion of the political order in central Europe established by the peace treaties. It lacked, however, a wider appeal: it could contribute nothing to Hitler's drive for 'acceptance', first for his régime and then for its expansion, by the Great Powers. Indeed, the Nationalist Socialist movement was lifted out of its exclusive parochialism only by the virtue of the 'international threats'—the Jewish and Bolshevik 'conspiracies'—it claimed to combat.

So long as Hitler's objectives remained limited to central Europe or, more precisely, to its German part, Nazi propaganda alone was sufficient to shatter the established order. But after the achievement of its most impressive victories, a certain exhaustion, a certain thinness, appeared in Nazi propaganda. In the summer of 1939, it was pursuing too many objectives: from having been ruthlessly concentrated, it was becoming diffuse.

And the publicity drive on behalf of the army marked the beginning of its decline. The army and military problems were fast becoming Hitler's main interests: there was room for nothing else in his mind. Although he had no intention of breaking up the apparatus Goebbels had carefully built up, civilian-conducted propaganda had to take a subordinate place. The *Promi* gave up some of its functions to the *Abteilung Wehrmachtpropaganda* in the *OKW*; central direction of the press was disrupted; the main function of Goebbels's Ministry was the dissemination of the material which was fed to it. Some of the secondary propaganda themes it initiated had to be either played down or abandoned. As far as occupied Europe was concerned, Nazi propaganda no longer operated in a vacuum, by remote control. The peoples of these countries came into contact with the realities of the German occupation, and their attitudes were affected by the direct contact rather than by the mellifluous outpourings of the propagandists.

Whereas Goebbels had succeeded in establishing some foothold for his Ministry in western Europe, he was unable to do so, until the end of 1943, in the occupied territories in the Soviet Union. Here, the propaganda of the National Socialist struggle against Communism was exposed as an empty sham. The Nazis were less able to establish a *modus vivendi* with the local population in the east than in western Europe. They came as superior conquerors, and they intended to exploit every advantage the situation offered.

Finally, the war broke the Nazi monopoly of information in the Reich itself: the process coincided with the reversal in Germany's military fortunes. It wasn't long before the defenders of the besieged fortress found the feeling of claustrophobia, heightened by the centralized system of information, unendurable. Through foreign broadcasts, they were able to re-establish contacts with the outside world. The last phase of Nazi propaganda, exhorting the Germans to a fanatic resistance, intensified the chaos that accompanied defeat.

BIBLIOGRAPHY

ORIGINAL SOURCES

1. *Unpublished*

PAPERS relating to propaganda from the *Reichspropagandaleitung*, now in the possession of the *Institut für Zeitgeschichte*, Munich; from the *Reichsrundfunkgesettschaft*, now at the Allied Document Centre, Berlin; diverse material filmed at the Alexandria (U.S.A.) repository, now at the Wiener Library; unpublished evidence submitted to the International Military Tribunal, Nürnberg, at the Wiener Library; speakers' directives, inserted into the *Promi* periodical, *Unser Wille und Weg*. A large part of the *Promi* papers was destroyed at the end of the war; most of the remaining material deals with the internal administration of the Ministry.

Documents from the archives of the Foreign Ministry (*Auswärtiges Amt*); film references were used throughout the book as additional indications to their placing.

2. *Published*

Documents on German Foreign Policy, Series C and D.

Documents on British Foreign Policy, 2nd and 3rd Series.

The Trial of the Major War Criminals before the International Military Tribunal, *Proceedings* (vols. I–XXIII), and *Documents in Evidence* (vols. XXIV–XLII). Nürnberg, 1947–9.

Trials of War Criminals before the Nürnberg Military Tribunals. Washington, 1951–3.

Domarus, Max: (ed.) *Hitler. Reden und Proklamationen.* Würzburg, 1962.

Mussolini, Benito: *Scritti e Discorsi.* Milan, 1938.

Der Hochverratsprozess gegen Dr. Guido Schmidt. Vienna, 1947.

Reichsgesetzblatt. A daily publication.

NATIONAL SOCIALIST PUBLICATIONS

ab Insulis, Geistiger Mensch und Nationalsozialismus. Ein Interview für den Gebildeten unter seinen Gegnern. Berlin, 1931.

187

Amt für Volksaufklärung (publisher), *Drei Jahre im Reich.* Protektorat Böhmen und Mähren, Prague 1942.

Anglo-German Academic Bureau. *Report on the activities of the AGAB during the first decade of its existence.* London, 1938.

Albert, Rudolf: Nationalwirtschaft. *Grundzüge deren Gestaltung im Dritten Reich.* Leipzig, 1932.

D'Alquen, Gunter, *Die SS. Geschichte, Aufgabe und Organisation der SS der NSDAP.* Berlin, 1939.

Arbeitsplan und Inhaltsübersicht zum Aktenverzeichnis des Reichsministeriums für Volksaufklärung und Propaganda. Berlin, 1936.

Arendt, Paul: *Die Hitler-Bewegung räumt auf—mit Bonzen, Prassern und Grossverdienern.* Sulzbach-Oberpfalz, 1933.

— *Eiserne Front oder Braune Front? Werbeschrift für die NSDAP.* Sulzbach, 1932.

— *Kampf dem Bonzentum! Die Grossverdiener in Ängsten!* Sulzbach, 1931.

— *Macht Deutschland von Bonzen frei!* Sulzbach, 1931.

— *Wo Bleibt der 2 Mann? jammert die SPD. 'Er geht zu Hitler'.* Sulzbach, 1931.

Bald, Gustav: *Die politische-satyrische Lyrik, ein publizistisches Kampfmittel.* Arnsberg, 1936.

Bang, Andreas: *Handgranaten. Waffen zur deutsche Freiheit!* Mingolsheim, 1931.

Bangert, Otto: *Deutsche Revolution. Ein Buch vom Kampfe um das Dritte Reich.* Munich, 1929.

Barth, Hans: *Nationalsozialistischer Geist im Wirtschaftsteil. Forderung zur Neugestaltung der Tagespresse.* Berlin, 1934.

Baum, Paul: *Zum Schutze der Republik. 3 Monate Gefängnis im Namen des Volkes.* Tostedt in Hann, 1930.

Bayer, Ernst: 'Die SA'. (In: *Schriften der Hochschule für Politik.*) Berlin, 1938.

Berg, Josef: *Siebzig Jahre Arbeiterbetrug! Ein Mahnruf an den deutschen Arbeiter.* Munich, 1928.

Berndt, Alfred-Ingemar: *Der Marsch ins Gross-Deutsche Reich.* Munich, 1939.

Best, Werner: *... wird erschossen. Wahrheit über die Boxheimer Dokumente.* Munich, 1932.

Biallas, Hans: 'Warum muss der Arbeiter nationalsozialistisch wahlen?' (In: *Schriftenreihe der nat.soz. Betriebszellen-Organisation.*) Diessen/Munich, 1932.

Bock, August: *Marxismus, Kapitalismus und Nationalsozialismus.* Berlin, 1931.

Bock, August: *Nationalsozialismus und Geldschöpfung, Beitrag zur wirtschaftl. Führerfrage.* Berlin, 1932.

Boehm, Max Hildebert: *Deutschoesterreichs Wanderschaft und Heimkehr.* Essen, 1939.

Bosch, Elisabeth: *Die Katholikin und das Hakenkreuz.* Munich, 1932.

Boesser, Friedrich: *Ideen für eine zu begründende Nationalsozialistische Praesidial-Partei Deutschlands.* Hannover, 1932.

Brackmann, Albert: *Krisis und Aufbau in Osteuropa.* Berlin, 1939.

Braun, Walter: *Heidenmission u. Nationalsozialismus.* Berlin, 1932.

Brehm, Bruno: *Glückliches Oesterreich.* Jena, 1938.

Brepohl, Friedrich Wilhelm: *Nationalsozialistische Revolution und Volksgemeinschaft.* Ponta Grossa, 1933.

Brombacher, Kuno: *Die nationalsozialistische Idee. Das Bekenntnis eines katholischen Dichters.* Munich, 1932.

Brugger, A.: *Jahrbuch für vorbildliche Anzeigenwerbung im nat.-soz Staate.* Dresden, 1935-6.

Buckner, Hans: *Die Goldene Internationale. Vom Finanzkapital, Tributsystem und seinen Trägern.* Munich, 1931.

— *Warenhauspolitik und National-sozialismus.* Munich, 1929.

Dachauer, Max: *Das Ende Oesterreichs. Aus der K.u.k. Monarchie ins Dritte Reich.* Berlin, 1939.

Dammert, Rudolf: *Zeitung. Unser täglicher Hausgast.* Leipzig, 1938.

Darre, R. Walther: *Landvolk in Not und seine Rettung durch Adolf Hitler.* Munich 1932.

Das Grosse Wunder. Reichspräsidentenwahl 1932. Hamburg 1932.

Das politische Bekenntnis von Nürnberg. Hanover, 1933.

Denkler, Werner: *Wie Halte ich eine Betriebsversammlung ab, oder einen Betriebsappell? Mit 150 Tageslosungen für Vertrauensmänner u. Betreibsführer.* Berlin, undated.

— *Der 9 November 1923. Die Wahrheit über die Münchener Vorgänge.* 1923.

d'Ester, Karl: *Die Presse Frankreichs im eigenen Urteil 1540-1940.* Stuttgart and Berlin, 1942.

'Die Wahrheit über Braunschweig', ed. by the Reichspropagandaleitung der *NSDAP.* (In: *Kampfschrift.*) Munich, 1932.

Dich ruft Deutschland. Dresden, 1933.

Diehl, Guida: *Die Deutsche Frau und der National-sozialismus.* Eisennach, 1932.

Dietrich, Otto: *Mit Hitler in die Macht.* Munich, 1935.

— *Nationalsozialistische Pressepolitik.* Rede geh. am 7/3/38 vor Diplomatie und Auslandspresse. Berlin, 1938.

Dietz, Heinrich: *Agitation Massenhysterie in England. Propagandamethoden historisch gesehen.* Essen, 1941.

Dierwerge, Wolfgang: *Der neue Reichsgau Danzig Westpreussen.* Berlin, 1940.

Dobiasch, Sepp: *Volk auf dem Amboss. Kampfabschnitt Oesterreich 1933–35.* Berlin, 1938.

Drechsel, Paul: (ed.) *Schaffende Deutsche! Deutsche Bauern ... Heraus! Schlagt das Elendssystem! Kämpft mit Adolf Hitler für Ehre, Freiheit, Brot, soziale Gerechtigkeit.* Planitz, 1932.

— *Wer hilft aus Wirtschaftsnot und Arbeitslosigkeit? Die 'Eiserne Front' oder die ' Front Adolf Hitlers'.* Planitz, 1932.

Dresler, Adolf: 'Der Führer und die Presse'. (In: *Zeitungswissenschaftl. Monatsschrift für internationale Zeitungsforschung.*) Essen, 1939.

— *Mussolini als Journalist.* Essen, 1939.

Eckart, Dietrich: *An alle Werktätigen! An alle, die arbeiten, ganz gleich, was und wo, wenn sie nur arbeiten. An alle vernünftigen Menschen.* Munich, 1919.

Ehrich, Emil: DieAuslandsorganisation der NSDAP. (In: *Schriften der dt. Hochschule f. Politik.*) Berlin, 1937.

Eich, Hermann: *Die Nachrichtenpolitik der franz. Presse, von der Emser Depesche bis zur Gegenwart.* Frankfurt, 1939.

'Ein Gedanke wird Tat. Vom Werden und Wachsen einer nat.-soz.' *Tageszeitung.* Hamburg, 1940.

Engel, Johannes: *Praktischer Leitfaden für den N.S. Betriebsfunktionär.* Berlin, undated.

Erste Tagung der nationalsozialistischen Freiheitsbewegung Grossdeutschlands in Weimar 15—17/8/1924. Weimar, 1924.

Everling, Friedrich: *Organischer Aufbau des Dritten Reichs.* Munich 1931.

Feder, Gottfried: *Die Wohnungsnot und die soziale Bau- und Wirtschaftsbank als Retterin aus Wohnungselend, Wirtschaftskrise und Erwerbslosenelend.* Munich, 1929.

Feder, Gottfried and Strasser, Gregor: *Reden im Reichstag Oktober 1930 nach dem amtl. Stenogramm.* Berlin, 1930.

Fiehler, Karl: *National-sozialistische Gemeindepolitik.* Munich, 1932.

— 'Wenn Hindenburg wiedergewaehlt wird, dann ... ja, was dann?' (In: *Kampfschrift.*) Munich, 1932.

Fischer, E. Kurt: *Dramaturgie des Rundfunks. Studien zum Weltrundfunk und Fernsehrundfunk.* Berlin, Magdeburg, 1942.

Frauendorfer, Max: *Der ständische Gedanke im National-sozialismus.* Munich, 1932.

Franke, Heinz: *Die Journaille lügt!* Munich, 1932.

— 'Die Partei der "Köpfe".' (In: *Kampfschrift.*) Munich, 1932.

Franke, Heinz: *Lügen über Coburg*. Munich, 1932.

— *Nieder mit der Hugenberg-Reaktion!* Munich, 1932.

— *Warum?* Munich, 1932.

Freisler, Roland: Kunisch, Siegmund: Spieler, Christian: (eds.) *Das Gemeinschaftslager 'Hanns Kerrl'*. Berlin, 1934.

Frick, Wilhelm: *Die Nationalsozialisten im Reichstag 1924–31*. Munich, 1932.

— *Wir bauen das Dritte Reich*. Oldenburg and Berlin, 1934.

Friedrich, Hermann: *Unter dem Hakenkreuz. Meine Erlebnisse als Agitator bei der NSDAP*. Karlsruhe, 1929.

Frisch, Hans von: *Die Gewaltherrschaft in Oesterreich 1933–38. Eine Staatsrechtliche Untersuchung*. Leipzig and Vienna, 1938.

Fritzsche, Georg: *Feuilleton und Kulturpolitik. Polit. Führer durch d. Feuilleton unter besonderer Beruecksichtigung der Zeit von 1918–33*. Radebeul, 1938.

Galera, Karl Sigmar: *Das junge Deutschland und das Dritte Reich*. Leipzig, 1932.

Gast, P.: *Das Schriftleitergesetz vom 4/10/33 nebst den einschlägigen Bestimmungen erläutert*. Berlin, 1944.

Geisow, Hans: *So wurde ich Nationalsozialist. Ein Bekenntnis*. Munich, 1931.

Germany. The Olympic Year 1936. Berlin, 1936.

Gerstel, Joachim, W.: *Die Antithese Sozialismus-Marxismus als Basis der Ideenwelt der NSDAP*. Heidelberg, 1931.

Geschäftsverteilungsplan des Reichsministeriums fuer Volksaufklaerung und Propaganda vom 10 Oktober, 1936. Berlin, 1936.

Girardet, Herbert: *Der wirtschaftliche Aufbau der kommunistischen Tagespresse in Deutschland von 1918 bis 1933. Unter besonderer Berücksichtigung d. Verhältnisse im Reg-bez*. Düsseldorf, Essen, 1938.

Goebbels, Joseph: 'Der Faschismus und seine praktischen Ergebnisse'. (In: *Schriften der dt. Hochschule f. Politik*.) Berlin, 1934.

— *Das Eherne Herz*. Rede vor der deutschen Akademie am 1 Dezember 1941. Munich, 1941.

— *Dreissig Kriegsartikel für das deutsche Volk*. Munich, 1943.

— and Mjoelnir: *Das Buch Isidor. Ein Zeitbild voll Lachen und Hass*. Munich, undated.

— *Der Bolschewismus in Theorie und Praxis*. Rede auf dem Parteikongress in Nürnberg 1936. Munich, 1936.

— *Der Blick nach vorn. Aufsätze aus den Jahren des Krieges*. Tornisterschrift des OKW 79, Munich, 1943.

— *Der geistige Arbeiter im Schicksalskampf des Reiches*. Rede vor der Heidelberger Universität am 9 Juli 1943. Munich, 1943.

Goebbels, Joseph: *Kampf um Berlin. Anfang.* Munich, 1936.
— *Nation im Aufbau.* Sonderlieferung der Aufklärungs—und Redner—Informationsmaterials der Reichspropagandaleitung. Munich, undated.
— *Nationalsozialistischer Rundfunk.* Munich, 1935.
— *Die Wahrheit über Spanien.* Rede auf dem Reichsparteitag 1937.
— *Die zweite Revolution.* Briefe an Zeitgenossen. Zwickau, 1927.
— *Das kleine abc des Nationalsozialisten.* Berlin, 1929.
— *Der Angriff. Aufsätze aus der Kampfzeit.* Munich, 1939.
— *Der National-sozialismus. Fragen und Antworten für die Nationalsizialisten!* Elberfeld, 1927.
— *Der Sinn der Revolution.* Rede am 24 April 1933 im Gürzenich zu Köln vor der westdeutschen Presse. Wolfenbüttel, 1933.
— *Die Zeit ohne Beispiel.* Reden und Aufsätze aus den Jahren 1939/40/41. Munich, 1941.
— *Eine Rede des Herrn Reichsministers Dr. Joseph Goebbels beim Kantate-Festessen 1933.* Leipzig, 1933.
— *Kommunismus ohne Maske.* Munich, 1935.
— *Lenin oder Hitler?* Eine Rede gehalten 19 Februar 1926 im Opernhaus in Könisberg. Zwickau, 1926.
— *Revolution der Deutschen 14 Jahre Nationalsozialismus. Goebbelsreden mit einleitenden Zeitbildern von Hein Schlecht.* Oldenburg, 1933.
— *Richtlinien für die Gesamthaltung der deutschen Presse.* Berlin, n.d.
— *Signal zum Aufbruch.* Rede eines Mannes, dem im Preussen das Reden verboten war. Geh. am 28 Marz 1931 in Danzig. Munich, 1931.
— *Signale der neuen Zeit 25 Ausgewählte Reden.* Munich, 1934.
— *Wege ins Dritte Reich.* Briefe und Aufsätze für Zeitgenossen. Munich, 1927.
— Wetterleuchten. *Ausätze aus der Kampfzeit.* Munich, 1939.
Grimm, Friedrich: *Hitlers deutsche Sendung. Oesterreich kehrt heim.* Berlin, 1938.
Grünbeck, Max: *Die Presse Grossbritanniens. Ihr geistiger und wirtschaftlicher Aufbau.* Leipzig, 1936.
Guerke, Norbert: *Der Nationalsozialismus das Grenz und Auslanddeutschtum und das Nationalitaetenrecht.* Vienna, 1932.
Haake, Rudolf: *Der Leipziger Stadtbankskandal. Eine Anklage gegen buergerl. marxist. Misswirtschaft.* Leipzig, 1932.
— *Der Versammlungsleiter.* Leipzig, 1931-32.
Haas, Werner: *Europa will leben.* Berlin, 1936.
Hadamovsky, Eugen: *Dein Rundfunk. Das Buch für alle Volksgenossen.* Munich, 1934.

Hadamovsky, Eugen: *Propaganda und nationale Macht. Die Organisation der öffentlichen Meinung für die nationale Politik.* Oldenburg, 1933.

Hardefust: 'Was hat uns die Revolution gekostet?' (In: *Kampfschrift*.) Munich, 1932.

Hart, Herbert: *Das Dritte Reich, wie es sein wird. Eine neue Wirtschaftsordnung für Deutschland. Die Hypothekenmark, Arbeitsbeschaffung, Fürsorgereform.* Hamburg, 1932.

Hartlieb, Wladimir von: *Parole: das Reich. Eine historische Darstellung der politischen Entwicklung in Österreich von März 1933 bis März 1938.* Vienna, 1939.

Hasselbach, Ulrich von: *Die Entstehung der nat.-soz. deutschen Arbeiterpartei 1919–23.* Breslau, 1931.

Haushofer, Karl: *Der nationalsozialistische Gedanke in der Welt.* Munich, 1933.

Hein, Theobald: *Nationalsozialismus und Philosophie.* Leipzig, 1932.

Heindel, Rudolf and others: Nat. soz. Denken und Wirtschaft. (In: *Kulturpolit. Schriftenreihe*.) Stuttgart, 1932.

Heiss, Friedrich: *Deutschland und der Korridor.* Berlin, 1933.

Henlein, Konrad: *Der Lebenswille des Sudetendeutschtums.* Karlsbad, 1938.

— *We want to live as free men among free men.* Speech delivered before the Annual Congress of the Sudetendeutsche Partei, Karlsbad 1938.

Herold, Martin: *Geschichte der französischen Saar-politik. Ausgangsstellung und Angriff—Von der Saar zum Rhein.* Bonn, 1934.

Heydrich, Reinhard: *Wandlungen unseres Kampfes.* Munich, Berlin, 1935.

Hiemisch, Max: *Der nationalsozialistische Kampf um Bielefeld.* Bielefeld, 1933.

Hitler, Adolf: *Mein Kampf.* (Translation by J. Murphy.) London, 1939.

— *Hitlers zweites Buch. Ein Dokument aus dem Jahre 1928.* Ed. by Institut für Zeitgeschichte. Stuttgart, 1961.

— *Der Weg zum Wiederaufstieg.* Munich, 1927.

— *Offener Brief an Herrn von Papen. Die Antwort des Führers der NSDAP an den Reichskanzler* .... Berlin, 1932.

Holzmann Arthur: *Die Tätigkeit der Nationalsozialisten für die Landwirtschaft.* Munich, 1931.

Itzinger, Karl: *Tagebuch vom 10 February bis zum 13 März 1938. Ein Überblick über die letzten Tage des Kampfes und die ersten Tage des Sieges.* Linz, 1938.

Joyce, William: *Dämmerung über England.* Berlin, 1940.

Jung, Rudolf: *Der nationale Sozialismus. Seine Grundlagen, sein Werdegang und seine Ziele.* Munich, 1923.
— *Nationaler oder internationaler Sozialismus.* Berlin, 1930.
— *Nationalsozialismus—der Aufbruch eines Volkes zu neuem Volkstum, Freiheit und sozialer Gerechtigkeit.* Aussig, 1931.
— 'Was wollen die deutschen National-sozialisten in der Gemeindestube?' (In: *Nationalsozialistische Schriften.*) Troppau, 1923.

Kampmann, Karoly, (ed.): *Die Volksfront. Mit dem Volk!—Für das Volk! Wahlflugschrift der NSDAP.* Berlin, 1932.
Karg, Max: *Kapitalismus, Marxismus und National-sozialismus.* Rede aud der Parteitag in Eger August 1923. (In: *S. Flugschriften.*) Aussig, 1923.
Keller, Hans: *Am Internationalismus gehen die Völker zugrunde.* Zürich, 1936.
Klagges, Dietrich: 'Kampf dem Marxismus.' (In: *Schriftenreihe der Reichspropaganda-Abteilung der NSDAP.*) Munich, 1930.
— *Reichtum und soziale Gerechtigkeit. Grundfragen einer nat.-soz. Volkswirtschaftslehre.* Leipzig, 1932.
Kniesche, Arno: *Deutschlands Zukunft unter der Hakenkreuz.* Bad Dueben-Mulde, 1930.
Krebs, Hans; *Kampf in Böhmen.* Berlin, 1937.
— *Redner-Fibel.* Leipzig, 1935.
— *Wir Sudetendeutsche.* Berlin, 1938.
Kremers, Hermann: *Nationalsozialismus und Protestantismus.* Berlin, 1931.
Krumm, Paul: *Der deutsche Sozialismus nach A. Hitler. Oswald Spengler u.d. Aufstieg des National-sozialismus.* Leipzig, 1932.
Kube, Wilhelm (ed.): *Almanach der nat.soz. Revolution.* Berlin, 1934.
Kuntze, Paul: *Entgiftete Brunnen. Zerfall, Abwehr und Gesundung der Nation.* Munich, 1936.
Kuptsch, Julius: *Christentum im Nationalsozialismus.* Munich, 1932.
— *Durch Wiedergeburt des Volkes zur Wiedergeburt des Reiches.* Soldin, 1932.
Kurth, Karl and Hollmann, Wolfgang: *Die Wirkungsgesetze der Presse. Gedanken über den Zusammenhang von Volkstum und Nachrichtengestaltung.* Berlin, 1941.

Lama, Franz Ritter von: Die Satire als Kampfmittel in der Bayerischen Publizistik. (In: *Zeitung und Leben.*) Munich, 1937.
Lang, Leopold: Hitler und Österreich. *Die Geschichte der Heimkehr Österreichs ins Deutsche Reich.* Vienna, 1938.

Lawaczeck, Franz: *Technik und Wirtschaft im Dritten Reich. Ein Arbeitsbeschaffungsprogramm.* Munich, 1932.

Leer, Johann von: *Bomben auf Hamburg. Vision oder Möglichkeit.* Leipzig, 1932.

Lehmann, Julius Friedrich: 'Warum wählt das nationale Deutschland im 2. Wahlgang Adolf Hitler?' (In: *Deutschlands Erneuerung.*) Munich, 1932.

Lehmann, Verlag: *50 Jahre J. F. Lehmann Verlag 1890–1940.* Munich, 1940.

Ley, Robert: *Die Deutsche Arbeitersfront. Ihr Werden und ihre Aufgaben.* Munich, 1934.

Löffler, Anton: *Benesch, Stalin, & Co. Der Weg eines Auch-Staates.* Berlin, 1938.

Lüdde, Karl: *Grundgesetze und Richtlinien für die Entwicklung der Wirtschaft im nat. soz. Staate.* Leipzig, 1932.

Maurer, Emil: *Die Brechung der Zinsknechtschaft.* Munich, 1932.

Max, Hubert: *Wesen und Gestalt der politischen. Zeitschrift.* Essen, 1943.

Metzner, Kurt: *Geordnete Buchbesprechung. Ein Handbuch für Presse und Verlag.* Leipzig, 1935.

Moravec, Emanuel: *Das Ende der Benesch-Republik, Die tschechoslowakische Krise 1938.* Prague, 1942.

Muchow, Reinhold: *Nationalsozialismus und 'freie' Gewerkschaften.* Munich, 1932.

— *Reichsleitung der NSDAP. Organisation der nationalsozialistischen Betriebszellen. Ziel und Systematik der Arbeit.* Munich, 1932.

— *Sind die Nationalsozialisten sozialreaktionär?* Miesbach, 1932.

Müller, George Wilhelm: Das Reichsministerium für Volksaufklärung und Propaganda. (In: *Schriften zum Staatsaufbau.*) Berlin, 1940.

Münster, Hans A.: *Geschichte der deutschen Presse in ihren Grundzügen dargestellt.* Leipzig, 1941.

— *Zeitung und Politik. Eine Einführung in die Zeitungswissenschaft.* Leipzig, 1935.

Nationalsozialismus und Kriegsopfer. Published by Reichsorganisationsabteilung—Referant Kriegsopferversorgung. Diessen vor Munich, 1931.

Pesl, Ludwig Daniel: *Nationalsozialismus und Bodenreform.* Berlin, 1932.

Pfaff, Alfred: *Der Wirtschaftsaufbau im Dritten Reich.* Munich, 1932.

Pfitzner, Josef: *Das Sudetendeutschtum.* Cologne, 1938.

Presse: Reichsverband der dt. Presse. Gliederung des RDP, Schriftleitergesetz, Satzung, Richtlinien, etc. Berlin, undated.

14

Presserecht: Ed. by Karl-Friedrich Schrieber and Anton Willi. Berlin, 1936.

Pressehandbuch: Gesetze, Anordnungen, Erlasse, Bekanntmachungen zusammengestellt und erläutert nach den Beduerfnissen der Praxis. Berlin, 1938.

Presse-Kameradschaftslager: das erste deutsche. Wiesbaden, 1934.

Rahm, Hans-Georg: *Der Angriff. Der nat.-soz. Typ der Kampfzeitung.* Berlin, 1939.

Raschhofer, Hermann: *Grossdeutsch oder kleinösterreichisch? Die Funktion der kleinösterreichischen Ideologie.* Berlin, 1934.

Raumer, Kurt: *Der Rhein im deutschen Schicksal. Reden und Aufsätze zur Westfrage.* Berlin, 1936.

Rebentisch, Willy: *NSDAP. Unsere Führer im Bild.* Leipzig, 1931.

Rehse, Sammlung: edited by Adolf Dreslir, Munich 1941.

Reichel, Karl-Ferdinand: *Die pazifistische Presse.* Würzburg, 1938.

Reinhardt, Fritz: *Achtung! Alarm!* Herrsching a. Ammersee, 1929.

— *Die rote Pest.* Herrsching a. Ammersee, 1930.

Reptau, Gustav: *Die Vernichtungspropaganda gegen das deutsche Volk.* Berlin, 1927.

Reupke, Hans: *Der Nationalsozialismus und die Wirtschaft.* Berlin, 1931.

Reventlow, Graf Ernst: *Nationaler Sozialismus im neuen Deutschland.* Berlin, Leipzig, 1933.

Richtlinien fuer den Unterricht über polit. Tagesfragen. Nur für den Dienstunterricht in der Wehrmacht. n.p. 1938.

Riehl, Walter: *Unser Endziel. Eine Flugschrift für den dt. Nat. soz.* Vienna and Leipzig, 1923.

Rintelen, Anton: *Erinnerungen an Österreichs Weg. Versailles-Berchtesgaden-Grossdeutschland.* Munich, 1941.

Roegels, Fritz Carl: *Der Marsch auf Berlin. Ein Buch vom Wehrwillen dt. Jugend.* Berlin, 1932.

Rosenberg, Alfred: 'Die Entwicklung der deutschen Freiheitsbewegung'. (In: *Die nat.-soz. Revolution.*) Ponta Grossa, 1933.

— *Nationalsozialismus und Jungdeutscher Orden. Eine Abrechnung mit A. Mahraun.* Munich, 1927.

Roskam, Karl: *Was sill die nat.-soz. Freiheitsbewegung und wie will sie die sozialen Fragen lösen?* Dortmund, 1924.

Rother, Kurt: Rüstzeug d.nat.-soz. Freiheitsbewegung Grossdeutschlands. Mit Genehmigung der Reichsführerschaft. Berlin, 1924.

Rust, Bernard: *Papen oder Hitler?* Munich, 1932.

Santifaller, Leo: *Deutschösterreich und seine Rückkehr in das Reich.* Weimar, 1938.

Sauer, Franz: *Unser Weg zum wirtschaftl. Aufstieg und zur sozialen Befreiung.* Berlin, 1931.

Schaafbausen, F. W., *Der Grossdeutsche Gedanke.* Cologne, 1934.

Schach, Eugen: *Nationalsozialismus und Genossenschaftswesen.* Munich, 1931.

Schauff, Rudolf: *Das sind Tatsachen!* Berlin, undated.

Schemm, Hans: *Der rote Krieg. Mutter oder Genossin.* Bayreuth, 1931.

— *Der rote Krieg. Mutter oder Genossin? Nationalsozialismus oder Bolschewismus?* Sulzbach, 1931.

Scherer, Joachim: *Manifest zur Aufrichtung des 'Völkischen Staats-Sozialismus'. Eine wirtschaftpolit. Auseinandersetzung.* Boeblingen, 1932.

Schirach, Baldur von: *Die Hitler-Jugend. Idee und Gestalt.* Leipzig, 1934.

Schirach, Karl (ed.); *Das zweite Gesicht. Werbeschrift der NSDAP.* Vienna, 1932.

— (ed.): *Die Frau als 'Zuchstute'. Werbeschrift der NSDAP.* Vienna, 1932.

— (ed.): *Religion in Gefahr. Werbeschrift der NSDAP.* Vienna, 1932.

— (ed.): *Was wollen die Nazi?* Vienna, 1932.

Schloesser, Robert, and Breuer, Walter: *Nationalsozialismus und Konsumgenossenschaftswesen.* Cologne, 1932.

Schmidt-Pauli, Edgar von: *Hitlers Kampf um die Macht. DerNational-sozialismus u.d. Ereignisse d.J. 1932.* Berlin, 1933.

Schmiedchen, Johannes: *Führer durch den National-sozialismus.* Berlin, 1933.

Schneefuss, Walter: *Deutsch-Böhmen. Schicksal und Weg der Sudetendeutschen.* Leipzig, 1938.

— *Oesterreich—Zerfall und Werden eines Staates.* Leipzig, 1937.

Schopper, Hans: *Presse im Kampf. Geschichte der Presse während der Kampfjahre der NSDAP (1933–38) in Oesterreich.* Munich, 1942.

Schuhmann, Walter: 'Wir Helfen dem Landarbeiter'. (In: *Schrif-tenreihe der nat.-soz. Betriebszellen-Organisation.*) Miesbach, 1932.

Schultze, Hannes-Heinz: *Der Schriftleiterverband der Landesver-baende Gross-Hamburg und Nordmark in Reichsverband der dt. Presse.* Hamburg, 1938.

Schwerber, Peter: *Nationalsozialismus und Technik. Die Geistigkeit der nat.-soz. Bewegung.* Munich, 1932.

Schwichow, Walther von: *Der Bauer von Morgen. Gedanken über die deutsche Landwirtschaft im Dritten Reich.* Bremen, 1932.

Sebottendorff, Rudolf von: *Bevor Hitler kam. Urkundliches aus der Frühzeit der nat.-soz. Bewegung.* Munich, 1933.

Seidl, Ernst: *Kampfgenossen des Führers*; *Hitler u.d. Männer seiner Bewegung. Ein Bildwerk*. Linz, 1932.

Silber, Paula: *Um das Gewissen der deutschen Frau*. Munich, 1932.

Springenschmid, Karl: *Der Donauraum. Österreich im Kraftfeld der Grossmächte*. Leipzig, 1935.

— *Österreichische Geschichten aus der ersten Zeit des illegalen Kampfes*. Munich, 1935.

Stark, Johannes: *Nationalsozialismus und katholische Kirche. Antwort auf die Kundgebung der dt. Bischhöfe*. Munich, 1931.

Stark-Berlin, G.: 'Moderne polit. Propaganda.' (In: *Schriftenreihe der Reichspropaganda-Abteilung der NSDAP*.) Munich, 1930.

Starcke, Gerhard: *Die Presse der deutschen Arbeiterfront Ihre politische Bedeutung nach der Umgestaltung*. Leipzig, 1936.

Steininger, Anton: *Rebellen für Deutschland*. Graz, Leipzig, and Berlin, 1939.

Stiewe, Willy: *Das Bild als Nachricht. Nachrichtenwert und Technik des Bildes. Ein Beitrag zur Zeitenkunde*. Berlin, 1933.

—- *Das Pressephoto als publizistisches Mittel*. Leipzig, 1936.

Stoltze, Willy: *Der Aufstieg*, 1934–35.

Strasser, Gregor: *Der Letzte Abwehrkampf des Systems*. Munich, 1931.

— 'Hammer und Schwert'. Kampf. (In: *Ausgewählte Reden und. Schriften eines Nationalsozialisten*.) Berlin, 1928.

Strasser, Otto: *Wissen Sie das auch schon? Eine interessante Sammlung von Tatsachen, Worten und Gedanken*. Berlin, 1928.

Strickner, Herbert: *Die geschichtliche Entwicklung der Sportberichterstattung und d. Sportteils im 'Völkischen Beobachter' (1920–36)*. Zeulenroda, 1938.

Sturminger, Alfred: *Politische Propaganda in der Weltgeschichte. Beispiele vom Altertum bis in die Gegenwart*. Salzburg, Vienna, Leipzig, 1938.

Suchenwirth, Richard: *Das tausendjährige Österreich*. Munich, 1938.

Tatsachen und Lügen über Hitler. Munich, 1932.

Thierfelder, Franz: *Sprachpolitik und Rundfunk*. Berlin, 1941.

Todt, Fritz: *Die Strassen Adolf Hitlers*. Berlin and Leipzig, undated.

Um Volk, und Reich. Zehn Jahre Arbeit des Volk und Reich Verlag. Berlin, 1935.

Unger-Winkelried, Emil: 'Brolatariat. Zum 60 jähr. Jubilaeum des Kommunistischen Manifestes' (In: *Kampfschrift*.) Munich, 1932.

Vogel, Wilhelm: *Volk oder Herrenklub? Der Kampf gegen Klassenwahn und Kastenwahn um die dt. Volksgemeinschaft*. Munich, 1932.

Volksgemeinschaft und Völkerfriede. Sitzungsbericht der Berliner Tagung. Zürich, 1935.

Wache, Karl: *Deutscher Geist in Oesterreich. Ein Handbuch des völkischen Lebens der Ostmark.* Munich, 1933.

Wachtmeister: 'Schlesisches Bonzenregister.' (In: *Schlesische Flugblätter.*) Breslau, 1932.

Wagener, Otto: *Grundlagen und Ziele der nat.-soz. Wirtschaftspolitik.*

Wagner, Joseph: *Der Kampf um die Macht im Staate.* Breslau, 1930.

Wahrmund, Adolf: *Gericht über Hugenberg.* Dillingen, 1932.

Waldenhagen, Peter: *Das dritte Reich. Unser zukünftiges Deutschland. Ein Tagebuch aus den Jahren 1926–33.* Leipzig, 1933.

Was will Adolf Hitler. Das Programm der NSDAP. Bautzen, 1930.

Wassenberg, Bernhard: *Deutschland einst und morgen. Ausführliche Idee eines nationalen Sozialisten zur Einrichtung eines dritten Reiches.* Barmen, 1932.

Weberstedt, Hans: *Die polit. Parteien und ihre Sünden.* Munich, 1932.

Weiss, Heinrich L.: Um des Volkes Zukunft. (In: *Deutschlands Erneuerung.*) Munich, 1932.

Welchert, Hans Heinrich: *Österreichs Weg ins Reich 1917–38.* Hamburg, 1938.

Wen sollen wir wählen? Neue Männer ins Rote Haus! Nationalsozialistische Wahlpropaganda. Berlin, 1929.

Welt vor der Entscheidung. Vom Kampf der nationalen Erneuerungsbewegung Europas. Munich, 1938.

'Wirtschaftliches Sofortprogramm der NSDAP. ed. by the Hauptabt. 4 der Reichsorganisationsleitung der NSDAP.' (In: *Kampfschrift.*) Munich, 1932.

Witzmann, Conrad (ed.): *Die Deutsche Feier. Eine Sammlung von Reden, Ansprachen, Gedichten, Sprechchören, Kernsprüchen des Führers.* Leipzig, 1933.

Ziegler, Hans (ed.): *Der Werbeabend. Gedenkfeiern u. Festabend-Veranstaltungen der NSDAP. Programmvorschläge und Anleitungen.* Munich, 1932.

Zwischen gestern und morgen. Wahlflugschrift der NSDAP. Leipzig, 1932.

AUTOBIOGRAPHIES, BIOGRAPHIES, DIARIES

Asch, Walter: *Walter Frank. A study in Nazi Historiography.* Chicago, 1950.

Bade, Wilfred: *Joseph Goebbels.* Lübeck, 1933.

Beneš, Eduard: Memoirs. *From Munich to New War and to New Victory.* London, 1954.

Borresholm, Boris: *Dr. Goebbels. Nach Aufzeichnungen seiner Umgebung.* Berlin, 1949.

Bouhler, Philipp: *Adolf Hitler. Das Werden einer Volksbewegung.* Lübeck, 1943.

Bullock, Alan: *Hitler: a Study in Tyranny.* London, 1959.

Burckhardt, Carl J.: *Meine Danziger Mission, 1937–39.* Munich, 1960.

Chesteron, A. K.: *Portrait of a leader.* London, n.d.

Czech-Jochberg, E.: *Adolf Hitler und sein Stab.* Oldenburg, 1933.

— *Reichskanzler Hitler.* Oldenburg, 1935.

— *Wie Adolf Hitler der Führer wurde.* Leipzig, 1933.

Daim, Willfried: *Der Mann der Hitler die Ideen gab.* Vienna, 1958.

Dodd, Martha: *Through Embassy Eyes.* New York, 1939.

Doenitz, Karl: *Zehn Jahre Zwanzig Tage.* Bonn, 1958.

Drozdzynski, Aleksander and Jaborowski, Jan: *Theodor Oberländer. A Study in German East Policies.* Poznan, 1960.

Ebermayer, Erich and Roos, Hans: *Gefährtin des Teufels, Leben und Tod der Magda Goebbels.* Hamburg, 1952.

Fechner, Max: *Wie konnte es geschehen? Auszüege aus den Tagbüchern und Bekenntnissen eines Kriegsverbrechers.* Berlin, 1946.

Feierabend, Ladislav Karel: *Ve vládách druhé Republiky* (In the government of the Second Republic.) New York, 1961.

Frank, Hans: *Im Angesicht des Galgens. Deutung Hitlers und seiner Zeit auf Grund eigener Erlebnisse und Erkenntnisse. Geschrieben im Nürnberger Justizgefängnis.* Munich, 1953.

Frischauer, Willi: *Himmler, The evil genius of the Third Reich.* London, 1953.

Fritsche, Hans: *Hier spricht Hans Fritsche.* Zürich, 1948.

The Goebbels Diaries. Translated and edited by Louis P.Lochner. London, 1948.

— *Vom Kaiserhof zur Reichskanzlei.* Berlin, 1934.

Greiner, Josef: *Das Ende des Hitler Mythos.* Vienna, 1947.

Haas, Werner: *Die nationalen Erneurungsbewegungen in Wort und Bild.* Berlin, 1936.

Hagen, Louis: *Evil Genius.* The story of Joseph Goebbels by E. Ebermayer and H. Meissner. (Based on the Original German *Gefährtin des Teufels.*) London, 1953.

Hanfstaengel, Putzi: *Hitler, The Missing Years.* London, 1957.

Hart, F.Th.: *Alfred Rosenberg, Der Mann und sein Werk.* Munich, 1939.

Heiber, Helmut: *Adolf Hitler, a short biography.* London, 1961.

– (ed.): *Joseph Goebbels. Das Tagebuch von J. Goebbels mit weiteren Dokumenten.* Stuttgart, 1961.

—*Goebbels.* Berlin, 1962.

Heiden, Konrad: *Der Führer. Hitler's rise to power.* London, 1944.

Hess, Rudolf: *Der Stellvertreter des Führers.* Berlin, 1933.

Heydrich, Reinhard: *Oh the reign of terror in Bohemia and Moravia under the régime of Reinhard Hedyrich.* Ed. by Czechoslovak Ministry of Foreign Affairs Department of Information, London, undated.

Heydrich, Reinhard: *7/3/04–4/6/42.* Ed. by Reichssicherheitshauptamt, Berlin, 1942.

Hierl, Konstantin: *Im Dienst für Deutschland 1918–45.* Heidelberg, 1954.

Hinze, Kurt: 'Dr. Joseph Goebbels.' (In: *Jungdeutschland Bücherei.*) Donauwört, 1934.

Hoffmann, Heinrich: *Hitler was my Friend.* London, 1955.

Hombourger, René: *Goebbels Chef de Publicité du IIIéme Reich.* Paris, 1939.

Hunold, Hans: *Adolf Hitler und seine Männer.* Berlin, 1933.

Johst, Hanns: *Fritz Todt. Requiem.* Munich, 1943.

Jungnickel, Max: 'Goebbels.' (In: *Männer und Mächte.*) Leipzig, 1933.

Kersten, Felix: *The Kersten Memoirs, 1940–45.* London, 1956.

Knesebeck-Fischer, Alfred: *Dr. Joseph Goebbels. Im Spiegel von Freund und Feind. Sein Werdegang.* Berlin, 1933.

Krause, Willi: *Reichsminister Dr. Goebbels.* Berlin, 1933.

Krebs, Albert: *Tendenzen und Gestalten der NSDAP Erinnerungen an die Frühzeit der Partei.* Stuttgart, 1959.

Kriesi, Hans: *Betrachtungen zu Goebbels Tagebüchern.* Frauenfeld, 1949.

Kuegelgen, Carlo von: Dr. Joseph Goebbels, Ein Charakterbild'. (In: *Die Fahne hoch!*) Berlin, 1934.

Langoth, Franz: *Kampf um Österreich. Erinnerungen eines Politikers.* Wels, 1951.

Leasor, James: *Rudolf Hess, The Uninvited Envoy.* London, 1962.

Lippert, Julius: *Im Strom der Zeit. Erlebnisse und Eindrücke.* Berlin, 1942.

— *Lächle und verbirg die Tränen. Erlebnisse und Bemerkungen eines deutschen 'Kriegsverbrechers'.* Leoni am Starnberger See. 1955.

Manvell, Roger and Fraenkel, Heinrich: *Joseph Goebbels.* London, 1960.

Mitford, Jessica: *Hons and Rebels.* London, 1960.

Moeller, Eberhard Wolfgang: *Der Führer.* Munich, 1938.

Muehlen, Norbert: *Der Zauberer. Leben und Anleihen des Dr. Hjalmar Horace Greeley Schacht.* Zürich, 1938.

Oven, Wielfried von: *Mit Goebbels bis zum Ende.* Buenos Aires, 1949–1950.

Papen, Franz von: *Memoirs.* London, 1952.

— *Der Wahrheit eine Gasse.* Munich, 1962.

Pick, F. W.: *The Art of Dr. Goebbels.* London, 1942.

Piotrowski, Stanislaw: *Hans Frank's Diary.* Warsaw, 1961.

Price, Ward: *I Know These Dictators.* London, 1937.

Rauschning, Hermann: *Hitler Speaks.* London, 1939.

Reed, Douglas: *The Prisoner of Ottawa: Otto Strasser.* London, 1953.

Renner, Karl, *An der Wende Zweier Zeiten. Lebenserinnerungen* Vienna, 1946.

Ribbentrop, Joachim von: *The Ribbentrop Memoirs.* London, 1954.

— *Zwischen London und Moskau. Erinnerungen und letzte Aufzeichnungen.* Leoni am Starnberger See. 1953.

Riedrich, Otto: 'Dr. Joseph Goebbels'. (In: *Deutsche Führer— Deutsche Taten.*) Frankfurt, 1933.

Riess, Curt: *Joseph Goebbels, a biography.* New York, 1948; Baden-Baden, 1950.

Rosenberg, Alfred: *Das politische Tagebuch.*

— *Memoirs of Alfred Rosenberg.* edited by Lang, S. & Schenk, E. V. New York, 1949.

— Letzte Aufzeichnungen. *Ideale und Idole der Nat.-soz. Revolution.* Göttingen, 1955.

Schacht, Hjalmar: *76 Jahre meines Lebens.* Bad Woerishofen, 1953.

— *Account Settled.* London, 1949.

— *Abrechnung mit Hitler.* Berlin and Frankfurt, 1949.

Schellenberg, Walter: *Memoirs.* London, 1959.

Schirach, Henriette von: *Der Preis der Herrlichkeit.* Wiesbaden, 1956.

Schmidt, Peter: *Josef Grohé. Zwanzig Jahre Soldat Adolf Hitlers. Zehn Jahre Gauleiter. Ein Buch von Kampf und Treue.* Cologne, 1941.

Schuschnigg, Kurt von: *Dreimal Österreich.* Vienna, 1937.

Seeler, Hans O.: Goebbels. (In: *Die Reihe der deutschen Führer.*) Berlin, 1933.

Seidel, Erich: *Dr. Goebbels. Von einem SA-Mann geschrieben.* Leipzig, 1933.

Semmler, Rudolf: *Goebbels, the man next to Hitler.* London, 1947.

Seraphim, Hans Günther: *Das politische Tagebuch Alfred Rosenbergs.* Göttingen, 1956.

Stephan, Werner: *Joseph Goebbels—Dämon einer Diktatur.* Stuttgart, 1949.

Strasser, Otto: *Hitler and I.* London, 1940.

— and Stern, Michael: *Flight from Terror.* New York, 1943.

BIBLIOGRAPHY

Vansittart, Lord: *The Mist Procession*. London, 1958.
Vaeth, Lore: *Johann von Leers. Ein Beispiel von pseudowissenschaftlicher Judenhetze.* Hamburg, 1960.
Viator: *Goebbels—Wer ist das?* Berlin, 1932.
Wahl, Karl: '. . . *es ist das deutsche Herz'. Erlebnisse und Erkenntnisse eines ehemaligen Gauleiters.* Augsburg, 1954.
Wenzel, Fritz R.: *Walter Darre und seine Mitkämpfer. Der Sieg von Blut und Boden.* Berlin, 1934.
Wighton, Charles: *Heydrich, Hitler's most evil henchman.* London, 1962.
Wulf, Josef: *Heinrich Himmler. Eine biographische Studie.* Berlin, 1960.

SECONDARY WORKS

Ball, Margaret M.: *Post-war German–Austrian Relations. The 'Anschluss' movement. 1918–36.* Stanford, 1937.
Bartlett, F. C.: *Political Propaganda.* Cambridge, 1940.
Bausch, Hans: *Der Rundfunk im politischen Kräftespiel der Weimarer Republik 1923–33.* Tübingen, 1956.
Beck, Joseph: *Dernier rapport Polonaise 1926–39.* Brussels, 1951.
Benedikt, Heinrich (ed.): *Geschichte der Republik Österreich.* Vienna, 1954.
Bierschenk, Theodor: *Die deutsche Volksgruppe in Polen 1934–39.* Kitzingen, 1954.
Bilek, B.: *Fifth Column at Work.* London, 1945.
Birch, Lionel: *Why they joined the Fascists.* London, n.d.
Bischoff, Ralph F.: *Nazi conquest through German culture.* Harvard, 1942.
Blake, Leonard: *Hitler's last year of power.* London, 1939.
Bodenstedt, Adolf: *'Sonderbericht der dt. Wochenschau' v. Überfall auf Jugoslawien und Griechenland. Ein Beispiel nat.-soz. Filmpropaganda im 2. Weltkrieg.* Hamburg, 1958.
Bohmann, Alfred: *Das Sudetendeutschtum in Zahlen.* Munich, 1959.
Bondy, Louis W.: *Racketeers of hatred. Julius Streicher and the Jew-Baiters' International.* London, 1946.
Braunthal, Julius: *The Tragedy of Austria.* London, 1948.
Breyer, Richard: *Das Deutsche Reich und Polen, 1932–37.* Würzburg, 1955.
British Union of Fascists and National Socialists, *Constitution and Regulations.* London, 1936.
Brook-Shepherd, Gordon: *Dollfuss.* London, 1961.
The Brown Network (Anon.): The Activities of the Nazis in Foreign Countries. New York, 1936.

203

Buttinger, Josef: *Am Beispiel Österreichs. Ein geschichtlicher Beitrag zur Krise der sozialistischen Bewegung.* Cologne, 1953.

Childs, Harwood Lawrence: *Propaganda by Short Wave.* Princeton, 1942.

— *Propaganda and Dictatorship.* Princeton, 1936.

Clark, R. T.: *The Fall of the German Republic.* London, 1935.

Cross, Colin: *The Fascists in Britain.* London, 1961.

Driencourt, Jacques: *La propaganda nouvelle force politique.* Paris, 1950.

Ducloux, Louis: *From Blackmail to Treason. Political Crime and Corruption in France 1920–40.* London, 1958.

Edwards, Violet: *Group Leaders Guide to Propaganda Analysis.* New York, 1938.

Eichstädt, Ulrich: *Von Dollfuss zu Hitler. Geschichte des Anschlusses Oesterreichs 1933–1938.* Wiesbaden, 1955.

Ettlinger, Harold: *The Axis on the Air.* Indianapolis and New York, 1943.

Fabricant, Noah D.: *13 Famous Patients.* New York, 1960.

Fellner, Anton: *Wie es kommen sollte... Dokumentarische Belege für den Verrat Schuschniggs.* Linz, 1938.

Franzel, Emil: *Sudetendeutsche Geschichte. Eine volkstümliche Darstellung.* Augsburg, 1958.

Frisch, Sepp: *Die Saar blieb deutsch. Ein Rückblick 1680–1955.* 1956.

Frischauer, Willi: *Twilight in Vienna.* London, 1938.

Fuchs, Martin: *A Pact with Hitler. The Death of Austria.* London, 1939.

Funder, Friedrich: *Als Österreich den Sturm bestand. Aus der erfsen in die zweite Republik.* Vienna and Munich, 1957.

Garratt, Geoffrey T.: *The Shadow of the Swastika.* London, 1938.

Gedye, G. E. R.: *Fallen Bastions. The Central European Tragedy.* London, 1939.

Golding, Claud: *From Versailles to Danzig.* London, 1940.

Gordon, Matthew: *News is a weapon.* New York, 1942.

Goette, Karl Heinz: *Die Propaganda der Glaubensbewegung 'Deutsche Christen' und ihre Beurteilung in der dt. Tagespresse.* Münster, 1957.

Gregory, J. D.: *Dollfuss and His Time.* London, 1935.

Hagemann, Walter: *Publizistik im Dritten Reich. Ein Beitrag zur Methodik der Massenführung.* Hamburg, 1948.

Hájek, Miloš: *Od Mnichova k 15. březnu.* Prague, 1959.

Hargrave, John: *Words win Wars.* London, 1940.

Hartmann, Mitzi: *Austria still lives.* London, 1938.

Heiden, Konrad: *Geschichte des Nationalsozialismus. Die Karriere der Idee.* Berlin, 1932.

— *Adolf Hitler,* vol. 2. Zürich, 1937.

Heike, Otto: *Das Deutschtum in Polen, 1918–39*. Bonn, 1955.

Hepp, Fred: *Der geistige Widerstand im Kulturteil der 'Frankfurter Zeitung' gegen die Diktatur des 'Totalen Staates'*. Augsburg, 1949.

Hirsch, Helmut: *Die Saar in Versailles. Die Saarfrage auf der Friedenskonferenz 1919*. Bonn, 1952.

— *Die Saar von Genf. Die Saarfrage während des Völkerbundregimes von 1920–35*. Bonn, 1954.

Ingrim, Robert: *Der Griff nach Österreich*. Zürich, 1938.

'Les Instructions Secretes de la Propagande Allemande'. Ed. by *Le Petit Parisien*. Paris, undated.

Iwo, Jack: *Goebbels erobert die Welt*. Paris, 1936.

Jaksch, Wenzel: *Europas Weg nach Potsdam, Schuld und Schicksal im Donauraum*. Stuttgart, 1958.

— *Rhum und Tragik der Sudetendeutschen Sozialdemokratie*. Malmö, 1946.

— *Sudeten Labour and the Sudeten Problem; A report to International Labour*. London, 1945.

Jedlicka, Ludwig: *Ein Heer im Schatten der Parteien. Die militärpolitische Lage Österreichs 1918–38*. Graz and Cologne, 1955.

Jenks, William A.: *Vienna and the Young Hitler*. New York, 1960.

Jong, Louis de: *The German Fifth Column in the Second World War*. London, 1956.

Kleinwächter, Friedrich F. G.; *Der Deutschösterreichische Mensch und der Anschluss*. Vienna, 1926.

Klepetar, Harry: *Seit 1918.... Eine Geschichte der Tschechoslowakischen Republik*. Moravská Ostrava, 1937.

Kluke, Paul: 'Nationalsozialistische Volkstumspolitik in Elsass-Lothringen, 1940–45'. (In: *Festgabe für Hans Herzfeld*.) Berlin, 1958.

Kochan, Lionel: *Pogrom, November 10th, 1938*. London, 1957.

Koerner, Ralf Richard: *So haben sie es damals gemacht.... Die Propagandavorbereitungen zum Österreichanschluss durch das Hitlerregime 1933–38*. Vienna 1958.

Koszyk, Kurt: *Des Ende des Rechtsstaates 1933–34 und die dt. Presse*. Düsseldorf, 1960.

Kracauer, Siegfried: *From Caligari to Hitler*. Princeton, 1947.

Kreibisch, Karl: *Des Volkes Sache ist nicht Henleins Sache. Das Aussiger Programm der SdP und die Kommunisten*. Prague, 1937.

Kreisler, Fritz: *Wer hat Dollfuss ermordet?* Bodenbach, 1934.

Kriss, Ernst and Speier, Hans: *German Radio Propaganda. Report on home broadcasts during the war*. London, 1944.

Kun, Bela: *Die Februarkämpfe in Oesterreich und ihre Lehren*. Moscow and Leningrad, 1934.

Kunschak, Leopold: *Österreich 1919–34*. Vienna, 1934.

Lambert, Margaret: *The Saar*. London, 1934.

Lavie, Harold and Wechsler, James: *War propaganda and the U.S.* New Haven, 1940.

Lean, Tangye: *Voices in the Darkness. The story of the European Radio War*. London, 1943.

Leubuscher, Walter: *Der grosse Irrtum. Ein Beitrag zur Geschichte der nat. soz. Bewegung in Oesterreich*. Vienna, 1937.

Lennhoff, Eugen: *Agents of Hell*. London.

— *Last Five Hours of Austria*. London, 1938.

— *Thousand and one Nazi Lies*. London.

Lisický, K.: *Československà cesta do Mnichova*. London, 1956.

Ludwig, Eduard: *Österreichsche Sendung im Donauraum. Die letzten Dezennien Österreichscher Innen–und Aussenpolitik*. Vienna, 1954.

Macdonald, Mary: *The Republic of Austria 1918–34. A Study in the Failure of Democratic Government*. London, 1946.

Mackenzie, J. A.: *Propaganda Boom*. London, 1938.

Maetzke, Ernst-Otto: *Die Deutsche-Schweizerische Presse zu einigen Problemen des zweiten Weltkrieges*. Tübingen, 1955.

Margolin, Leo, J.: *Paper Bullets, a Brief Story of Psychological Warfare in World War II*. New York, 1946.

Martin, Kingsley: *Fascism, Democracy and the Press*. London, 1938.

Mayer, Hans: *Frankreich zwischen den Weltkriegen*. Frankfurt, 1948.

Meerloo, A. M.: *Total War and Human Mind. A psychologist's experiences in occupied Holland*. London, 1944.

Micaud, Charles: *The French Right and Nazi Germany 1933–39. A study of public opinion*. Durham, North Carolina, 1943.

Mirbt, Karl Wolfgang: *Methoden publizistischen Widerstands im Dritten Reich*. Berlin, 1958.

Mullally, Frederic: *Fascism inside England*. London, 1946.

Mueller-Sturmheim, E.: *99.7%. A Plebiscite Under Nazi Rule*. London, 1942.

Münch, Hermann: *Bömische Tragödie. Das Schicksal Mitteleuropas im Lichte der tschechischen Frage*. Braunschweig, 1949.

Münzenberg, Willi: *Propaganda als Waffe*. Paris, 1937.

Murphy, Raymond E.: *National Socialism, Basic Principles. Their application by the party's Foreign Office and the use of Germans abroad for Nazi Aims*. Washington, 1943.

Nationale Frage und Österreichs Kampf um seine Unabhängigkeit.
Paris, 1939.

Neusüss-Hunkel: *Die SS.* Hannover, 1956.

Niedermeyer, Albert: *Wahn, Wissenschaft und Wahrheit. Lebenserinnerungen eines Arztes.* Innsbruck, 1956.

Nobecourt, R. G.: *Les secrets de la propagande en France occupée.*
Paris, 1962.

Österreich unter dem Reichskommissar. Bilanz eines Jahres Fremdherrschaft. Paris, 1939.

Pezet, Ernest: *Fin de l'Autriche—Fin d'une Europe.* Paris, 1938.

Pitt-Rivers, George: *The Czech Conspiracy—a phase in the World War plot.* London, 1938.

Pleyer, Wilhelm: *Europas unbekannte Mitte. Ein politisches Lesebuch.*
Munich and Stuttgart, 1957.

Pohle, Heinz: *Der Rundfunk als Instrument der Politik. Zur Geschichte des dt. Rundfunks 1923–38.* Hamburg, 1955.

Pozorny, Reinhard: *Wir suchten die Freiheit. Weg einer Volksgruppe.*
Munich, 1959.

Prago, Ladislas (ed.): *German psychological warfare. Survey and Bibliography.* New York, 1941.

Preidel, Helmut: *Die Deutschen in Böhmen und Mähren.* Ein historischer Rückblick, Gräfelingen bei Munich, 1952.

The Press in Authoritarian Countries. Ed. by the International Press Institute. Zürich, 1959.

Presse in Fesseln. Eine Schilderung des NS-Pressetrusts. Gemeinschaftsarbeit des Verlages auf Grund authentischen Materials. Berlin, 1947.

Propaganda Analysis: Ed. by the Institute for Propaganda Analysis. New York, 1938–40.

Quinn, Edward: *Mission of Austria.* London, 1938.

Radl, Emanuel: *Der Kampf zwischen Tschechen und Deutschen.*
Reichenberg, 1928.

Raschhofer, Hermann: *Die Sudetenfrage. Ihre völkerreichtliche Entwicklung vom ersten Weltkrieg bis zur Gegenwart.* Munich, 1953.

Rauschning, Hermann: *Die Revolution des Nihilismus.* Zürich, 1938.

Renkel, Rudolf: *Staat und Nation.* Bonn, 1957.

Renner, Karl: *An der Wende Zweier Zeiten. Lebenserinnerungen.*
Vienna, 1946.

Rieser, Max: *Österreichs Sterbeweg.* Vienna, 1953.

Rogerson, Sidney: *Propaganda in the next war.* London, 1938.

Roennefarth, Helmuth K. G.: *Die Sudetenkrise in der internationalen Politik.* Wiesbaden, 1961.

Rudlin, W. A.: *The Growth of Fascism in Great Britain*. London, 1935.

Rudolf, Karl: *Aufbau im Widerstand. Ein Seelsorgebericht aus Österreich 1938–45.* Salzburg, 1947.

Ruehl, Manfred: *Der Stürmer und seine Herausgeber.* Nürnberg, 1960.

Scanlan, Ross: 'The Nazi Rhetorician.' (In: *Quarterly Journal of Speech*.) New York, 1951.

Schaefer, Wolfgang: *NSDAP*. Hanover, 1956.

Schmeer, Karlheinz: *Die Regie des öffentlichen Lebens im Dritten Reich*. Munich, 1956.

Schneidmadl, Heinrich: *Grüner Weg in die braune Hölle*. Vienna, 1946.

Schumann, Wolfgang: *Oberschlesien, 1918–19, Vom gemeinsamen Kampf deutscher und polnischer Arbeiter*. Berlin (East), 1961.

Schuschnigg, Kurt von: *Austria must remain Austria*. n.p. 1938.

— *Austrian Requiem*. New York, 1946.

— *Farewell Austria*. London, 1938.

Seabury, Paul: *Wilhelmstrasse*. University of California Press, 1954.

Searchinger, C.: *Voice of Europe*. London, 1938.

Serant, Paul: *Le Romantism Fascist*. Paris, 1959.

Servaes, Franz: *Grüsse an Wien*. Vienna, 1948.

Shepherd, Gordon: *The Austrian Odyssey*. London, 1957.

Sington, Derrick and Weidenfeld, Arthur: *The Goebbels Experiment. A Study of the Nazi Propaganda Machine*. London, 1942.

Skalnik, Kurt: *Der Mann zwischen den Zeiten: Karl Lueger*, Vienna and Munich, 1954.

Soják, Vladimir: *O Československé zahraniční politice 1918–39*. Prague, 1956.

Starhemberg, Ernst Rüdiger: *Between Hitler and Mussolini*. New York, 1942.

Stránský, Jaroslav: *K otázce česko-německé*. London, 1955.

Taylor, A. J. P.: *The Origins of the Second World War*. London, 1961.

Teeling, William: *Youth on the Rhine. The Problem of the Saar*. London, 1934.

Turnwald, Wilhelm K.: *Renascence or Decline of Central Europe. The Sudeten German–Czech problem*. Munich, 1954.

Veale, F. J. P.: *Der Barbarei entgegen*. Hamburg, 1954.

Veuillot, François: *La Rocque et son parti. Comme je les ai vus*. Paris, 1938.

Wandruszka, C. F. A.: *Geschichte einer Zeitung. Das Schicksal der 'Presse' und der 'Neuen Freien Presse' von 1948 zur Zweiten Republik*. Vienna, 1958.

BIBLIOGRAPHY

Webster, Nesta H.: *Germany and England*. London, 1938.
Weinberg, G. L.: *Germany and the Soviet Union*. Leiden, 1954.
Wieser, Georg: *Ein Staat Stirbt. Oesterreich 1934–38*. Paris, 1938.
Weizsäcker, Ernst von: *Erinnerungen*. Munich, 1950.
West, Rebecca: *The Meaning of Treason*. New York, 1947.
White, Amber Blanco: *The new Propaganda*. London, 1939.
Williams, Chester S.: *Ways of Dictatorship*. Evanston, Illinois. 1941.
Wiskemann, Elizabeth: *Czechs and Germans*. Oxford, 1938.
— *The Rome–Berlin Axis*. Oxford, 1949.
Zeder, Heinrich: *Judas sucht seinen Bruder. Schicksale aus dem Freiheitskampf Österreichs*. Vienna, 1948.
Zeman, Z. A. B.: *The Break-up of the Habsburg Empire 1914–18. A Study in National and Social Revolution*. London, 1961.
Zernatto, Guido: *Die Wahrheit über Österreich*. New York, Toronto, 1938.
Zoellner, Erich: *Geschichte Österreichs von den Anfängen bis zur Gegenwart*. Vienna, 1962.

NEWSPAPERS AND PERIODICALS

Die Aktion: Kampfblatt für das Neue Europa (Monthly).
Der Angriff: Tageszeitung der Deutschen Arbeiterfront (Daily).
Der Aufbau: Alleiniges amtliches Organ des Hauptamtes für Handwerk und Handel der NSDAP und der DAF (Fortnightly). First Year of Publication, 1933.
Der Auslandsdeutsche: Mitteilungen des dt. Auslandinstituts (Monthly).
Der Berliner Lokalanzeiger: (Daily), owned by Hugenberg.
Die Bewegung: (Weekly).
Der Blitz: Kampfblatt der deutschen Aktion (Weekly).
Böhmen und Mähren: Blatt des Reichsprotektors in Böhmen und Mähren (Monthly) First Year of Publication, 1940.
Die Brennessel: Satyrische Zeitschrift des NSDAP (Weekly).
Deutsche Allgemeine Zeitung: (Daily),
Deutsche Forschung Im Osten: Mitteilungen des Instituts für Deutsche Ostarbeit (Quarterly).
Deutsche Rundschau: (Monthly).
Der Deutsche Weg: Kampfblatt der Deutschen in Polen (Weekly).
Deutsches Wollen: Zeitschrift der Auslandsorganisation der NSDAP (Monthly).
Erzieher im Braunhemd: Gaublatt des N.S. Lehrerbundes (Monthly).
Handbuch des deutschen Rundfunks: (Annual publication).

Die Hitlerjugend: (Weekly).

Der Illustrierte Beobachter: First Year of Publication, 1926 (Weekly).

Die Junge Welt: Reichszeitschrift der Hitlerjugend (Monthly).

NS Landpost: (First Year of Publication, 1930).

Der SA Mann: (Weekly).

Monatshefte der Auswärtigen Politik: (Monthly).

Nationalsozialistische Monatshefte: First Year of Publication, 1930. (Monthly).

Rasse: Monatsheft der Nordischen Bewegung. First Year of Publication, 1934. (Monthly).

NS Rechtsspiegel: Organ des Reichsrechtsamtes der NSDAP.

Das Reich: (Weekly).

Der Reichswart: (Weekly).

Das Schwarze Korps: Organ der Reichsführung SS (Weekly).

Der Stürmer: (Weekly). First Year of Publication, 1923.

Der Tag: (Daily), owned by Hugenberg.

Unser Wille und Weg: Monatsbläetter der Reichspropagandaleitung der NSDAP (Monthly).

Volk und Reich: Politische Monatszeitschrift (Monthly).

Völkischer Beobachter: Kampfblatt der nationalsozialistischen Bewegung Grossdeutschlands (Daily).

Völkische Kultur: Monatszeitschrift für die gesamte geistige Bewegung des neuen Deutschlands (Monthly).

Der Volksdeutsche: Organ des Volksbundes für das Deutschtum im Ausland.

Die Woche: (Weekly), owned by Hugenberg.

Die Zeit: Amtliche Tageszeitung der NSDAP Sudetenlandes (Daily).

INDEX

Abroad, propaganda: *see* Foreign propaganda
'Acceptance' theme in propaganda, 55–56, 142–9
Action Committee . . . , 12
'Active propaganda', 39, 42
Africa, *AO* department, 70; broadcasts, 112, 113; *Grossraum* projects, 164; North, 175
Agricultural policy, 30–31
Aircraft, use for electioneering purposes, 35
Air-force, daily reports, 160–1
Air-raids on Germany, 161, 175, 176
Air space, broadcasting and sovereignty, 104; violation by leaflet raids, 130
Aktion, Die, 89
Albrecht, 167
Allgemeiner Deutscher Schulverein, 63
Alliance Raciste Universelle, 73
'Allied' countries, propaganda in, 162, 164; German fear of propaganda from, 176
Alpenwacht, Die, 125
Altkampfer (old Nazis), 3
Altona, 33, 70
Amann, Max, 10, 44, 46, 47, 51
America, Central, broadcasts to, 111–13
America, North, Germans in, 62, 63, 67, 70
America, South, broadcasts to, 111–13; Germans in, 62, 63, 67, 70; Nazi organization, 67, 69
Anglo-German Fellowship, 151–3
Anglo-German Review, 152
Angriff, Der, 23, 25–26
Anonymous letters produced by *Promi*, 161

Anti-Communist propaganda: *see under* Communism
Antifaschistischer Kampfbund, 21
Antikomintern, 75, 87–92
Antisemitism and antisemitic propaganda (*see also* Jews; *and* under countries), 7, 72, 77–82, 102, 184
Antikomintern department for action, 88
British attitude to, 78–80
Congress, 73
Films, 49
Hitler and, 77–78
'Idiot's Socialism', 82
Leading party antisemite (Streicher), 60
Ministry section, 42
Press treatment of, 25
Unofficial organizations, 72–74
Value for propaganda, 77–79, 82, 83
AO (Auslandsorganisation): *see* Foreign Organization.
Arbeitertum, Das, 31
Architecture, 39
Armament parity, 135
Army, publicity campaign on behalf, 156, 159, 186; daily reports, 160
Arndt, Ernst Moritz, 62
Art, party programme, 22; protection of works of art, 42
Arts, creative, 42
Aryans, 73, 74, 81
Asia, broadcasts, 112, 113; frontiers with Europe, 166–7
Atrocities propaganda, 89–90
Attachés abroad for propaganda, 57
Audience research, 39, 183
Auflkärungsausschuss, 149
Auslandsdeutsche: *see* German minorities abroad

15

211

Auslandsorganisation: see Foreign Organization
Aussenpolitisches Amt: see Foreign Political Office
Australia, *AO* department, 70; broadcasts, 112, 113
Austria:
   Anschluss, 118, 123, 132; Hitler-Schuschnigg meeting, 137; annexation of Austria to the Reich (1938), 138–41, 154, 185
   Antisemitism, 122, 137
   AO department, 70
   Broadcasting, 106, 116–17, 124, 128–31, 154; Nazis force entry to studios, 131
   Chancellor murdered (1934), 131
   Christian-Socialists, 121, 123
   Civil War (February 1934), 130, 132
   Constitution suspended (1933), 123
   Customs Union with Germany, proposed, 121
   Elections (1930), 121; (1932), 121, 123
   Germans in, 62–65, 105, 118–19, 154; party: see National Socialists, below
   Intelligence network set up by Nazis, 124
   Italy, relations with, 127, 132
   'National' parties, 123
   National Socialists, early organizations, 119–20; party incorporated into Reich organization, 120; progress, 120–22; propaganda campaigns, 122–5; measures against, 123; party banned (1933), 106, 123–4; underground organization, 124–6, 130–1; Reich functionaries expelled, 125–6; headquarters transferred to Germany, 126; abortive *putsch* (July 1934), 8, 131–6, 141, 143, 185; *Landesleitung* disbanded, 134; recovery of movement, 136–7; plot for another *coup d'état*, 137, 138; *Anschluss* (1938) 138–9 *(and see Anschluss,* above
   'Ostmark', 13
   Peasants, 136
   Press, newspapers printed in Germany made available, 125, 136; use for propaganda, 126–8, 132–4, 136, 139
   Propaganda campaigns, 122–34, 184; contraband material from Germany, 125; leaflet raids, 130; end of first phase, 131–2; second phase after 1934 *putsch,* 132–7; before and during the *Anschluss,* 138–41, 154
   Refugees in Germany, 130–1
   SA and *SS* units, 15, 122, 124, 126, 130–1, 136
   Social Democrats, 121–3, 130
   Treaty with Germany (1936), 135, 138
Austrian Legion, 130–1, 133
Auswärtiges Amt: see Foreign Ministry
Axis Powers, 81

Baltic States, 84, 100, 170
Bank deposits, citizens urged to withdraw, 124
'Barbarossa' operation, 165
Barmat, 23
Barrington-Ward, R. M., 150
Bartlett, Vernon, 149
Bauer, Captain Hans, 35
Bausch, Hans, cited, 36
Bavaria:
   Communists, 83
   Nazis, ban on party lifted (1925), 9; Hitler forbidden to make speeches, 12; ban lifted, 13; main strength concentrated in, 19; press, 24; activities, 26; party organization, 29
   Ostmark, 19, 29
   People's Party, 21
   Soviet Republic (1919), 3
Bayer, Ernst, cited, 17, 20
Bayernwacht, 21
Bayrische Ostmark, 19, 29
Beaverbrook, Lord, 5
Beiträge zur Vorgeschichte und Geschichte der Julirevolte, cited, 120, 122, 124–5
Benedikt, Heinrich, cited, 120
Beneš, Eduard, 155
Berger, Erich, 123
Berlin:
   Gauleiter, Goebbels appointed, 26–29

Berlin—*continued*
    Nazis, party banned (1927), 13,
    19; party members march to
    Bavaria, 14; *SA* tactics, 19–20;
    party organizations, 29
    Pharus-Saele battle (1927), 19, 26–
    28
    Press, 23
Berliner Arbeiterzeitung, 23
Berliner Börsen-Zeitung, 90
Berliner Lokalanzeiger, 29
Berndt, Alfred-Ingemar, cited, 164
Bertrand, Louis, 74
Bessarabia, 100
Biegler (Austrian Nazi), 126
Binnendeutsche, 64
Bischoff, R. F., cited, 63, 64
Bismarck, Prince, 151, 153
Böckmann, Kurt, 112
Bodyguard for Hitler, 18
Bohemian Germans, 119–20
Bohle, Ernst-Wilhelm, 67–72
Bolshevism, 60, 79, 84–86, 90–92, 101
    'British Bolshevik conspiracy', 165
    Campaign against: *see* Communism:
    Anti-Communist propaganda
    Germany bulwark against, 149, 162
    Hitler's views on, 76, 84–86
    'Jew-Bolshevik conspiracy', 85,
    93–94, 100, 166, 170, 185
    Russian Bolsheviks: *see under*
    Russia
    Unity against Bolshevism cam-
    paign, 165–7, 169
Bombes plastiques, 125
Bondy, L. W., cited, 73
Bormann, Martin, 162, 178
Bouhler, Philipp, cited, 17
Bräutigam, Otto, cited, 171
Bramstead, C., cited, 25
Braunschweig, 12
Brazil, broadcasts, 113, 115
Britain: *see* Great Britain
British Legion, 61–62
British Union of Fascists, 152–3
Broadcasting (*see also* under coun-
    tries):
    Antikomintern activities, 91–92
    Community listening, 108
    Compulsory listening, 52
    Control, by Government, 28, 36;
    by Nazis, 41, 47, 50–52, 182–3

Disturbances at functions being
    broadcast, 36
Example of script, 91–92
Foreign countries, from: German
    ban on listening, 176; monitoring
    service, 177; listening becomes
    accepted habit, 177–8
Foreign countries, to: 104–17;
    table, 113
Germans abroad, to, 105–9, 112, 114
Hitler's speeches, 51
Hugenberg's efforts to gain control,
    28
Language courses, 110, 112, 117
Ministry department, 42, 43, 105,
    175, 182–3
Party propaganda department sec-
    tion, 39, 42, 43
Personal contact technique, 114–15
Plays, 129
Political broadcasts, 51; controller
    appointed, 175
Propaganda medium, as, 7, 104,
    108–9
Receiving sets, cheap (*Volksemp-
    fänger*), 51–52, 108, 176, 177
Short-wave system, 111–17
Stations, new controllers, 162
Unavailable to Nazis during rise to
    power, 28, 35–36; facilities gran-
    ted, 50; control gained, 41, 50
War, during, 175–8
Zoning, 112, 113
Brown House, Munich, 13
Brown Network, The, cited, 61
Brüning, Heinrich, 33, 36
Bryant, Arthur, cited, 148
Bukovina, 100
Bullock, Alan, cited, 11
Bülow, Bernhard von, 56, 133
Bürckel, Josef, 106

Capitalism, Western, 85
Carinthia, 65
Carroll, C. E., 152
Casement, Sir Roger, 76
Caspar, C., cited, 84
Catholics, 4
Celebrations (State), regulation, 42;
    organization, 43
Cell-leader, 39
Censorship, 45, 159

Centralization of all propaganda activities, 42–43
Christian-Socialists, 4
Christoph, Friedrich, 62
Churchill, W. S., 161, 173
Cinema: see Films
Civil liberties, 40
Clark, R. T., cited, 21
Coburg, Nazi march (1922), 17, 60
Codreanu, Corneliu, 81
Coercion, use of, 8, 40, 52
Colonies, Bolshevization of Colonial Empire, 95; former German, 70, 71
Comintern, 91, 94, 101, 152; German–Japanese Anti-Comintern Pact, 95, 98
Commando tactics, 20, 157
Communism:
    Anti-Christian basis, 146
    Anti-Communist propaganda, 83–103, 182, 184; international campaign, 87–96, 102; achievement, 102–3; during war, 168
    German Communist Party (KPD), 16, 18, 20–21, 26–27, 36, 86–87
    Nazi attitude to, 36, 74, 153
    Parties outside Soviet Union, Goebbels's attack on, 94
    Press banned in Germany, 44, 46
    Reichstag fire plot, and, 40–41
    Threat to Germany exaggerated by Nazis, 86–87, 89–90, 102, 142–3
Communist International, 74, 88
Concentration camps, 40, 52, 147
Condor Legion, 97
Congregatio de Propaganda Fide, 2
Congresses, party: see Rallies
Constitution, sections suppressed, 40
Contemporary Review, 149
Contra Komintern, 89
Co-operatives, 31
'Culture' activities, 39, 42, 66
Cuza, Professor, 81
Czechoslovakia:
    Antisemitism, 81, 82
    Armed assault on planned, 158
    Broadcasting, 117
    Germans in (see also Sudetenland), 62–64, 155
    National Socialists, contingent at Nürnberg rally, 15; organization, 119, 120

Occupation by Germans (1939), 143, 155–6, 162, 185
    Propaganda, 154–5, 158
    State created, 118, 120
Czechs, 119, 120, 181
Czibulka, Alfons von, 129

Dachau, 147
Daim, W., cited, 119
Dallin, A., cited, 168–71
D'Alquen, Gunter, cited, 18
Danubian area, 60, 119
Danzig, 100, 154
Darre, Walther, 31
Defeatism in high places, 172, 177
de Jong, Louis, cited, 67, 71
Deutsch-Englische Gesellschaft, 151
Deutsch-Europaeischer Kulturbund, 146
Deutsche Akademische Austauschdienst, 151
Deutsche Allgemeine Zeitung, 127–8
Deutsche Arbeiterpartei Österreichs, 120
Deutsche Hochschule für Politik, 86
Deutsche Tag, 17
Deutscher Fichte-Bund, 73
Deutsches Auslandsinstitut,, Stuttgart, 63
Deutsches Nachrichtenbüro, 44–45, 161
Deutsches Schutzbund, 63
Deutschlandsender, 92, 105, 169
Deutschnational party: see German National Party
Dictatorial powers, 41
Dietrich, Otto, 126, 160, 162
Diewerge, Wolfgang, 175
Diplomacy, propaganda preferred to, 7, 55–57, 184; expenditure on, 59
Diplomatic service, 56, 57, 69
Directives to the press: see under Press
Dirksen, Ambassador, 79
Disarmament of Germany, 142
Discontented, propaganda aimed at the, 31, 37, 55, 182
District director of propaganda, 39
DNB (news agency), 44, 45, 161
Dodd, Martha, cited, 57
Dollfuss, Engelbert, 106, 123, 126, 127, 129–33; assassinated (1934), 131

Domarus, Max, cited, 1, 86, 94, 137, 142, 154
Dresler, Adolf, cited, 22
Dressler-Andress, 36
Düsseldorf, party organizations, 29

Eagle (Nazi symbol), 15
Eastern problem, 42, 55, 60, 85; Germany's expansion plans, 61, 169–72
Eckart, Dietrich, 15, 22
Economic motif in propaganda, 143
Economic-political department, 31
Economic slump, Nazi party growth during, 28, 31–32, 37, 55, 182
Economics, Ministry of, 66
Eher (Franz) Verlag, 46
Ehrich, Emil, cited, 70
Ehrt, Dr. Adolf, 89, 90
Eichstädt, U., cited 118, 123, 131, 133
Ein Volk, ein Reich, ein Führer (slogan), 162
Einsatzgruppen, 156
El Alamein, 175
Elections, (1924), 30; (1928), 29; (1930), 23, 30–32; (1932), 34–36; (1933), 40–41, 183; (1936), 92
Emigration, German, 62
Enabling Law (1933), 41
Enemy countries: see 'Allied' countries
Engels, Friedrich, 84
Erfurt, 72, 74
Espionage activities, 57, 148
Essen, party organizations, 29
Eugenics institute, 73
Europe:
Central, 143–4, 154; German minorities, 64, 80, 154, 185; nationalism, 63
Decline of prominence in world affairs, 54–55
Eastern, 98, 100; German minorities, 62, 80, 104; Jewish problem, 80, 82, 102; nationalism, 80
Frontiers, 166–7
Nazi propaganda campaign, 80, 143–4, 166–7
North-eastern, *AO* department, 70
Reorganization plan, 162–4
South-eastern, 143; German minorities, 62

'Third Europe', 74
Western, *AO* department, 70
Exhibitions, travelling, 162
Ex-servicemen, 21

Fabricant, N.D., cited, 11
Far East, 70
Farmers, party and, 30–31
Feder, Gottfried, 36
Fichte League, 73
Films:
Company controlled by Hugenberg, 28, 29, 34, 49
Control of industry, 47–50, 182–3
Law, 48–49
Ministry department, 42
Nazi-produced, 34
Nazi tendencies in pre-Hitler films, 47–48
Newsreels, 28, 29, 49
Occupied territories, in, 170–1
Party propaganda department section, 39
Propaganda, as, 49–50, 162
Finance Ministry, 66
First World War, propaganda in, 5, 71
'Fist and the propaganda arm' (*SA*), 20
FitzRandolf, Sigismund-Sisso, 148
Flags, Nazi, 15, 18
Fleischhauer, Colonel, 72–74, 151
Foreign affairs, leading Nazis ignorance of, 54, 76, 184
Foreign countries, popular images created, 95
Foreign Ministry (*Auswärtiges Amt*):
Cultural Policy Department, 66
Expenditure, 58–59
Germans abroad, and, 66, 67
Hitler's attack on, 55
Nazis and changes in organization, 55–72
Party Foreign Organization taken over by, 59, 68–69, 72
Press Department, 57–59, 62, 66
Propaganda, organization, 42; control given up, 42; top men hold similar posts in party organization, 42; functions bestowed on Ministry of Propaganda, 58; co-operation agreement with Ministry, 59–60; conflict between

Foreign Ministry—*continued*
   ministers, 75, 184; role in sub-
   versive propaganda drive, 155;
   issues directives, 160; monitoring
   service, 177
   Rosenberg's scheme for, 60–62, 145
   Secret Circular (1933), 143
Foreign Organization (*Auslandsorga-
   nisation*) of the party, 59, 67–72,
   111; departments, 70
Foreign policy:
   Acceptable at home, 76
   Attacks on conduct of, 55–57
   Broadcasts and, 104, 106
   Party office created: *see* Foreign
   Political Office
   Propaganda and, 72, 95–96, 141,
   149, 159
   Responsibility for, 66, 184
Foreign Political Office (*Aussenpoli-
   tisches Amt*) of the party, 60–62,
   68
Foreign propaganda, Nazi (*see also*
   under countries), 7–8, 54–75, 87,
   142–3, 153–7, 184–6
   Absence of basic directives, 76
   Aimed at making the régime accep-
   table abroad, 55, 142–3
   Conference of heads of departments
   (1933), 57, 58
   Control, Foreign Ministry relin-
   quishes to Propaganda Ministry,
   42, 58; co-operation agreement
   between ministries, 95
   Effectiveness, information lacking,
   102
   Financing, 57–59
   Lessons of Austria, 141
   London reactions, 153–4
   Preference for employment of
   Germans, 54
Fraenkel, Heinrich, cited, 28
France:
   Anglo–French mission in Moscow
   (1939), 98
   Broadcasting, 109
   Position in Europe, 143–4
   Propaganda, during war, 164
   Saar, and, 108–9
   Vichy régime, 163–4
   War in, 81, 161–4
Franco, General, 93

Franconia, 29
Frank, Hans, 123, 128–9
Fränkische Tageszeitung, 81
Frauenorden, 30
Frederick the Great, 41
Freemasons, 73, 88
Freikorps, 15, 67
Frendenverkehrsabteilung, 42
Frick, Dr. Wilhelm, 13
Fritzsche, Hans, 169, 175; cited, 156
   180
Funk, Walther, 57

Gajda, General, 82
Garmisch-Partenkirchen, 110
Gaupropagandaleiter, 39
General Union of German Schools, 63
Geopolitics, 64–65
German citizenship, Hitler lacking, 1;
   Jews deprived of, 52; Nazi con-
   ception of, 70–71
German Institute in London, pro-
   posed, 151
German minorities abroad (*see also*
   under countries), 54, 55, 62–75,
   80, 154
   Broadcasts to, 105–9, 111
   Hess's record of a decision, 65–66
   Ministerial responsibility, 66–67
   Nazi attempt to control, 64–65,
   67–75
   Nazi groups, 67–70
   Societies, 63, 66–67, 72–75
   Study of, 64
German National Party, 29, 41, 86
German Workers' Party, 4
'Germany Awake' (Nazi battle-cry),
   15
Gesamtmarxismus, 83, 84, 86, 92, 101
Gestapo, 71
Gleichschaltung, of political activity,
   41; of the press, 43, 47; of the
   means of mass communication,
   162, 164
Gleiwitz broadcasting station, sham
   attack, 156–7
Goebbels, Dr. Joseph, *Gauleiter* for
   Berlin (1926), 26; *Reichpropa-
   gandaleiter* (1929), 26, 38; Minis-
   ter of Popular Enlightenment
   and Propaganda (1933), 40, 41;
   Reich Trustee for Total War

Goebbels, Dr. Joseph—*continued*
(1944),179; Chancellor (1945),179
(and mentioned *passim*)
Angriff, Der, launches (1927), 23;
technique in, 25
Austria, visit to (1932), 122; press
and, 126, 134; and treaty with
Germany, 135
Berlin, *Gauleiter* (1926), 26–29
Bolshevism, and, 85–86, 94
Broadcasting, and, 7, 50–51, 109,
116
Chancellor (1945) 179
Defeatism in high places, on, 172,
177
Diaries, cited, 72, 85, 160, 172–3,
177
Election campaign, 34–35
Enemy propaganda, fears of, 176
Films, and, 48–50
Foreign affairs, and, 54, 55
Foreign Ministry, animosity to-
wards, 61, 72, 75
Foreign propaganda, and, 57–59, 72,
75
Hitler, full support to, 23, 26, 37;
image of 'the young Chancellor',
38, 41; critical of, 86, 159, 172–3;
reads Hitler's last speeches,
179
Influence, on Nazi propaganda,
25–26; decline in, 156, 159
Kampf um Berlin, cited, 27
Minister of Popular Enlightenment
and Propaganda (1933), 40;
work as, 40–53, 182–3; last con-
ference as, 180 (*passim*)
Nationalsozialistischer Rundfunk,
cited, 109
Orator, as, 26
Party office, Hitler's offer of, 86
Pessimism propaganda, 173–4
Press, and, 24, 43–46, 50
Reich Trustee for Total War (1944),
179
Reichspropagandaleiter (1929–33),
work as, 26, 38; reorganizes
party propaganda administra-
tion, 38–40
Rosenberg, conflict with, 61, 170–1
'Stage management' of meetings,
on, 39–40

Vom Kaiserhof zur Reichskanzlei,
cited, 24, 33–35, 38, 41
War, attitude to, 159; effect on
propaganda, 159–60, 173; activi-
ties during, 161–2, 172–3, 175–6,
180–1
Goga, Octavian, 81
Gömbös, Julius, 81
Gooch, Professor G. P., 149
Göring, Hermann, 18, 55, 120, 151,
171, 172
Graeschke, Walter, 123
Gramophone records of speeches, 35
Great Britain:
Anglo–French mission in Soviet
Union (1939), 98
Anti-Nazi literature, 148, 150
Antisemitism, attitude to, 78–80,
153
AO department, 70
'British–Bolshevik conspiracy
against Germany', 165
Broadcasting, 150
Europe, position in, 144, 162–4
Fascists, British, 152–3
First World War propaganda, 5
Germany, relations with, 144–6;
desire for understanding, 153
Jewish immigrants, 79
'Maturity' of the English people, 46
Ministry of Information in First
World War, 5
Press, and antisemitism, 79; Nazi
efforts to influence, 148–50;
German correspondents in
Britain, 148–50
Pro-German societies, 151–2
Propaganda, Nazi, 144–53, 164;
Ambassador's report, 146;
authors' impressions, 146–8;
controlled through Embassy in
London, 148–9; unsuccessful be-
fore the war, 150–1, 153; during
war, 164
Rosenberg's visit to London (1933),
61–62, 144–5, 153
Soviet Union, negotiations with
(1939), 96
Sponsored visits to Germany, 146,
151
Gregory XV, Pope, 2
Grenzdeutsche, 64, 65

Grimm, Jacob, 62
Gritzbach, Dr., 151
Grossdeutsche Reich, 105, 123, 128, 129, 135
Grossveranstaltungen, 39, 43
Grothe, Willy, 67
Gutterer, Leopold, 43, 161

Haas, Werner, cited, 152
Habicht, Theodor, 121–3, 125–7, 129, 131, 134, 141
Habsburg Empire, 5, 55, 63, 82, 118, 120–1, 181
Hadamovsky, Eugen, 16, 36
Haegert, Wilhelm, 43
Hagemann, Dr. Walter, cited, 8, 43–47, 50, 100–1, 160–1, 165, 174, 177
Hakenkreuz insignia, 125, 137
Hardinge, Lady, 79
Haushofer, Karl, 64–65
Hegel, G. W. F., 147
Heiber, H., cited, 85, 159, 161, 162, 177
Heiden, Konrad, cited, 10, 129
Heil greetings, 15
Heimkehr ins Reich (slogan), 105
Henlein, Konrad, 82, 155
Hess, Rudolf, 44, 55, 64–67, 112, 134; biographical, 64–65; foreign background, 54, 64, 68, 75; interest in Germans living abroad, 65–72; 'mentally sick', 162; 'Record of a decision', 65–66; *SA* leader, 17
Himmler, Heinrich, 18, 156, 171
Hindenburg, Field-Marshal Paul von, 34, 36, 40, 41, 56
Hitler, Adolf, biographical, 1–5; release from Landsberg prison (1924), 6, 9, 36; candidate in presidential election (1932), 34–36; Chancellor (1933), 36, 40; plenary powers given (1942), 172; attempt on life (1944), 179 (and mentioned *passim*)
Antisemite by conviction, 77–78
Attempt on life (1944), 179
Austria, and, 132–4, 137–8; announces incorporation into Reich (1938), 138–9; visits to, 4, 120, 140
Bolshevism, and, 84–86, 93–94
Broadcasting, attitude to, 50, 51
Chancellor (1933), 36, 40
Communism, and, 83–87, 93–94
'Defender of peace', 155
English image of, 166
Europe's frontiers, on, 166
Hugenberg, alliance with, 28–30, 34, 182
Jews, on, 23, 84
Limited acquaintance with outside world, 54
Masses, attitude to the, 6
Mein Kampf, 2, 26; cited or quoted, 3–6, 76, 83–86, 143; poster appendix, 84; copies given to newly-married couples, 183
Military superiority of Germany, on, 168–9
Mussolini, meeting with (1934), 131
Nationality, Austrian, 119; German citizenship lacking, 1; ranked as foreigner, 13
Orator, rather than writer, 10–12, 21, 181; failure on radio, 51; decline as, 173, 179
'Peace speech' (1933), 142
Personal bodyguard, 18
Plenary powers, given (1942), 172
'Political Education Officer' to Bavarian Regiment, 3
Presidential election, candidate (1932), 34–36
Propaganda, views on, 3–7, 76–77; 'command' concerning (1938), 159–60
'Reactionary' attitudes, 86
Reichstag, speeches (1938), 154; (1942), 172–3
Release from Landsberg prison (1924), 6, 9, 36
Revival of party (1925), 9–10
Rise to political power, 1, 36
Russia, and, 85, 86; on German attack on (1941), 100, 165; on war against, 168–9
Speeches, forbidden to make public speeches (1925–8), 12–13, 18; printed in pamphlet form (1925), 12, 21; recorded, 35; broadcast, 51; read by Goebbels, 179
Terror and violence, views on, 6, 16
Voice frequency, 11

Hitlerjugend: see Youth organization, Nazi
Hoesch, Leopold von, 146
Hoffmann, Heinrich, 9
Holidays (State), regulation, 42
Holland, 177
Holy Roman Empire, Imperial insignia, 162-3
Horst Wessellied, 15, 16
Hugenberg, Alfred, 28-30, 34, 41, 47, 49, 182
Humanité, 164
Hungary, antisemitism, 81-82; *AO* department, 70; German settlements, 62, 63

Ideological differences, directives regarding, 98, 99, 101
Illustrierte Beobachter, 23, 24
Industrial cells, organization of, 31
Industrialists, support for Nazis, 32, 34
Inkeles, Dr., cited, 8
Inseldeutsche, 64
Insignia, Nazi, 15, 125, 137
Institut für Auslandskunde . . ., Leipzig, 63
Institute of Propaganda Analysis (American), 116
Intellectuals, and propaganda, 6, 11
Interior, Ministry of the, 42, 66
International Union of Nationalists, 73
Intimidation, use of, 6, 16, 122
Ireland, *AO* department, 70
'Iron curtain', 42
Italy:
　AO department, 70
　Austria, relations with, 127, 132
　Fascists, 74
　Jews, 78
　Political system, 147
　Propaganda in, 78
　War declared on United States, 172

Japan, Anti-Comintern pact with Germany (1936), 95, 98; Soviet treatment of Olympic team, 93
Jefferson, Thomas, 6
Jews (*see also* Antisemitism):
　'Cement' of Russia-Western alliance, 166

Deprived of German citizenship, 52
German treatment of, 10, 45, 77-80, 88, 109, 147, 171, 181
Hitler and, 23, 77-78, 84
'Jew-Bolshevik conspiracy', 85, 93-94, 100, 166, 170, 185
Minorities in eastern Europe, 80-82
Non-Aryan, 74
Nürnberg laws, 52
Johannsen, Dr., 149
Journalists, 22, 24, 35, 43-47, 126, 138; image of ideal editor, 45
Judenkenner, Der, 73
Jung, Rudolf, 120

Kaganovich, L. M., 91
Kampfring der Österreicher, 131, 133
Kampfzeit (period of struggle), 7, 19, 45, 181
Keitel, General Wilhelm, 159
Keller, Hans, 73-75
Kitson, Mr., 151
Klein, Dr. (of the *Antikomintern*), 88, 91
Klein, Fritz, 127-8
Kluke, Paul, cited, 163, 166
Knirsch, Hans, 120
Koch, Erich, 123
Kochan, Lionel, cited, 79
Koerner, R. R., cited, 126-7, 132, 134-5, 138-40
Kommass, Dr. R., cited, 92
Kowalevski, Colonel, 80-81
KPD (Communist Party of Germany), 86-87
Kracauer, Siegfried, quoted, 47-48
Krebs, Hans, 120
Kreispropagandaleiter, 39
Kriegler, Hans, 43, 105
Krupp's, 28
Kube, Wilhelm, cited, 71
Kulturamt, 42
Kutisker, 23

Lainzer Zoo raid, 122
Land reform, demand dropped, 30
Landsberg prison, 6, 9, 36, 65
Lang, Serge, cited, 61
Laqueur, Walter, cited, 84
Latin America: *see* America, South
Lau, Alfred, 104
Laval, Pierre, 144, 164

League of Nations, 51, 118, 149
Leipzig, treason trial (1929), 13
Lenin, V., 8
Ley, Robert, 123
Liberal parties, 40
Lies, counter by bigger lies, 6
Lines, Charles, 152
'Link, The' (pro-German organization), 152, 153
Literature, party programme, 22
Locarno pact, 85
Lochner, L. P., cited, 72, 160, 172
London treaty (1942), 172
Loudspeakers, use of, 34, 35, 52, 177
Lueger, Karl, 4–5
Luitpoldhain, 14
Lunn, James B., cited, 81
Lyle, Sir Leonard, cited, 153

Machtergreifung (seizure of power), 3
Manvell, Roger, cited, 28, 156
Marching, effect of, 20
Marx, Karl, 84
Marxism and Marxists, 17, 26, 42, 72, 90, 103, 119
  Campaign against Gesamtmarxismus, 83, 84, 86, 92, 101
  Hitler and, 17, 23
  Propaganda, and, 2, 4
Masaryk, T. G., 82
Mass communications, 28, 43, 47, 164, 181
'Masses', attitude to the, 6
Mecklenburg, 12
Mediterranean, 164
Meetings (see also Rallies), 10, 13–14, 33, 39–40, 43, 182; broadcasting, 51; compulsory attendance, 52; conduct of, 13–18; 'stage-management', 10, 40; use of microphones and loudspeakers, 34
Meier-Benneckenstein, Paul, 86
Memorials, protection, 42
Merchant seamen, Nazi organized, 69
Microphones, use of, 28, 34
Middle-classes, 26–27, 31, 55
Military activities, reporting of, 156, 158–9, 165; spreading of 'false but credible information', 158
Milner, Lord, 146, 153

Ministries, conflict between, 75, 170–1, 184
Minorities abroad: see German minorities abroad
Mitteilungsblatt des Kampfringes ..., 125
Mjoelnir (cartoonist), 25
Molotov, Viacheslav, 98, 100
Moravia, 120
Mosley, Sir Oswald, 79, 152
Mosse (publisher), 28
Mueller (M.) and Son, 126
Müller, Adolf, 56
Münchener Beobachter, early title of Völkischer Beobachter (q.v.), 22
Munich:
  Bürgerbräukeller meeting (1925), 10, 12
  Hitler in, 3, 4, 10, 12, 17
  Hofbräuhaus meeting (1921), 17
  Nazi movement in, 13, 15–17, 84
  Putsch (1923), 10, 14, 23, 60, 65, 120
  Rally (1923), 18
Munich agreement (1938), 82, 154
Münster, Hans A., cited, 23, 24, 32
Music, 42
Mussolini, Benito, 78, 127, 132, 163

Napoleon, 50
National Socialism:
  Authors' impressions, 146–8
  Export, 69, 94
  First organization of that name, 119
  Ideology, 2
  International appeal, lacking, 54, 76
  Origins, 119–20
  Party: see Party, Nazi
National Socialist German Workers' Party (NSDAP): see Party, Nazi
Nationalism, Austria-Hungary, 119; central Europe, 63; eastern Europe, 80; Germans abroad, 64; international Union of Nationalists, 73–74
Nationalist International, 73, 74
Nationalsozialistische Partei-Korrespondenz, 33
Naval agreement, Anglo–German (1935), 151
Navy, daily reports, 160
Near East, 70

Neurath, Baron Konstantin von, 55–59, 61, 66, 68
Neusüss-Hunkel, cited, 18
New Pioneer, The, 79
News agencies, 33, 44, 45, 161
News Chronicle, cited, 153
Newspapers: see Press
Niederbayern (province), 19
Nineteenth Century and After, The, 149
Nobility, German, 56
Northcliffe, Lord, 5
NSDAP: see Party, Nazi
NS Landpost, 31
Nürnberg, laws, 52; local organizations, 29; party rallies: see under Rallies; trials: see War crimes trials

Oberfranken (province), 19
Oberpfalz (province), 19
Occupied countries, 161–2, 164, 167–72, 177–8, 186
Ödenburg (Sopron), 66
Österreichische Pressedienst, 126
OKW: see Wehrmacht
Olympic Games (Berlin, 1936), 92, 93; broadcasting, 109–12, 116; films, 49
One-party state, 8, 102
Operation Green, 158
Ortsgruppe, 67, 69
Ortsgruppenpropagandaleiter, 39
'Ostmark', term used for Austria, 13
Ostministerium, 170, 171

Pan-Aryans, 73
Papen, Franz von, 50, 106, 133–5
Paraguay, Nazi organization, 67
Para-military organizations, 18, 21, 30 (*see also* under title of organization)
Parliamentary institutions, Nazis and, 40
Parteigenossen (regular party members), 3
Parteitag: see Rallies, party
Parties (political), organization, 2–3
Party, Nazi (NSDAP) (*see also* subject headings throughout index):
  Anniversaries, celebration organization, 43
  Bans on party or activities, 9, 13, 18, 19
  Foreign Organization: see that title
  Foreign Political Office: see that title
  History, 3–4
  Local organizations, 29
  Membership, 20, 29; 1928–32 (table), 32
  Organization, 7, 29–30, 38
  Propaganda department: see *Reichspropagandaleitung*
  Rallies: see that title
  Re-establishment (26 February 1925) after Hitler's release from prison, 9–10, 18, 23, 30
  Rise to power analysed, 1, 29–37
  State, and the (memo., 1943), 178
  States governments' measures against, 9, 13, 18, 19, 36
Peace, speech by Hitler (1933), 142
Peace treaty, 1919: see Versailles treaties
Peasantry, party and, 30, 31, 136
Period of struggle (*Kampfzeit*), 7, 19, 45, 181
Periodicals: see Press
Persuasion, use of, 8, 40
Pessimism, propaganda of, 173–4
Pétain, Marshal, 164
Pfeffer, Franz von, 18
Photographs, regulation, 99; of Red Army prisoners-of-war, 169
Pistor, Ernst, 73
Plenary powers for Hitler (1942), 172
Pohle, Heinz, cited, 50–52, 105–6, 108, 110–11, 115
Poland:
  Antisemitism, 80–82
  Austria, and, 119
  British guarantee, 156
  Broadcasting, 104–5
  German invasion and occupation (1939), 59, 97, 100, 105, 185
  Germans in, 62, 65, 105
  Propaganda, 156–7
  Russian invasion and occupation, 100
  Treaty with Germany (1934), 104–5
Political parties: see Parties

Political repression, Nazis use *Reich-stag* fire as pretext, 40–41
'Political troops': see Para-military organizations
Popular Enlightenment and Propaganda Ministry: see Propaganda Ministry
Potsdam, garrison church, 41
Pottere, de, 74
Pravda, 99
Presidential election campaign (1932), 34–36
Press (*see also* under names of newspapers):
Active propaganda section's newspaper, 39
Austria: see *under* Austria
Censorship, 45, 159
Conferences, official, 44–45, 58, 180
Directives to, 96–99, 101, 131–2, 134, 140, 159–60, 165; co-ordination during war, 160
Foreign, 22, 42
Freedom of opinion, 46, 127–8
Fund, 23
German correspondents in Britain, 148–50
Hitler's views on, 21–23
Hugenberg's newspapers, 29, 34, 47
Image of ideal editor, 45
Journalists: see that title
Law (1933), 45–46
Mass-circulation, 28, 50
Nazi press, newspaper acquired by party (*see Völkischer Beobachter*), 22–23; early history, 22–24, 28; analysis, 24–25; newspaper reappears after banning (1925), 9–10, 23; circulation growth, 32, 33; number of newspapers, 33, 43, 47; compulsory purchase, 52; new newspapers, 162
Non-party, 127–8
Number of newspapers, 43, 47
Party programme, 22, 44
Political movements and ownership of newspapers, 21
Press Chamber, 46
Priority in bringing news, 51
Propaganda, as means of, 33–35, 181–3, 186

Publishers, 46, 47
Supervision, 42
Suppression and banning of newspapers, 9–10, 40, 43, 44, 46, 128
Unfriendly to Nazis, 16–17
Uniformity, 43–47
Preussische Zeitung, 104
Prisoners-of-war, 164, 171; photographs of Russians in German press, 169; names of Germans broadcast by Soviet, 178
Proksch (Austrian Nazi), 126
Promi (abbreviation for Propaganda Ministry, *q.v.*), 58
Propaganda (word), 2
Propaganda (*see also* subject headings throughout index), functions and basic principles (1943 memo.), 178; three phases reviewed, 181–6
Propaganda abroad: see Foreign propaganda, Nazi
Propaganda department, party: see *Reichspropagandaleitung*
Propaganda Ministry (Ministry of Popular Enlightenment and Propaganda) (*Promi*), creation (1933), 40, 52; Goebbels appointed Minister, 40–42, 182–3
Broadcasting department, 42, 43, 105, 175, 182–3
Building planned, new, 161
Expenditure, 58–59
Film department, 49
Foreign Ministry, delimitation of duties, 57–58, 66; agreement on co-operation (1941), 59–60; conflict between ministers, 75, 184
Foreign press section, 156
Germans abroad, and, 66
Importance declines, 161
Last conference, 180
Organization, 42–43
Ostministerium, conflict between ministers, 170–1
Party propaganda organization, co-operation with, 42–43
Press department, 44, 45, 126
Wehrmacht, co-operation with, 159–61, 186
Propagandists, Nazi preference for employment of Germans, 54
Protestants, 4

Prussia, ban on party and *SA* (1927), 19; ban on Hitler lifted (1928), 13; ministries and Germans abroad, 66

Public speaking, Hitler's main propaganda weapon, 10–12; ban on Hitler (1925–1928), 12–13, 18; direction of, 39

Publishing, control, 46, 47

Putsch (November 1923): see Munich putsch

Radio: *see* Broadcasting

Rallies, party, 14–15, 33, 39, 48, 153, 182
Films of, 49
1923 (Munich), 14, 18
1926 (Weimar), 14, 18, 23, 24, 30
1927 (Nürnberg), 14, 19, 20
1936 (Nürnberg), 1, 70–71, 89, 92, 93
1938 (Nürnberg), 162

Ramsay, Captain A. H. M., 79

Raskin, Adolf, 106–7, 161

Rauschning, H., cited, 76–78, 143

Red Front fighting organization, 27

Redeverbot, 12, 21

Rednerwesen (*see also* Public speaking), 39

Refugees, from Nazi Germany, 71; from Baltic provinces, 84; from Austria, 130–1

Regional governments: see States

Rehse, Sammlung, cited, 13, 14, 20, 23, 29, 34, 129

'Reich', concept of the, 163

Reich, Das, 162–3, 175, 177

Reichmann, Dr. E. G., cited, 77

Reichsbanner, 21

Reichsgesetzblatt, cited, 45, 48, 58

Reichskulturkammer, 73

Reichsorganisationsleitung, 38

Reichspressekammer, 46

Reichspropagandaleitung (party department of propaganda), 38–40, 42–43, 86, 95–96, 98, 127

Reichsrundfunkkammer, 43

Reichssendeleitung, 88, 91

Reichstag, 13, 28; elections: see Elections; fire (1933), 40, 44, 46; Hitler's speeches, 142, 154; meeting in Potsdam church, 41

Reimesch (playwright), 129

Reparations, Young Plan, 28, 29, 36

Reschny (Austrian Nazi), 126

Rheinbaben, Freiherr von, 149–50

Rhineland, 26, 92, 135, 153

Ribbentrop, Joachim von, 98, 100, 171; Foreign Minister, 56, 59, 155, 184; on Germans abroad, 69

Riehl, Walter, 120

Rintelen, Dr., 131

'Ritual murder', 25

Roden, Max, 90

Roosevelt, President F. D., 51, 69

Rosenberg, Alfred, 72, 75, 84, 151; biographical, 60: editor of *Völkischer Beobachter*, 22, 60; and foreign affairs, 54, 55; head of Foreign Political Office (1933), 60–62, 68; London visit, 61–62, 144–5, 153; appointed to *Ostministerium*, 170–1; cited, 62, 153

Rote Adler, Der, 125

Rotfront-Kaempferbund, 21

Rothermere, Lord, 5

Ruhr, 19

Rumania, antisemitism, 80–82; Austria, and, 119; Fascist Iron Guard 81; German-Rumanian relations, 81; German settlements, 62–63

'Russia' (word), replaced by 'Soviet Union', 168

Russia:
Anglo–French military mission (1939), 98
Bolsheviks, 1–3, 54–57, 76, 85, 170
Broadcasts, 116, 167, 170, 178
Communism, 83, 84, 90
German settlements, 62
Germany, diplomatic relations with, 95, 96; negotiations and events after Pact, 100–3
Economic relations with, 96–98
Invasion of Soviet Union: see War, below
Pact with (August 1939), 88, 95–99, 156, 162, 165
Great Britain, anti-Soviet attitude in, 153; negotiations with (1939), 96
Institute for Scientific Research on the Soviet Union, 88
Marxist Socialism, 55, 83

Russia:—*continued*
'Masses', attitude to the, 6
Nazi attitude towards, 84–85
Party congress (1939), 96
Poland, invasion of, 100
Propaganda, Russian: technical equipment lacking, 28; loud-speakers introduced, 52
Propaganda *about* the Soviet Union, 72, 87–88, 90; campaign, 93–97; after German attack, 165–9, 172
Propaganda *to* the Soviet Union, 87, 167; leaflets dropped, 168
Revolution, 60, 90
Social Democracy, 2
War (1941–5), German attack (June 1941), 100–1, 164–6; volunteer units from other nations, 166; German confidence of military superiority, 168–9; German advance halted, 172; struggle for Stalingrad, 174, 178; last days, 180
Rust, Bernard, 177

SA troops (*Sturmabteilungen*), 14–15, 17–21, 27–28, 30, 33–34, 40 53,
Saalschlacht, 17, 19–21, 27
Saarland, 135, 185; broadcasting campaign (1934), 7, 106–9, 116, 117, 126, 153; Plebiscite (1935), 106, 108–9
Saxe-Coburg and Gotha, Duke of, 151
Saxony, 13, 18
Schacht, Hjalmar, cited, 11
Schaefer, Wolfgang, cited, 29, 31, 32
Scheffer, 78
Scheiner, Dr., 91
Schenk, Ernst von, cited, 61
Scherl Verlag, 28, 29, 47
Scheubner-Richter, Max, 84
Schleicher, Kurt von, 56
Schleswig-Holstein, 24
Schmeer, Dr. Karlheinz, cited, 8, 15–16, 20, 39–42, 68
Schmidt, Dr. Guido, 135–7
Schönerer, Georg, 4–5, 121
Schools, General Union of, 63
Schreck, Julius, 18
Schriftleitergesetz, 45
Schuschnigg, Kurt von, 137–40, 154
Schutzstaffeln: see SS troops

Schwerin-Krosigk, von, 58
Seabury, Paul, cited, 55, 59
Searchinger, C., cited, 116
Secret State Police, 134
Semmler, Rudolf, cited, 167, 169
Seton-Watson, Hugh, cited, 80
Sex, treatment in Nazi press, 25
Seyss-Inquart, Arthur, 138, 140, 162
Sima, Horia, 81
Slav *Untermensch* propaganda, 166–7, 169–70
Slovakia, 82
Social Democrats, 2, 16, 20, 40, 56, 83–84, 86–87; hold on workers, 20, 26, 87; press, 6, 24, 44, 46
Socialists, 29; press, 24
Solf, Wilhelm, 111
Songs, Nazi, 15
Sopron: see Ödenburg
Soviet state, Lenin's dictum, 8
Soviet Union: see Russia
Spahn, Walter, 123
Spain, 164; Civil War, 93, 95, 101
SPD: see Social Democrats
SS troops (*Schutzstaffeln*), 14, 15, 18, 27, 30, 33, 171
Stage management of meetings and rallies, 10, 15, 20, 40 122
Stahlhelm, 21
Stalin, Joseph, 3, 87, 90, 94, 96, 102, 167
Stalingrad, 174, 178
State, and propaganda, 38–53; and party, 178
State visits, organization, 43
States, German, governments' attitude to Hitler, 12, 13; measures against Nazis, 9, 13, 18, 19, 36; party organizations in, 29; central government's powers in, 40
Steinacher, Dr. Hans, 65, 66, 134
Steinert, Fritz, 123
Stern, Michael, 20–21
Stieve, Friedrich, 66
Stosstrupp Hitler, 18
Strasser, Gregor, 23, 26, 85; head of department of party organization, 38
Strasser, Otto, 20–21, 23, 26, 85
Streets, domination of the, 16, 17; battles, 20–21, 33; 'loudspeaker pillars', 52

INDEX

Streicher, Julius, 12, 23, 25, 60, 67, 72–73, 75, 81, 109
Stresemann, Gustav, 28
Streudeutsche, 64
Sturm, Sturm, Sturm (song), 15
Sturmabteilungen: see SA troops
Stürmer, Der, 23, 25, 109
Stützpunktpropagandaleiter (cell-leader), 39
Subversive propaganda, 143, 154–5
Sudetenland, 59, 82, 105, 120, 157; propaganda campaign, 155, 158–9, 185
Suendermann, 160
Sunday Graphic, 145
Supreme Command, 159–61, 174
Switzerland, *AO* department, 70; Germans in, 64

Tag, Der, 29
Tannenberg anniversary, 99–100
Tavs, Leo, 138
Taylor, A. J. P., cited, 64
Technical equipment for propaganda, 28, 33–34, 37
Television, 28, 154
Terror, use of, 6, 16, 33, 40, 122, 125, 137, 157
Teutonia, 67
Theatre, 42, 49
Third International, 91
Thost, Dr., 149
Thüringia, 12, 18
Tiroler Volksbund, 63
Times, The, 79, 150
Timoshenko, Marshal, 168
Torgler, 167
Total War, Reich Trustee for, 179
Totalitarian countries, Sir A. Wilson's views, 146–8
Tourist traffic, 42
Trade treaties, offers of, 143
Trade unions, 31, 32
Trotsky, L., 91, 167
Tyrol, South, 63, 65

Überseedeutsche, 64
UFA (film company), 28, 29, 49
Uhland, Ludwig, 62
Ullstein (publisher), 28
Unemployed, as recruiting ground for Nazis, 30–33, 182

Uniforms (political), first use by Nazis, 18; banned, 19–20, 33; ban lifted, 33
Union of German Anti-Communist Societies (*Antikomintern*), 75, 87–92
Union of Germans Abroad: see *VDA*
United States:
Broadcasts, 111–13, 115, 116
German emigrants to, 62, 63, 67
Nazi organization, 67
Propaganda, 166, 176
War (1941–1945), Germany and Italy declare war, 172; conducted against Nazis not German nation, 176
Unser Wille und Weg, 39, 86
Untermensch: see Slav

Vansittart, Lord (*earlier* Sir Robert Vansittart), 61, 145
VDA, the Union of Germans Abroad, 63, 65, 134
Versailles treaties (1919), 29, 36, 42, 63, 106, 118–19, 142
Vienna, siege of workers' quarters (February 1934), 130; abortive Nazi *putsch* (July 1934), 8, 131–6, 141, 143, 185; Hitler visits, 4, 6, 120, 140
Violence, use of, 6, 16, 37, 71, 182; Hitler's views, 6, 16; treatment in Nazi press, 25
Voice frequencies, 11
Völkischer Beobachter, 10, 15, 28, 60, 81, 93, 149; acquired by party (1920), 22; history, 22–24; re-appears after ban (1925), 10, 23; circulation, 23, 24, 32; differences in two editions, 127–8
Volksbund (also *Verein*) *für das Deutschtum in Ausland*: see *VDA*
Volksdeutscher Rat, 65–67
Volksempfänger (radio set), 51–52, 108, 176, 177
Volkstimme, Die, 125

Wagener, Otto, 31
Wagner, Adolf, 93
Wahrmund, Dr. Adolf, cited, 29
Wandervogel, 15

INDEX

Wandruszka, Adam, cited, 120, 123, 136
War, Hitler on propaganda and, 77
War (1939–1945), propaganda during, 159–81, 186; propaganda of pessimism, 173–4; Nazi monopoly of information broken, 177–8, 186; closing stages, 180–1, 186
War crimes trials, 59, 67, 168
Washington treaty (1942), 172
Wehrmacht, 156, 159–61, 167–8, 174, 186
Weimar rally (1926), 14, 18, 23, 24, 30
Weimar Republic, 16, 31, 47, 51; broadcasting, 105, 111, 112; German minorities abroad, and, 63, 64, 105; Nazi campaign against, 1, 37, 90, 182
Weinberg, G. L., cited, 96
Weinberger, A., 129
Weiss (editor), 45
Weiss, Dr. (deputy police chief), 25
Weizsäcker, Ernst von, cited, 56
Weltanschauung, 74, 94
Weltdienst, 72, 73, 151
Westdeutsche Gemeinschaftsdienst, 106
Weyh, Gerhard, 123

Wiener Library, vii; *Bulletin* cited, 22, 79
Wilson, Sir Arnold, 146–9
Wilson, Woodrow, 118
Winterhilfe, 125
Wireless exhibition (Berlin, 1932), 36
Woche, Die, 29
Wolff Telegraphenbüro, 44, 78
Women's organization (*Frauenorden*), 30
Working classes, and Nazis, 26, 31–32, 136; in Austria, 83, 119, 120
World Review, 149
World revolution, 90–91
Wright, Elwin, 152
Writing, Hitler and, 10, 21; Nazi lack of writers, 24; Ministry section dealing with, 42
WTB agency, 44, 78

Young Plan for reparations, 28, 29, 36
Youth organization, Nazi (*Hitler-jugend*, 30, 49, 180
Youth textbook, quoted, 16–17
Yugoslavia, 62, 119, 136

Zeman, Z. A. B., cited, 76
Zürich, 73